W9-DGB-394

THE BEST OF THE AMISH COOK

VOL 2, 1991-1996

By Elizabeth Coblentz

Editor: Kevin Williams

Visit "The Amish Cook" on the web at www.theamishcook.com

1996 – 1997

This was a time of turmoil in the United States. TWA Flight 800 inexplicably exploded off the coast of Long Island on a quiet July evening, sending hundreds to their death. Several weeks later the peace and competitive spirit of the Summer Olympics in Atlanta were shattered by a bomb explosion. Security guard Richard Jewell was named the suspect, but was eventually cleared. Eric Robert Rudolph was later linked to the bombing, he remains at large. While Rudolph remained elusive, another notorious bomber was captured. Ted Kaczynski was arrested. Kaczynski was identified as the UnaBomber, responsible for a years-long campaign of terror. Meanwhile, voters went to the polls and elected President Clinton to a second term, defeating Kansas senator Bob Dole. 1997 saw the death of Princess Diana in a tragic accident top the news.

While the world grappled with terrorists and elections, the Coblentzes quietly dealt with their own changes and turmoil. December of 1996 saw The Amish Cook's mother pass away at age 90. That's also the month that Elizabeth's daughter, Lovina, and her husband, Joe, moved into a home of their own. They had been living in a trailer across the driveway from Elizabeth and Ben. Elizabeth missed her daily visits with Lovina.

Elizabeth's grandson Paul Jr. underwent emergency open-heart surgery in Indianapolis to correct a serious birth defect. He stoically stayed in the hospital for six weeks, while the family kept an anxious vigil. Paul Jr. recovered and grew stronger after he returned home. Paul Jr's return home was greeted with tragedy, though, when his 6-year-old sister Mary died suddenly from diabetic complications.

November brought healing to the Coblentzes with the birth of granddaughter Rosa, born to Elizabeth's daughter, Liz.

Could use some rain, but the good Lord will provide. We are having a lot of goodies from the garden, which makes meal-planning easier. Lots of salads can be prepared, especially with the plentiful lettuce in the garden (oakleaf and prizehead lettuce). The hot and sweet peppers have advanced and tomatoes, pickles, green beans, red beets, sweet corn, carrots - and you name it - are on the menu. I took out the onions now for later use.

To the Cambridge, Minnesota reader about canning chunk beef. Chunk the beef and add 1 teaspoon of salt and 1/4 teaspoon pepper to a quart of beef chunks. Process in pressure cooker for 90 minutes at 10 pounds of pressure. Good luck!

To the Fort Wayne, Indiana reader, here is my recipe for rhubarb jam: 5 cups rhubarb (cut fine), 4 cups sugar, 6 ounces of strawberry Jello or whatever flavor you prefer. Mix rhubarb and sugar and let set overnight. In the morning, boil for five minutes. Then add gelatin. Put in jars and seal.

A Cortez reader has requested a recipe for tofu cheesecake. Anyone out there have a recipe for it?

To the Bowling Green, Ohio reader: the recipes of homemade salsa and hot peppers are included in this column. Good luck! All our family are fond of canned or raw hot peppers.

To the Battle Creek, Michigan reader: I included a recipe as you being diabetic.

To other readers who have asked. Ben and I have eight children: two boys and six girls. All married except for two girls. We have 20 grandchildren. The girls are taking the lead, as we have 12 granddaughters and 8 grandsons. Everyone is so precious to us. It means so much when everyone seems healthy - at least thus far. Good we don't know our future.

We took supper in Sunday evening for my aged mother. My older sister, Leah and her husband, cared for her during the day - taking dinner along. Then when they left we took over until 9 a.m. I sent breakfast along with my sister for my mother when they drove past in the morning.

Daughter Lovina and her two little girls are here today. We canned some cucumber salad which always tastes to good. Would've hated to seen them pickles go to waste. Lovina can't use all of hers as they've done so well.

Will share some recipes with you great readers out there.

SEPTEMBER 1996

𝕿he weather has been ideal. The temperatures haven't been so hot, but we are in need of a bit of rain. Garden goodies need the rain badly, but it still seems so plentiful. I didn't want to can anymore this year, but I hate to see it go to waste. The second batch of corn stalks were tossed over the fence for the cattle to eat. So another batch is almost ready to eat, but it needs a good rain. Good thing we can't rule the weather.

Daughters Lovina and Susan and I were to my sister's house on Wednesday to help get ready for the wedding of their youngest daughter. So we baked 62 pies and lots of pie crusts. The pies included: Bob Andy pie, cherry, raisin, and peanut butter pie. We made nine batches of "nothings" - a traditional Amish wedding pastry. These were all made under a tent. They had rented a tent to put over the area where the kerosene stoves and tables were to prepare the meals for the wedding. The ceremonial wedding tables were set up in their shed. What less work to not have the wedding in the house and to rearrange the furniture, etc. The wedding services were held at a neighbor's in a big, cleaned out tool shed.

On Saturday, we went to the Columbus, Ohio zoo with some of the family. This was a certificate we purchased at the recent benefit auction in our area. A non-Amish man donated his nice van to haul 11 Amish people to the zoo (Amish people are not allowed to own automobiles, but can ride in them for special occasions if a non-Amish person is driving). At the same benefit auction we put in our own donation for people to bid on: breakfast for 12 at our home. So a certificate was purchased by a local family for the meal. Also we put in a donation for a Saturday evening chicken barbecue for 18, so this was also purchased by a local family. So one of these Saturday mornings and Saturday evening's we'll be serving those meals. The auction was to raise money for an area Amish family with huge hospital bills. The benefit auction was well-attended and much appreciated by the family.

Well it is about time I rush to my kitchen and start a batch of cinnamon rolls so it can rise and cut into rolls, rise again, and then bake in a hot oven. Naturally making frosting for them. So they'll be topped with frosting for a special occasion. We are also making peanut butter cookies this afternoon. Following is a recipe for the breakfast meal we will serve the auction bidders and for the cookies:

BREAKFAST PIZZA

1 package pizza crust mix or prepared crust
Salt, pepper to taste
1 pound bulk sausage
2 tablespoons grated Parmesan cheese
1 cup frozen hash-brown potatoes
4 eggs
1 cup shredded Cheddar cheese

3 tablespoons milk
Yield: 6 servings
Prep time: 30 minutes
Baking: 30 minutes

Preheat oven to 375 degrees. Meanwhile, brown sausage and drain well. Cool.
Prepare pizza dough for crust as directed on package, or use a prepared crust. Spoon cooled sausage over crust.

Sprinkle with thawed hash browns and the Cheddar cheese.
Beat eggs to blend, then beat in milk, a dash of salt and pepper to taste. Pour over potatoes and cheese. Bake pizza 30 minutes at 375 degrees.

SEPTEMBER 1996

This is Saturday noon and some of the married children are here for dinner as the menfolk were helping unload hay which we bought from a friend of ours. Be good to have our own hay now. Hay is at a good price this year. Don't know if we should sell cattle.

The highlights of this week included a baby girl being born to daughter Emma and Jacob on Thursday evening at 8:45 p.m. Guess what the name is? Elizabeth. This makes the sixth Elizabeth in this family, as we have six marrieds. What a good feeling for Grandma that her name keeps in the family. Some ask how do we keep or call them apart - so far, no problems. Guess we aren't the only family who names after the parents. So many others do too. Emma and baby are doing good and I reckon Daddy is too. She weighed five pounds, twelve ounces, and was 19 1/2 inches in length. It is so sweet to have a cute bundle in this household once more.

This week has been many happenings. Monday, Tuesday, and Wednesday we cooked dinner for my husband's carpenter crew as they weren't working far from here. They tore off a house roof and put a new one on it. So the three dinner meals seemed to be enjoyable to them all. Then we had visitors all week and most of all Thursday evening when Emma and Jacob became parents for the first time. Reckon I'll be cooking Sunday dinner and supper with the help of my daughters.

So good to have so much from the garden. We have tomatoes, lettuce, red beets, sweet and hot peppers, cucumbers, and we used the last of our sweet corn this week. So thankful we can still feast on the garden.

Should get this in the mail, so hope to beat the mailman to the box. Maybe I will have more news next time.

I will share some recipes. The rest are all eating dinner and here I sit writing this task which can't be neglected. That's right all my six daughters are here for dinner. Three daughters are married and have families. Always glad to prepare a meal for them. Son Albert and his boys have left for home already. See you all next week.

This is the dish I prepared for dinner tonight:

FRIED CUCUMBERS: Take big cucumbers and peel and slice lengthwise. Roll in flour and fry in a skillet with lard until golden. Season with salt and pepper. We also had beef, noodles, salad, sliced tomatoes, sweet and hot peppers, wieners, cake, peaches, and home-baked bread that I made this week. Everyone likes home-baked bread!

OCTOBER 1996

So many changes when we are in this season of autumn. Aren't the colors magnificent: yellow, orange, and red leaves are gradually falling from the trees. Looking towards the woods from my window, the leaves are in their autumn splendor. With no killing frost as of yet, we're still having garden eats, such as endive, red beets, and carrots that should be taken care of before it freezes. It is a good feeling to have all of those empty jars filled once more for those cold winter months ahead. It was such a nice wash day. I enjoy such days as to hang out the laundry in a short time, they're dry and ready to be ironed. October has so many memories on my part. It'll be 38 years that Ben and I took up our life sentence - marriage. We moved here 32 years ago,
October 29, having two children. Leah was four and Amos turned --two the next day. It was a change for them to move to a different. place, but they got adjusted.

Also, October 2 was the wedding anniversary of son Albert and October 4 was the wedding anniversary of daughter Liz. We had my mother's family reunion one year on October 30, with towards 300 people here for dinner. Of all things it was our first snow of the season on that same day. The occasion was meant for an early Christmas gathering, which probably brought on the snow and colder weather. Ha!

So Albert's and Joe's were here for supper tonight as the menfolks were digging up the floor tiles that are hooked up to our sink drain. It is hard work after coming home from a hard day's work They are quite sluggish for quite some time after coming home. Glad when the kitchen is in good working order again. Daughters Verena and Leah made some good pizza for supper tonight. They made the dough. They rolled the dough out and put on pizza pans. They also fried some hamburger and chopped onions to put on the rolled out dough in pans. Top with pizza sauce, mushrooms, and then chopped up sweet peppers. and grated cheese. It was yummy!

Those homemade pizzas made from scratch are quite filling. The girls enjoy making it in different ways. We like it topped with some chopped up hot peppers.

We received the book "A day in the Life of an Amish Kitchen" in the mail today. It has some good recipes, kitchen chats, and pictures. I found it to be very interesting. It's companion book, "A Day in the Life of the Amish" is also very interesting. I suppose some of you readers out there have these books.

I dug up our bulbs from the ground tonight. They can't survive the cold winter, I will plant them again next Spring. Then there's some bulbs I would like to get in the ground tomorrow.

You readers try this recipe for "snoozer sandwiches," they are a delicious ham treat.

SNOOZER SANDWICHES

1 cup ketchup
1/2 cup water
1/2 teaspoon mustard (wet)
2 tablespoons vinegar
1-1 1/2 pounds of ground ham
1/3 cup of brown sugar
YIELD: 6 servings
PREP TIME: 15 minutes
BAKING TIME: 1 hour

Stir all together the ketchup, water, mustard, vinegar, ground ham and brown sugar. Turn into a casserole and bake at 250 degrees for 1 hour. Spoon onto bread and serve as a sandwich.

OCTOBER 1996

𝔉armers in the area are in full swing harvesting soybeans and corn.

Tuesday was just another one of those days with lots going on. Daughter Emma missed a day from work at the sewing factory as to go along with her husband Jacob to the hospital. Losing his balance, Jacob fell 12 feet off a roof while on construction work the evening before. Results: a broken heel. Gets around with the aid of crutches. So I reckon he won't be climbing up on a roof for sometime. Emma and Jacob have lived here with us since their June 15 marriage.

Daughters Leah and children, Liz and children, and Lovina and her daughter came to spend the day here today. Plans had been made to have a sewing day, but the girls went on with the sewing while I - and Jacob's mother also - went along with Jacob and Emma to the hospital. The girls like to sew on my good, old Singer treadle sewing machine which has been in use for many, many years.

We arrive back here from the hospital later for dinner, but we still got in on the leftovers. The girls had a dinner which consisted of fried chicken, mashed potatoes, gravy, corn, and more. Always tastes better when someone else does the meal. Sister-in-law Betty, who took us to the hospital, also stayed for the late dinner.

It seems impossible that we have seven grandchildren in school now. How these years slip away. We have 19 grandchildren now, including one set of twin girls. Also, when I took up this task of writing in August of 1991 we had five unmarried girls in our care yet and two sons and a daughter who were married. Now we still have two unmarried girls here with us.

When you think back, how nice it would be if all eight of our children could still be in our care in these troubled times we are in. Do we appreciate good health enough when you read and hear of so many losing their good health? So, I guess we are just living one day at a time, right?

Well, I must get with it and let you readers out there rest yours eyes until next week if you happen to be reading this column.

NOVEMBER 1996

Such a lovely autumn day. This brings back memories of 39 years ago today, when we got what you'd call a life sentence. Ha! Today is Ben and my anniversary.

We invited all our family for supper tonight for our wedding anniversary, plus a few more couples who have their anniversary coming up.

The huge wash is drying outside and the ironing has been completed. I was out in the garden gathering vegetables as we're going to have a "haystack" for supper for tonight's meal. Some might not know what a haystack is. You put hamburger on your plate, then top it with whatever you want and then pour cheese sauce on top. You soon have a plateful. Some cook rice and mushrooms in with the hamburger, it is a very good meal. So there's to be cut-up lettuce, chopped-up tomatoes, peppers, celery, carrots, radishes, crushed crackers, and also crushed-up corn chips - all to pile on top of the hamburger. Then pour over the cheese sauce. The hamburger is to be fried for it. Also there will be peas, kidney beans, cheese sauce, and hot sauce. As side dishes we will have buttered red beets, green beans, and hot peppers from the garden. How thankful we are for such a plentiful garden. I pickled cucumbers yesterday, our cucumber crop looks like history for 1996. But to think that this is October 17 and no killing frost yet. I'll probably be one of these days soon.

Well, there goes the mailman and really I don't have time to write with all that work ahead. I will write more later.

This leaves it later in the evening and all my company has left. Turned out to be stormy and wonder if any of the children got wet on their way home. We have the open buggies in this area (buggies without a roof). But the umbrella helps a lot. Then winter comes, you just had better bundle up while traveling in the buggy. Winter: I always dread to see that coming up.

That means keeping those stoves in high gear once more,. They take more work to keep going.

Well, I had best hike to bed. We had 49 here for supper. It was good to see all our family together again tonight, plus the others who came. Singing and yodeling took place after supper which always makes a relaxing feeling.

7

Verena grilled 27 pounds of pork steak for supper, which means leftovers. We had cake and ice cream plus what everyone brought in made more than a table-full, which was casserole, salad, pies, brownies, cottage cheese, peas, and fruit salad.

SWISS CUSTARD PEACH PIE

6 fresh peaches or canned peaches, drained
1/2 cup sugar
2 eggs
1/4 teaspoon salt
2 tablespoons melted oleo
1/4 cup condensed milk

Place peaches in unbaked pie shell. Mix eggs with oleo, sugar, and salt. Beat a few minutes. Then add milk. Beat once more, pour mixture on peaches in shell. Bake for 15 minutes at 375. Reduce heat to 300 until custard is firm - about 40 minutes longer

NOVEMBER 1996

Today we washed clothes, and then I canned 78 quarts of grape juice. I want to can some more. With those long winter months ahead, a glass of grape juice with popcorn in the evening by the warm stove will taste good.

The girls and I assisted daughter Lovina on Tuesday in making the remainder of her garden. We cooked and canned the red beets and canned her hot peppers. Then Wednesday we assisted daughter Liz with her cleaning. Those were two enjoyable work days.

I must get to bed. Time goes on and the clock keeps on striking one hour after the other. It has been a long work day especially with Ben being on the sick list. He didn't work on his carpenter duties all week. But glad he is feeling better. Guess we just don't appreciate good health enough while we have it. Right? Good night.

It is now Saturday morning and I'm here alone, as Verena and Susan went to help son Albert's. Albert's is having a church service at their place tomorrow. So Ben decided he felt well enough to hitch up our Belgian team of horses to get the bench wagon where the church services were held on Sunday and take it to Albert's. The enclosed wagon holds the benches, song books, etc. The bench wagon goes from place to place. Jacob's (daughter Emma's husband) went to help his folks today as they are remodeling their kitchen.

There were so many readers who sent in the "coal flowers" recipe. A reader in Eaton, Ohio asked for it. There were different names to call it, "coal flowers", "depression plants," etc. I must say, I received 59 letters in three days from readers, mostly about the coal flower recipe. Which recipe should I use in this column?

This is now later on Saturday evening. I am ready for bed, but I will try and complete this letter. I was out in the garden all morning picking green beans, tomatoes, radishes, pickles and jerked out the red beets to can. My niece and husband have bought the trailer home from Joe and Lovina which sits here across the driveway from our house. They are now in the process of moving it. Joe and Lovina lived there before they moved into their present home a couple of miles from here. It just seems a short time ago that Joe's lived in it.

A miniature potted rose plant here on the porch has had two red roses on it for quite sometime now. The wind and rain never made them fall off. They still are a pretty red. We want to plant it in the ground before too long.

Following is the coal garden recipe, this one was sent in by Jane Abbott, a Cincinnati Post reader. This is a change of pace, not a food recipe, so don't try eating it!

DEPRESSION GARDEN

Six small stones or lumps of coal (no larger than an egg)
Place stones in the bottom of a shallow, glass bowl. Mix together:
6 liquid tablespoons of liquid bluing (not powder)
6 tablespoons of salt
1 tablespoon of household ammonia

Pour over the coal or stones. Do not cover. Keep solution at same level by feeding with equal parts water and ammonia. Pour down the sides of the bowl, not over the stones. A drop of food coloring on each stone will add color. The flowers will grow out of the bowl. This solution will damage furniture so watch closely.

DECEMBER 1996

Here is a diary for last Monday:

4 a.m. Ben and Jacob go out to do milking and do rest of barn chores. Emma, Susan, and I are getting breakfast, joining us is Emma and Jacob's baby, Elizabeth, who wants to be here in the kitchen with us. She attracts so much attention, being born just in September.

4:50 a.m. We're seated for breakfast and Jacob is leaving for his job, having ate a rushy breakfast as usual.

5:30 a.m. Verena leaves for the sewing factory and we're washing breakfast dishes.

6 a.m. Ben leaves for his job as a carpenter. Dishes have been done.

6:30 a.m. I put water over to do the laundry in wash house. It is so easy to have those two one-burner heaters which each have a 20 quart canner in them. So it doesn't take long to get that water hot for the washer. A neighbor man stopped in to see how Ben is. Ben was a sick man last week. Ben went back to work today, don't know if he can hold out all day.

8:30 a.m. All the laundry hangs out on the clothesline It is somewhat different to see those many pieces of baby clothing on the line once again. The girls are mopping the floors. The weather is so ideal. Vegetables were doing great in the garden until early November, it was a good feeling to share with others. Late lettuce is still so tender as I have some coming up yet.

Noon. We had dinner, and I wrote a little bit of this column. Baby Elizabeth is sleeping after her daily bath. It seems a person can spend so much time in the garden.

1 p.m. Daughter-in-law Sarah Irene (son Albert's) and children drive in with horse and buggy. She's on her way to school where their two children attend. Girls are taking laundry off the line and are folding it, to be put back in their place. It is always good to bring those fresh smelling clothes in from the line.

2:30 p.m. Daughter-in-law and children stopped in on the way home, but missed her sister who was also returning from school with her kids. They were going to meet here and ride their buggies back home together. So since Sarah wasn't in a rush, I told her to go get your laundry and we'll wash it here. She leaves the children at my place while she to her place to get her laundry. While she was away I quickly put the two canners of water on and by the time she came back with her clothes, the water was good and hot and we were ready to wash. Thought this would help her since she will be busy preparing for church services in her home this Sunday.

5 p.m. Verena and Susan come in from milking the cows and daughter-in-law and children are ready to leave for home. We hung some of her laundry on our clothesline and it seems to be drying well. Ben and Jacob also came home from work. They're glad the milking has been completed.

5:30 p.m. No supper was made as Ben and I got a "secret pal" anniversary card today saying that our supper will be catered in tonight and to our surprise here a lady from a local restaurant brought our supper which looked so delicious and made up so neat. It consisted of tenderloin sandwiches, each a bowl (for all of us) of so delicious looking salad, French dressing, French fries, lemonade and a cherry pie (good-tasting pie) and a container of ice-cream. So it makes us wonder who is our "secret pal." Thanks anyways whoever it may be. This made our day. Easy way - no supper dishes to wash tonight.

8 p.m. - 8:30 p.m. All in bed. Was a long, hard-working day. Son-in-law Joe was here after supper to get some more of their things they hadn't got since they moved from here. I will share a recipe. Good night and Happy Thanksgiving!

SPEEDY ROLLS

1/2 cup of sugar
2 packages of yeast
6 1/2 cups of flour
2 eggs
1/3 cup of shortening or butter
1 tablespoon of salt

2 cups of lukewarm water

Place water, sugar, salt, yeast, and 2 cups of flour in a bowl. Beat 2 minutes. Add eggs and shortening and beat 1 minute. Gradually add 4 1/2 cups of flour, stir until firm. Allow dough to set at least 20 minutes for easy handling.
Then roll out and spread with melted butter. Sprinkle with brown sugar and cinnamon. Roll up like a jelly roll and slice vertically. Put in greased pans and let rise. Bake at 375 for 25 to 30 minutes or until done.

DECEMBER 1996

Tuesday at 9 a.m. was the funeral of my aged, 90-year-old mother. She peacefully fell asleep on Saturday, November 2 at 9:25 a.m. It's been a blessing that she could leave this wide, wicked world. She had longed to be in God's care since father's death, but there's a purpose for it all.

There were 55 or 56 horse and buggies and 8 vans that went to the graveyard where dear mother was laid to rest. Father was laid to rest seven years ago in the same graveyard. Dear parents are gone, but not forgotten.

Mother left behind 7 living children, 80 grandchildren, and 302 great-grandchildren. She had her husband, a daughter, 5 grandchildren, and 7 great-grandchildren deceased.

Mother came from a family of 15 and has four sisters living. We were glad for the nice weather we had over the funeral. Meals were prepared in a shed and everyone ate out there. Everyone who attended the funeral were invited for lunch at noon, as that's the usually way. The funeral was largely attended. We'll miss her, but glad she won't have to survive the cold winter ahead.

Viewing was from Sunday evening until the time of services.

As if that wasn't all enough, my husband, Ben, has been under doctor's care. Hasn't been well the last couple of weeks, but was glad he was able to go all those days before the funeral .

Otherwise, this is a nice autumn day. Looks like the trees in our nearby woods lost their colorful leaves. The trailer home across our driveway, that Joe and Lovina lived in for a couple of years, is now on wheels and one of these days it'll be moving out of our driveway. Lots of memories when Joe and Lovina and the two daughters lived in it.

I share a recipe for this week, something quick?

MOTHER'S CHICKEN SALAD

8 cups diced chicken
8 eggs, hard-boiled and cut-fine
2 cups of salad dressing

4 cups diced celery
3/4 cup chopped olives
1 teaspoon salt

Toss ingredients together, except dressing. Add dressing after it is tossed. Chill and serve on a lettuce leaf.

DECEMBER 1996

$\mathfrak{B}$en and I have now been in our farm house 33 years. Three years ago this month, we had mother's family here for a reunion dinner We had our tool shed cleaned out so we could all eat out there. We had everything set up in it and of all things we had our first snow that day, a day which also turned colder. The women and small children went inside and enjoyed being in the house where it felt warmer. We had 279 present. There was a lot of sickness at the time, which meant some families couldn't attend. It was good in the evening to have the tool shed, house cleaned and back in order again. They are happy memories, glad we could have that reunion since mother passed away.

Let me answer some reader mail.

To the Queensbury, New York reader: Yes our daughters use electric irons, sewing machines, etc. while working away from home at the sewing factory.

To the Quincy, Illinois reader: I never made chicken and dumplings that you roll out the dough. I usually make apple dumplings. I roll out the dough, cut into pieces and put 1/2 peeled, cored apple in the middle and press the edges of the dough and bake.

To the Tipton, Indiana reader who requested a root beer recipe. Here's one: 2 cups sugar, 4 1/2 teaspoons root beer extract, 1/2 teaspoon yeast dissolved in warm water. Put into a gallon jar and fill with lukewarm water. Let stand in a warm place for 12 hours, then refrigerate. Don't turn the lid on too tight.

To the Albany, Indiana reader who requested my recipe for sandwich spread, here it is: 12 green tomatoes, 12 sweet peppers, 12 colored peppers, 2 large onions ground fine, 1 cup prepared mustard, 1/2 cup sugar, 1/3 cup salt, 1 tablespoon celery seed. Put tomatoes and the peppers through a food grinder. Boil all ingredients 15 minutes, take off heat and add 1 quart salad dressing. Keep on low heat so it doesn't burn. Pour into jars and seal.

To the Cincinnati, Ohio reader about how to cook tapioca. I usually like to soak the tapioca in cold water several hours before I cook it. Here is my recipe for tapioca

TAPIOCA

1 quart water   1 cup tapioca
3 ounce box Jell-O (strawberry, or whatever you prefer)
1 1/2 cups sugar

Cook tapioca and water for 10 minutes. Remove from stove. Add sugar and Jell-O. Stir well. Let it cool and set. If too thick, add water. Stir a few times while cooking, as tapioca will settle to the bottom. When cold, I add Cool Whip or any other topping will do. Add the amount of tapioca you desire. Good luck!

JANUARY 1997

𝕴t is such a lovely sunshiny Sunday afternoon and I thought I'd quick write for all you great readers out there.

We attended church services and then were invited to go back there for supper. We might give it a try, it depends on whether my husband feels like going as he lies passed out on our bed sleeping. Ha! Seems such a relaxing Sunday afternoon here at home. Quiet! A nap would seem good now on this Sunday afternoon, but I need to write to you great readers out there.

Last night was an enjoyable event. At the Eicher Benefit Auction several weeks ago we donated a breakfast for 12 and a Saturday evening barbecue chicken supper for 18. It was auctioned off to go to the Eicher fund. Being such a busy fall, we haven't gotten a chance to serve the supper yet. So Monday morning I sat down and wrote to my nephew and wife (who bid for the supper) to have it Saturday evening, and of all things we each got the same nation and had it both planned for Saturday evening. Remarkable! I thought it might be hard to barbecue chicken outside if the weather might be cold but how lucky the weather wasn't that cold. So we barbecued 72 pieces of chicken and 24 wieners on Saturday afternoon for that barbecue chicken supper. We were 38 in all to feast on it. Had plenty for all and leftovers.

This morning when I prepared breakfast, I realized: Oh, no! We forget to set out some salads for that supper last evening. There were full containers of potato salad and Waldorf salad which were on the menu, but we forgot to put out on the table. I don't believe that we forgot! But we did serve a lettuce salad.

I guess we were just overwhelmed to see all those people coming in. Ben's uncle who's 88-years of age were among the people who showed up. I was glad he was included. Guess I was so overtook that the two prepared salads weren't included. I was shocked when I saw them in the ice chest this morning. My husband must be counting how many times I have repeated: "How could I have forgotten?" But I guess so it goes in this busy, rushy life. Just a good lesson on me for the next time to see that all is out that
we have prepared. How many of you ever done this? What a feeling!

The evening was spent in singing and yodeling. Hey, this was such a relaxing and enjoyable evening. Was good to hear my two married nephews sing again. We just don't get together that often anymore. So this was an enjoyable event. So glad those two donated meals are over now. Was enjoyable, though.

Well I must sign off for now as everyone is ready to go back for supper where church services were held today. The weather being great and none of the married children coming home for supper the way it looks. We'll take advantage of the weather to go.

Tomorrow, son-in-law Jacob goes in to have his cast removed. Hopefully his heel is on the mend. With best regards we must be on our way. So will share a few recipes with you readers out there.

SMALL DONUT BALLS

2 cups flour
1/4 cup sugar
3 teaspoons of baking powder
1 teaspoon of salt
1 teaspoon nutmeg
3/4 cup milk
1 egg
1/4 cup vegetable oil

Mix sugar, eggs, and oil together. Add rest of ingredients and mix well. Drop by teaspoon in hot fat (275). Roll in sugar or glaze.

HOT ROLLS

1 package of dry yeast, dissolved in 1/2 cup warm water
1/2 cup sugar
2 eggs
1 1/2 cup water, warm
3 tablespoons of oil
2 teaspoons salt
6 cups flour

Stir 2 cups flour with the other ingredients. Slowly add the additional 4 cups. Rise in covered bowl. Punch down. Put in refrigerator or basement. Shape into rolls and place on baking sheet. Bake at 350 until brown.

JUNE 1997

𝕿oday was the Coblentz reunion with a good attendance. Lots of food! In the afternoon, the children of Ben's brother Melvin surprised their folks for their 30th anniversary. A table was decorated with a three tier cake, ice cream (mixed with 7-UP and pineapple sherbert), and candy. It sure was a great surprise on them. Balloons decorated the table. It looked neat! So we all got in on the cake and ice cream.

We had a severe thunderstorm with hail during the reunion dinner. Son Amos had their new, open two-seater buggy and they didn't bring a canvas to cover it with.. The whole buggy, blankets, bonnets, etc were all wet. The rest of the buggies were well-covered but with such a wind, we were thankful all the canvases covering the buggies stayed on. Some Amish communities have the top buggies (enclosed buggies), but in this area its an open buggy pulled by a horse. Usually at these hot summer gatherings, the day ends with a water battle, but we had plenty of rain so no one thought of it.

The garden looks wet again. Things are growing well, but some places in the area had so much hail that some of the gardens were ruined. Tomato plants broke, some vegetables were knocked to the ground. Corn fields were stripped. Some people around here used the hail in their yards to fill their ice chests which are used to keep food during the summer. Ice is usually bought at the ice house, but the hail saved some people the trip. I wonder how we ever did without ice chests years ago. When Ben and I were first married, Ben dug a hole in the ground beside the house and set half of a 50 gallon barrel in it. Then he made a lid to cover it. There's where we kept our food, as we had no basement. Now, however, we have a nice, cool basement and several ice chests which hold the ice and keep food fresh during the summer.

I will share some of the reunion recipes that we took.

HAMBURGER CASSEROLE

2 pounds of hamburger
1/2 teaspoon of black pepper
1/2 teaspoon of salt
16 ounce can of tomato sauce
1 cup of cooked rice

1/4 cup of chopped onion
3/4 cup of chopped green pepper
1 tablespoon of chili powder
2 cups of shredded cheese

Cook hamburger and drain excess grease. Mix cooked hamburger and the rest of the ingredients together in a large casserole dish, save one cup of cheese to spread on top. Bake at 350 for 20 minutes.

CRYBABY COOKIES

3/4 cup of shortening
1 cup of sugar
2 eggs, beaten
1 cup of light molasses`
4 cups of flour
3/4 cup of strong, cold coffee

1 teaspoon of salt
1 teaspoon of baking soda
2 teaspoons of cinnamon
2 teaspoons of ginger
1/2 teaspoon of cloves

Mix all together. Drop by teaspoon onto a greased cookie sheet. Bake at 350 for 10-15 minutes. Makes about 7 dozen.

AUGUST 1997

𝔑ice breezy morning after several hot days.

Paul Jr. seems to be a happy little boy after being at Riley's Children's Hospital in Indianapolis for another five days. A touch of pneumonia in one lung. Tomorrow, he's to have another check-up at Riley's. Just hope he can return home in the evening.

Our hearts still ache for our five-year-old granddaughter, Mary. But what could you wish her more than Heaven? Heaven is a good place to be, where there is no pain, no worry, only peace at heart. So why wish her back into this wicked world?

Gardens seem to be doing their duty. Frequent rains help the crops, hay, and gardens. Makes meal-planning easier.

We want to clean some more of the house where Jacob and Emma will be moving to on August 2. It has been packing and moving items over to their place. We'll miss them so much after being here with us since marriage, which was two years last June. Their baby, Elizabeth, is so cute. Such a sweet, tender age.

Emma is ironing, which is one huge stack of ironing. The girls are working at the sewing factory, Ben is at the dairy farm. The employees and families of the dairy farm were served a good meal, last Thursday evening with steak, wieners, and hamburgers on the grill. Lots of food, was very enjoyable.

This seems such a busy spring and summer. So different! It seems its go-go-go. But what more can you ask for than to be healthy?

Well, if we want to get more of Emma's new place cleaned up, I had best hurry and be with it.

Last night, we attended a "grocery shower" at Paul and Leah's. The people sure have been good to Paul's and us all. Thank you readers for all the cards and money, but most of all, for the encouraging letters. It has meant so much to me. I can't imagine receiving over 300 sympathy cards as of now. Encouraging letters and money was well-spent to pay someone to take us to and from Riley's Hospital which is two hours away. What helpful readers we have our there. Words can't express the appreciation.

AUGUST 1997

This is a lovely Thursday morning, with lots of memories of this month of August. Six years ago, I took up this task of writing a column. Life goes on. Right? Then, August 15, is when Ben and I had our first child, daughter Leah, 37 years ago. Seems impossible how these years take place. Anyone out there Leah's twin with an August 15 birthday? She now has her own family of five: three boys and two girls. Three of her children are now in school. Their oldest boy, Ben (named after Grandpa Coblentz), became a teenager in April. It will seem somewhat different on Ben being in school with older kids this year. It seems impossible it used to be my children were taught in school and now some of the teachers told me I have your grandchild in class this year. Where does that put us?

The weather has been dry and the garden goodies are longing for rain, and so are we. A good rain would do the duty.

The huge laundry is drying very well. I've been taking it off the clothesline as it dries as those birds can cause messes on them.

It is so good the windows and frames were cleaned and the curtains washed and ironed once again. It just keeps you busy to keep everything cleaned. I am glad for the help of my daughters.

Verena is now on a four-week leave from the sewing factory with her swollen heel. We really enjoy having her home with us. Home life is the best! She was also born in August - August 22, 1966. She has a niece and a nephew born on that date. The niece will be nine years old. Verena's foot seems to be mending quite well now.

The girls are busy outside cleaning and washing our wash house after mopping the floors in our home. I should get some dinner for the girls, as they have been hard at work. Meal-planning is so much easier with such a bountiful garden this year. Last night's meal out of the garden consisted of sweet corn, tomatoes, green beans, hot and sweet peppers, cucumbers fixed in salad, lettuce, and onions with sloppy Joe sandwiches, and potatoes (with jackets). That made a good meal. It won't be long until the garden of 1996 is history. Well, I best get dinner for my hard-working girls who are giving the shed a thorough cleaning.

Will share some recipes with you great readers out there. Thanks to all who sent me birthday cards last month - so many encouraging letters. It just keeps me up with this task of writing. Thanks for all of your time. How about a zucchini casserole recipe?

ZUCCHINI CASSEROLE

4 cups zucchini (cubed, peeled)
2 carrots (shredded)
1 can cream of chicken soup (low-fat, reduced sodium, undiluted)
1 (12 ounce) package of chicken stuffing mix
1/2 seasoning package in the stuffing mix
1 teaspoon vegetable oil
1 onion (cut-up fine)
1/2 cup low-fat cottage cheese

Lightly cook and drain zucchini. Mix stuffing and seasoning with oil. Mix together carrots, onion, zucchini, stuffing mixture, cottage cheese, and soup. Put in 9X12 casserole dish. Bake at 350 for 25-30 minutes or until it is heated thoroughly. Feeds eight people.

Try this one for raisin cookies.

RAISIN COOKIES

3/4 cup margarine
3 eggs
1 teaspoon baking soda

1 1/2 cups brown sugar
2 tablespoons molasses
2 1/2 cups flour (sifted)

1 cup raisins

Cream margarine with brown sugar. Add eggs, mixing well. Pour molasses into a separate bowl and stir in soda. Combine with first mixture. Add flour. Stir in raisins. Drop by teaspoon onto greased cookie sheet and bake 12 minutes at 350.

SUGAR COOKIES

1 cup margarine	1 cup brown sugar
1 cup white sugar	3 eggs
1 cup buttermilk	2 teaspoons vanilla
4 cups flour	3 teaspoons baking powder
1 teaspoon baking soda	1 teaspoon salt

Beat margarine, sugars, and eggs until creamy. Stir in the other ingredients and mix well. Drop by teaspoon or tablespoon onto a greased cookie sheet. Sprinkle with sugar or cinnamon and bake at 425 until golden.

AUGUST 1997

4 a.m. Ben and son-in-law Jacob go out to the barn to do the chores and daughter Emma and I prepare breakfast. Daughters Verena and Susan get ready to leave for the sewing factory.

4:45 a.m. We're all seated at the table to eat our first meal of the day, which consists of fried eggs and potatoes, bacon, toast, cheese, bananas, peaches, coffee and tea.

5 a.m. Son-in-law leaves for work.

5:10 a.m. Ben leaves for work at the dairy farm and the girls and I are washing breakfast dishes.

5:35 a.m. Girls are off to the sewing factory and I put water over to do laundry. Two 20 quart canners are filled with water on two one-burner kerosene heaters. The water gets hot in a hurry, it seems.

8 a.m. Laundry hangs out on the clothesline, the breeze is drying the laundry. The trash is being burned while the grass is wet. Putting trash on a brush pile that has to be burned in our little woods. Emma's baby, Elizabeth, wakes up and breakfast is prepared for her. She is such a sweet doll. I'm cleaning the five-burner kerosene stove of Jacob's. Is always so good to have a clean stove.

Noon: A quick lunch is prepared. Was in the garden picking up tomatoes, zucchini, pickles, green onions. Have green beans to can. The laundry brought in and folding and lots of ironing awaits.

3:45 p.m. The girls are home from work. The yard is being mowed and we're packing dishes as Jacob and Emma will be moving out soon. They recently bought a five-acre property. We'll really miss them, but they are only two miles away. Baby Elizabeth will be one-year old in September. She is so sweet to have around here. We'll really miss her and also the help of Jacob and daughter Emma. They were always willing workers around here, but we'll get adjusted., all of us, I reckon. It was two years in June they got their life sentence: marriage. Ha! Where did the time go? Busy life. Maybe too busy.

9 p.m. Tomorrow will be a busy day as we will continue to prepare for Jacob and Emma's move. Joe and Lovina and their two little girls were here this evening. Everyone is tired. It was a hard day of working Our wheat straw was baled today. More to bale tomorrow. I started to write this column at 3 a.m. this morning, as won't have time to write during the day tomorrow. Too much going on and this task has to keep in gear.

Try this recipe to use you fresh zucchini.

ZUCCHINI PATTIES

1 cup grated, fresh zucchini
1 egg
1 tablespoon chopped onion
1/2 teaspoon salt
2 tablespoons cracker crumbs

Mix all together. Drop by teaspoonful into greased frying pan. Let brown on both sides. Sprinkle tops with grated cheese. Makes 5 patties.

AUGUST 1997

Today, Wednesday, was Paul Jr.'s check-up day at Riley's Children's Hospital in Indianapolis, so Ben and I went with daughter Leah and family. It was so good to hear positive reports about him. He seems to be advancing in health. I just think back to the shape he was in. He seems so happy.

A "sunshine box" was taken to Paul and Leah's on Monday evening which was a day brightener for them. They miss little Mary, but she's at peace. The report shows that she died of diabetes. They will give more details later this week, I will share them when I get them. They didn't know Mary was diabetic.

We've been kept busy cleaning the house where Jacob and Emma will be moving. Packing is in full gear. The house will seem empty when they leave. The whole house of Jacob's has been given a thorough cleaning with washing off walls, ceilings, and windows. Makes a good smell now. Emma and Jacob have lived with us since they got married two years ago.

It was a rushy morning as at 8 a.m. a van driver picked us up to take us to Indianapolis for Paul Jr's check-up. Before we left, we did a huge amount of laundry. My brother Chris and his wife also went along with us to Indianapolis, it was nice to visit with them as we hardly see them. We used to be together a lot when both our children were young, but both having married children makes it different. We both have families of our own.

Well, I must get this written. Didn't get it finished the other evening. Too tired, I guess.

It is Sunday evening now, I have returned from church services. The services were largely attended at one of our friend's in another district. The churches are divided into sections. A good bunch was served at noon. People came to the services from Illinois, Michigan, LaGrange and Milroy, Indiana, and Ohio. Lots of visiting was done after lunch. It was such an enjoyable day.

I am looking for some of my children to come for supper tonight. Jacob and Emma just drove in. They moved on their property yesterday. Was a busy day of moving. The house feels empty without them. But they only live a couple of miles away. Their baby, Elizabeth, will be one-year-old next month. I missed her this morning as to feed her fried eggs and potatoes.

We have zucchini to prepare, how about a jam using the zucchini that is in season now?

ZUCCHINI JAM

6 cups peeled zucchini
5 cups sugar
1/2 cup lemon juice (Real Lemon brand)
1-20 ounce can crushed pineapple
6 ounces Jello (any flavor you want - apricot or orange works well)

Cook zucchini 20 minutes. Add next three ingredients and cook 10 more minutes. Take off of heat and add Jello.

A reader requested a cream cheese frosting recipe:

CREAM CHEESE FROSTING

3 ounce package cream cheese, softened
1/3 cup oleo, softened
1 tablespoon milk
1 teaspoon vanilla
2 cups powdered sugar

Beat first 4 ingredients until creamy. Stir powdered sugar until smooth.

𝕴 will try to write a quick column tonight.

Paul Jr. seems to be doing great thus far. He turned two years old on Friday, August 22. That is the same birthday as our daughter Verena, who turned 31. We also have son Albert's daughter Elizabeth's birthday on the same date. Verena planned a taco supper for all the family and some others on her birthday. So our shed was cleaned out and everything was held in there. Was good to all be in one big room together. Then with everyone bringing some food, the big table was well-filled.

On August 20, our sweet, loving granddaughter Mary (Paul Jr.'s sister) would've turned six years old. The final report of her death hasn't been fully announced. It must've been a sad time for the family when they spent some time at the grave of Mary on her birthday in the evening. Daughter Leah and children spent some of the day here as it seemed such a hard day on them to think of Mary's birthday. It at times seems like a dream, we had Paul and Leah's four children with us for 5 weeks and four days while Paul Jr. was in the hospital. Often, I think how their three oldest children went to school and Mary was here with me, my daughter Emma and her baby Elizabeth during the day. She must've been lonesome at times, but surely never showed it. She often took care of little Elizabeth.

She would often say to me: "Since I can't take care of Paul Jr., I can take care of Elizabeth", which she did. She was such a sweet little girl, I never had to scold her. So easy to care for her. Now that we think back she had such heavenly eyes. She was always such a little willing worker and took care of Paul Jr. while daughter Leah did her laundry. I often think back to when the undertaker brought Mary back home to be laid to rest. I put up her hair. It was so fluffy! The same hair I took care of for all those weeks. But I know God knew best for this Angel now in Heaven. How wonderful on her part!

Well I've got tomatoes , pickles, and hot peppers to can. Should pick them tomorrow. I am so glad for daughter Verena's help as she quit her job at the sewing factory after being there over 13 years. She says she wants to help me with the work here at home and get job only a couple of days a week. So it is a change in this household now that Jacob and Emma have moved out and Verena is here during the day. Verena is good help.

Thursday we want to attend a quilting at one of my nieces. She has a quilt in frame to donate at the benefit auction on Saturday, September 14 for Paul and Leah. She told me to bring my girls along, so hopefully we can all go and get some completed for my niece.

Well it is bed time, I need to hike off to bed where everyone else is resting peacefully.

Thank you to all those readers for the sympathy cards, encouraging letters, money, that has been sent to us. It has been so comforting to see all those readers with such encouraging letters. A hearty thank you to you all.

Here are some recipes

GRAPE JELL-O DESSERT

4 cups whipped topping
2/3 cup Jell-O dissolved in 2 cups hot water
1/4 cup powdered sugar
8 ounces of cream cheese
2 tablespoons sour cream

Beat together cream cheese, powdered sugar, and sour cream. Add whipped topping into cream cheese mixture. Add partly thickened Jell-O. When set, top with Jell-O. Any flavor of Jell-O can be used.

PIZZA BURGER

2 pounds hamburger, cooked and drained and cooled
1/2 medium-sized bottle of chili sauce
1/4 cup Parmesan cheese
1/2 teaspoon garlic powder
1 small package of Mozzarella cheese
1 small can tomato soup.

Mix all of the above with the hamburger. Form into patties and put on buns. Wrap in foil and bake for 25 minutes at 350. These may be frozen ahead and then heated. Bake longer if frozen.

SEPTEMBER 1997

Labor Day weekend is over with for 1997. This year on Labor Day, my sister and family had our Dad and Mom's reunion where they had lived till both went to rest in their Heavenly Home. Haven't heard of the count, so I know there were hundreds of them who attended. Had a beautiful day for it! A tent was set up for the occasion. Visiting, singing, and yodeling was done in the afternoon before everyone parted for their homes. A carry-in dinner was held at noon. Each family was to take like pies, some cakes, casseroles, fruit, relish plates, salads, and desserts. Our family was to take the fruit. Our family made seven different fruit dishes. So you can imagine how much food was on those tables. Such a variety! It was food, food, food and plenty of it
 all. It made a sad feeling to not see the parents around and then to think how deathly sick grandson Paul Jr. was, and he attended, yet healthy granddaughter, Mary, wasn't with us. She is in a much better place. God makes no mistakes. Guess we shouldn't question why.

Daughter Verena wasn't there either. She is enjoying a trip to the Smoky Mountains and various places of interest. She left Saturday morning with a van-load and will be gone eight days.

My parents had eight children (7 girls and 1 boy). All were present for the reunion except my oldest sister who died from a freak self-buggy accident on Sept. 12, 1973 and died on Sept. 18, 1973. Her husband also died sometime ago. So it must be quite a feeling for those children to see the rest of us there and not their parents. My sister at that time left 10 children behind, which a daughter was born the day after her accident, on Sept. 13, 1973.

Most of our married children left their horses and buggies at our house and walked over to the reunion. So towards evening they all returned back here and till it was done all our married children and families were here for supper.

A quick meal was planned for all 37 of us. Everyone but daughter, Verena. It is always good to prepare a meal for the family. Glad to see them come home even if it was a long day at the reunion. The evening before (Sunday) the dairy farmer that Ben works for had all his workers invited for a cook-out supper. So we got in on that. Had an enjoyable evening! It was really for a farewell for one of the workers. Homemade ice cream and cake was also being served.

Will share a recipe with you great readers out there.

ZUCCHINI CASSEROLE

4 cups sliced zucchini
2 cups boiling water
2 eggs
1 cup mayonnaise
1 onion, chopped
1/4 cup chopped green peppers
1 cup grated Parmesan cheese
salt and pepper to taste
1 tablespoon oleo
2 tablespoons buttered bread crumbs.

Cook zucchini in water till tender. Drain. In a large bowl, beat eggs. Stir in onion, mayonnaise, green pepper, cheese, salt, and pepper. Add zucchini. Pour into greased 1 1/2 quart baking dish. Dot with butter and sprinkle with bread crumbs. Bake in 350 oven for 30 minutes or until bubbly. Serves six.

SEPTEMBER 1997

The rush of the morning has come to a halt. Emma is sewing on the treadle sewing machine and Susan is out weeding in the garden. She had joined me after Emma and her had swept and mopped the floors. Lots has taken place since 4 a.m. today. Ben and son-in-law Jacob went out to do the milking which is done by hand; the rest of us getting breakfast and packing lunches for the menfolk. Son-in-law Jacob leaves for construction work at 4:50 a.m. We all get seated for breakfast before he leaves. After breakfast dishes are washed, Ben and daughter Verena leave for work around 5:30 a.m. Ben has been working for the same construction company since 1959, and Verena has been working over 12 years at the sewing factory.

Also this morning, the lamps and lanterns had to be taken care of. They need to be kept filled with kerosene and the wicks cleaned. It is not just like turning on a switch for light - same with the oil kerosene oil stoves. The burners and wicks need to be cleaned daily and every once in awhile the pipeline needs to be drained as to keep it clean. The list can go on and on with these daily household duties.

One of our highlights of this week was son Amos and wife Nancy Jean had an eight pound baby girl named Lovina - born on Monday, August 26. This makes them parents of six girls and they also have one boy. About two and a half years ago they had a set of twins named Arlene and Marlene. Their three oldest girls are in school now as they schools are in gear for another term. Ben and I now have 21 grandchildren. The girls taking the lead by 13. We can be so thankful that they are all healthy so far.

It is now seven years that my father has left for that Great Beyond. He died on a Saturday and the funeral was the following Tuesday. By the next Saturday his brother, Reuben, died unexpectedly and his funeral was also that following Tuesday. So we never know what the future holds. Life goes on. Right?

Will share some recipes. Want to can some hot peppers today So I had best hurry along. I'll can the hot peppers like my daughter Leah's recipe - it is a good recipe. She boils 3 cups vinegar, 3 cups water, 1 cup sugar, and 1/4 cup salt and pours over the hot peppers in jars and seals.

Awhile back some readers requested a recipe for salt-rising bread. This is a recipe for "salt-rising bread" sent to me by a reader in Lawrenceville, Illinois.

GRANDMA'S SALT RISING BREAD

3 medium potatoes
3 tablespoons corn meal
2 tablespoons sugar
4 cups boiling water
2 cups lukewarm milk
1 cup water
2 teaspoons salt
3 tablespoons melted shortening
7 cups of flour

Peel and grate potatoes. Add corn meal, sugar, salt, and boiling water. Cover and set in pan of hot water. Allow to stand (overnight) until sufficient fermentation to hear gas escape and can see bubbles. Add milk, water, salt, and shortening. Add flour to make stiff dough to knead. Knead till smooth and elastic. Form into three loaves and put into greased loaf pans. Cover and let rise until double. Knead about 10 minutes. Bake in 350 oven for 10 minutes, then at 300 for a total of 35 to 40 minutes.

This is recipe for salt-rising was sent to me from a reader in Addison, Michigan.

SALT RISING BREAD

1 cup scalded milk
1/2 cup coarse corn meal
3 cups milk
3/4 teaspoons salt
1 tablespoon sugar
5 tablespoons lard or butter
3 cups bread flour, sifted
2 1/2 cups all-purpose flour, sifted

Pour scalded milk over corn meal. Let stand in a warm place until bubbles rise to surface (about 2 1/2 hours) Then heat 3 cups of milk until lukewarm, then add salt, sugar, and shortening. Dissolve completely. Add corn meal mixture and set bowl in a dish of lukewarm water until bubbles rise throughout mixture. Work in sifted bread flour. When blended work in sifted all-purpose flour and knead until dough is very elastic. Divide into three parts and work into loaves. Place in greased pans and let rise until double in bulk. Bake for 15 minutes at 350. Increase baking temperature to 425 and bake an additional 25 minutes.

OCTOBER 1997

The largest benefit auction ever in these parts was held on Saturday, September 13 for Paul and Leah (my daughter) Shelter's two-year-old child, Paul Jr. The auction was to help pay hospital and medical bills resulting from Paul's heart surgeries over the summer.

Just the baked and canned goods brought in over $4000. Paul Neuenschwander of Berne, Indiana and 12 other area auctioneers donated their time. A hearty thank you to all!

It started at 9 a.m. in the morning and sold all day till after 5:30 p.m., with two rings going on. Neuenschwander said this was the largest benefit auction he remembers ever held in the area. The number of items for sale totaled 980 with 266 buy numbers given out. Some of the high-priced items sold included a $900 hand-made quilt and a $1300 grandfather clock. Even two candy suckers were auctioned off at $75. A 24 can case of Pepsi sold for $50.

A wide variety of items being donated from livestock to homemade quilts were auctioned off. Those attending the auction were not asked to pay a specific amount for their meal, but to donate whatever amount of money they chose. This helped raise more than $9000. There was 800 pounds of barbecued chicken. The soups consisted of chicken-noodle, vegetable, and pot pies. Cole slaw, macaroni salad, and lettuce salad were also served along with ham sandwiches, hot dogs, pickles, catsup, mustard, and sliced tomatoes. There was also a root beer float stand and a lemonade stand. Coffee, pop, chips, and popcorn were also served. Plenty of food everywhere!

Neuenschwander, a well-known auctioneer in the area, has conducted 15 benefit auctions for the Amish in his 52 years as an auctioneer, with this auction being the biggest in terms of profit. He has been inducted into the Reppert Auction Hall of Fame in Indiana. He graduated from Reppert Auctioneering School in 1945.

One of the unique aspects of Phil's auctioneering skills is that he can conduct auctions in both English and Swiss, which is the language of many of the Amish around here. So both Amish and non-Amish were able to participate in this auction. He did a wonderful job to take on this benefit auction for Paul and Leah's family.

It was so good to meet some of my readers of various places and to think one reader even brought a gift for me. Greatly appreciated. The auction day was so beautiful, couldn't have been nicer. And to top it all off, Paul Jr. seems to be doing better and better. Thanks to God!

It was an early start for a lot of us in the morning of the auction. Baking was done all day Friday and sending help to get ready for the auction. A lot of time was spent filling cups with Jell-O (17 boxes). Then Saturday morning was spent making spaghetti and meatballs (20 quart and 16 quart cookers) and making a big batch of potato salad really put us on the run and the day had just begun.

So the food consisted of soups, crackers, salads, sandwiches, barbecued chicken, sliced tomatoes, home-baked bread buns, a variety of chips, Jell-O, ice cream, popcorn, coffee, pop, pickles catsup, mustard, butter, apple butter, cake, and the beverage stands. Most all was donated, except for some items from the lunch-stand.
One item sold for donation was our one-horse mower, which sold for $500. We had a horse which pulled it so well and every Friday or Saturday I would mow our yard with it. It could get in close corners. That was around 25 years ago. I well remember when I was mowing the yard, daughter Leah was baking a birthday cake for my 36th birthday as to surprise me. Good old days are not forgotten. Leah was 12-years-old at the time, being 13 the next Monday. She was so happy to surprise me with a cake. Good old memories.

This is what I made for spaghetti and meat sauce for the benefit auction:

25 lbs. hamburger
9 gal. tomato juice
6 lbs. uncooked spaghetti
4 32-oz. jars spaghetti sauce
salt and pepper to taste

Divide the 25 pounds of hamburger in two 20-quart cookers*, cook until meat is no longer pink, and then drain. Divide 4 1/2 gallons tomato juice between the two cookers of meat, and let come to a boil. Next, add the 6 lbs. of spaghetti to the boiling sauce.

After the meat sauce again reaches a boil, let it cook for about 10 minutes, until spaghetti is tender. Divide remaining 4 1/2 gallons tomato juice between the two cookers. Finally, pour two jars of spaghetti sauce into each cooker. Sample meat sauce, adding salt and pepper to taste. Allow meat sauce to simmer for at least 20 minutes, until flavors have had time to blend.

Note: You may also use one 16-quart and one 18-quart cooker if you don't have two 20-quart cookers.

OCTOBER 1997

To the Ft. Wayne, Indiana reader who wants the recipe of green tomato pie: 6 green tomatoes, sliced; 1 apple, thinly sliced; 1 cup sugar, 3/4 tsp. cinnamon, 1/4 tsp. cloves, 1 tsp. butter, 1 tbsp. of tapioca, and 1 tbsp. of lemon juice. Arrange half of the fruit in the pie crust. In a separate bowl, mix ingredients, then sprinkle over the fruit in pie crust. Add the rest of the fruit. Put top of the pie crust on and dot with lemon juice. Makes 1 pie. Bake at 400 for 35 minutes.

To the Bridgman, Michigan reader who wants an oatmeal cookie recipe: one cup brown sugar, one cup white sugar, 1 cup lard, 2 eggs, 3 cups oatmeal, 2 cups sifted flour, 1/2 tsp. salt, 1 tsp. baking soda, 1 tsp. vanilla. Cream sugars thoroughly with lard until fluffy and no granules remain. Beat in the eggs until light. Stir in oatmeal. In a separate bowl, sift the measured flour with salt, soda and baking powder. Work into the oatmeal mixture. Mix in vanilla. Drop by teaspoon onto a cookie sheet. Bake at 350 for 10-12 minutes.

To the Richmond, Kansas reader who wants the recipe of a green tomato relish: 1 peck (8 quarts) green tomatoes and six red peppers. Put through grinder and let lay in mild salt brine for 3 hours. Drain and add: 1 tsp. cloves, 1 tsp. cinnamon, 1 tsp. ground allspice, 1 tsp. turmeric, 1/2 tsp. nutmeg, 1 ounce mustard seed, 6 cups white sugar, and 1 pint vinegar. Let this simmer until poached. Put in jars and seal.

Would any of you readers share a recipe of pineapple bread pudding? A reader from New York would like a recipe of it. Sorry, I never heard of it.

We had our first 30 degree autumn weather on October 15. We covered some of the garden last night with tarps and blankets. Maybe not enough. Well, we'll take a look at it when it warms up. I picked some garden goodies last night. Hopefully, the weeds helped the vegetables to survive. Yes, weeds, plenty of them. Many days of sweating was put into the garden.

Yesterday, my daughters and I went to spend the day with daughter Liz as she was having a former classmate, her daughter, and her mother there for dinner. Her former classmate now lives in Utah and her mother in Kokomo, Indiana. It is so interesting to hear how she located her birth mother. She was so glad to have her mother with her. Now having a baby daughter of her own, life seems so much more enjoyable to her.

We went to daughter Liz's at 9 a.m. I said: "Why not clean windows and wash your curtains," beings that the weather was so nice. So a laundry was quickly done, dried, ironed and hung back up again. Also, the kitchen walls were washed off and rooms were swept. Everything was completed by the time the guests arrived. A good noon meal was prepared and served to all. The afternoon was spent in washing dishes, visiting, singing, and yodeling.

Daughter Verena and Susan joined us after getting off work and we then all ventured to our homes. It was good to have all our six girls together, which seemed a work day together and also being with Liz's classmate and daughter and her mother for a noon meal.

Joe's and Jacob's are having supper with us tonight. Ben and my 40th wedding anniversary will appear on the calendar on October 17. Anyone out there on October 17 for 40 years?

Sunday was such a beautiful autumn day with several of the married children and families here to spend Sunday. In the evening, till it was done, all our married children and families were here for supper except one daughter and family. Folding tables and benches were set up outside for both noon and evening meals. How enjoyable to see the children and families come home.

Grandson Paul Jr. seems to be gaining strength every week. Remarkable, as all the surgery he had gone through. We so miss little Mary, not being with the family. But God makes no mistakes, and guess we shouldn't question why. She was such a sweet, helpful little girl. So easy to handle. Her sweet ways are a good remembrance.

NOVEMBER 1997

Our first killing frost came on October 23. Temperature at 28. Last night we gathered tomatoes, peppers, and more goodies. We covered some vegetables with blankets. Looks like all our crops are harvested for `97.

We attended a wedding today, where I was a cook. It was held in a nice, clean shed where the cooks prepared dinner and supper. The wedding tables were set up so that over 100 people could be seated at one time. It was largely attended. It was nice touch for the young mothers to be able to stay in the house and care for their kids. The food was set out for them also. The weather stayed ideal for the day. Well, I had best hike off to bed. It has been a long day, although enjoyable. Good night!

It is now another day. Ben and the girls are at work and I did the laundry only to see and feel some sprinkles. Some of the clothes had already dried, but some were almost dry, so I brought them in to the clothes dryer in the house (non-electric). Ha! The clothes were put by the warm stove.

Winter days will arrive soon: rainy, snowy, and cold. I dread these nasty days, but that's life. Good we can't judge the weather. We'd never be satisfied. Right?

The stove is in gear again for the cold weather season. So this means more work in another way: wood to carry in and ash-pans to be emptied when full. But without heat in the house it would be uncomfortable.

Looks like an all day rain now. Autumn weather. Leaves are falling fast from the trees.

Here are some recipes in case you'd like to use up those apples:

SKILLET APPLES

Fill a skillet with peeled and cored apples. Meanwhile, in a separate bowl, mix 1/2 cup sugar with 1 tablespoon flour. Sprinkle over apples. Add 1/2 cup water. Cover and simmer until done. Remove from heat and add 2 teaspoons margarine and 1 teaspoon vanilla to the apples and stir. You can add a dash of cinnamon. Serve warm or cold.

APPLE CAKE

4 cups sliced and diced apples (any kind)   2 eggs
2 teaspoons cinnamon   2 teaspoons soda
pinch of salt   1/2 cup vegetable oil
2 cups flour   1 teaspoon vanilla
2 cups brown sugar

Put apples in a bowl, add eggs and stir well. Then stir in vanilla, salt, soda, and cinnamon. Then stir in sugar. Finally, stir in the flour. Pour the mixture into any small or medium-sized, lightly greased loaf pan. Bake at 350 until golden brown and toothpick inserted in center comes out clean (about 45 minutes).

NOVEMBER 1997

Our 40th wedding anniversary is now history for 1997. Ben and I celebrated our special day, October 17.

Lots of memories of all those by-gone years. There were happy times, and, also, sad times. We are blessed with 8 children (two sons and six daughters). We had 23 grandchildren, now 22, since the death of granddaughter Mary, who is in such a better place.

All our family (a total of 38) went out for supper for our anniversary on Friday evening at a place called The East of Chicago Pizza Company, which was planned by the children. Also for our anniversary, daughter Leah had sewed eight pockets on a dishcloth and all eight children were to fill the pockets with money, we received a nice sum. She presented it to us while eating. The owner of the pizza place also gave us a fruit pizza for our 40th anniversary. The evening was what you would call an enjoyable and relaxing one.

Yes, 40 years ago - as I have written about before - was a time when Asian flu struck our area. It was a severe epidemic! My temperature went up to 105 degrees a week before our wedding. All our family came down with the flu except Ben, my Dad, and sister. There were so many sick in the area at the time. Mother was still sick the Tuesday before our Thursday wedding. But an Amish lady came by with a home-remedy called "tobacco salve" to rub into mother's chest. It took hold right away and she immediately recovered. I often wonder how the salve was made. You had to watch to not get the salve in the stomach area, only the chest.

Daughter Leah, and her husband, Paul, had all our family invited for the following Sunday evening (October 19) for a barbecue supper, which every one of the family attended. So we all got together on Friday and Sunday evening. Paul Jr. seems to be really improving from open-heart surgery. He was two years old on August 22.

We had a light frost last night. Time of year to expect a killing frost. We still have vegetables and flowers to be taken from the garden. We made 24 jars of sauerkraut, a double batch of hot pepper butter, and sandwich spread the other day. Have more cabbage to make more sauerkraut.

A reader misplaced the recipe for hot pepper butter, so here it is again:

HOT PEPPER BUTTER

42 hot peppers
2 c. prepared yellow mustard
1 qt. vinegar
6 c. sugar
1 Tbsp. salt
1 c. flour
1 1/2 c. water

Grind hot peppers. Place in a large cooker and add mustard, vinegar, sugar, and salt. Placing over medium heat, bring pepper mixture to a boil, lowering heat while you do the next step.

Combine flour and water to make a paste, and add to pepper mixture. Bring all to a boil once more and cook for five minutes, stirring occasionally. Pour into sterilized pint-sized jars and seal. Makes 7 pints. Great on sandwiches!

Now try this recipe for a different type of brownie!

ZUCCHINI BROWNIES

4 eggs
2 c. sugar
2 tsp. baking soda
1 tsp. salt
1 tsp. Vanilla
1 c. chopped nuts, walnuts or pecans

1 1/2 c. oil
2 c. flour
2 tsp. cinnamon
4 Tbsp. cocoa
3 c. shredded zucchini

Preheat oven to 350 degrees. Combine eggs, oil and sugar. In a separate bowl, sift together flour, soda, cinnamon, salt and cocoa. Slowly add flour mixture to sugar mixture. Finally, add vanilla, zucchini and nuts to batter. After mixing thoroughly, spread onto a 15 by 10-inch jelly roll pan. Bake in preheated oven for 30 minutes, or until center is set. Cooled brownies may be frosted, if desired.

NOVEMBER 1997

The calendar has turned into November. What is our first thought when we think of November: Thanksgiving Day. Right?

The highlight of our family this week was the birth of a baby daughter to my daughter Liz and her husband, Levi. Rosa A. was born Thursday, October 30 at 7:48 p.m. weighing 7 pounds, length: 19 1/2 inches. She welcomes a sister, Elizabeth and brother, Levi.
Daughter Verena has been doing the housework duties until Liz recuperates for several days now, in addition to her regular job. I took care of the duties on Friday.

It is a year now that mother has left us for that Great Beyond. God makes no mistakes. My sister had a quilting bee on Wednesday and Thursday where (my folks had lived in a portion of my sister's home in their later years) and what a sad feeling not to see how it used to be in the other part of the house where mother lived. But, I guess, life goes on.

So much going on this week, it seems. Our family got together at son Amos's house on Sunday evening for his birthday. We had a barbecued chicken supper for the occasion. Little Rosa was born on Amos's birthday.

Adding to our busy schedule, daughter Lovina had a Tupperware party on Wednesday evening.

And then Thursday we were helping daughter Emma prepare for church services which is to be held in their home Sunday. Also canned her red beets for her as red beets and pickles are always on the menu where church services are to be held. Lots of cleaning at such a time. One way the house and everything gets a thorough cleaning.

It is good to take the church services in our home, but always glad when it is over again, as next day seems like a clean-up day.

Now, I will answer some reader mail.

Thank you readers for sharing the pineapple bread pudding recipe for the New York reader who requested it. Thanks for your time and bother. I hope this is what you were looking for. This one comes from a reader in Hudson Falls, New York:

PINEAPPLE BREAD PUDDING

6 slices of bread, cubed
1/2 c. margarine, melted
1 c. sugar
1/2 c. flour

20 oz. can crushed pineapple, undrained
3 eggs, lightly beaten

Preheat oven to 350 degrees. In a mixing bowl, stir together bread, margarine, sugar, flour and crushed pineapple. Add eggs. Pour into a greased 2-qt. casserole and bake in preheated oven for 1 hour, or until knife inserted in center comes out clean.

HONEY BREAD PUDDING WITH PINEAPPLE

1 c. crushed pineapple
2 c. soft bread crumbs
2 c. milk, scalded
1/2 tsp. salt
2 eggs, beaten
1/3 c. honey
1 Tbsp. fresh lemon juice

Preheat oven to 325 degrees. Drain pineapple, reserving juice. Add just enough water or fruit juice to the pineapple juice to make 1/4 cup. Place the 1/4 cup juice in a large mixing bowl and add pineapple, bread crumbs, milk, salt, beaten eggs, honey, and lemon juice. Mix well. Pour into a greased 2-quart baking dish and bake in preheated oven for about 40-45 minutes, or until knife inserted in center comes out clean.

To the Bridgeport, Illinois reader who wants a butterscotch pudding for pie.

BUTTERSCOTCH PUDDING PIE

3 cups brown sugar
3 tablespoons margarine
10 tablespoons cream

Cream together and boil the following for five minutes and add to first mixture: 4 cups of milk, 4 tablespoons of flour, 3 beaten eggs, and 2 tablespoons cornstarch. Stir all over heat and cook until thickened. Put into cooked pie shells. It fills three crusts.

A reader asked about gooseberry pie: we used to grow them in our garden and mother would process them with mulberries. I, however, have never made a pie with them.

To the Bradenton, Florida reader who asked for my coconut cream pie recipe:

2 eggs
1/2 cup sugar
1/2 cup margarine
1/2 cup milk
1 cup coconut
1/4 cup flour

One unbaked pie shell

In a bowl, beat eggs and stir sugar in till lemon-colored. Add rest of ingredients. Mix until smooth. Pour into an unbaked pie shell. Bake 45-50 minutes at 350.

To the Niles, Michigan reader: if you can't have cheese in your diet, just omit the cheese from my zucchini casserole recipe.

A South Bend, Indiana reader wants a recipe for a hot sandwich called "hot brown." I have never heard of such a sandwich. How about you readers?

To the Bradenton, Florida and South Bend reader about dressing (stuffing). I really don't have a set recipe for dressing. I will share, however, the method that I use to make it, it isn't really a recipe, I just do it by feel. You can take a loaf of bread (cubed), 1 cup of celery, diced; 1/2 cup onions, chopped; 1 cup chicken broth or couple tablespoons chicken soup base and add 3 eggs to it. Stir and moisten well with the water from cooked potatoes. Add salt and pepper to your taste. Sometimes I add 1/4 cup diced carrots. For the color I usually fry this in a skillet. Don't bother to put in oven. Use margarine to fry it. Good luck!

DECEMBER 1997

Some readers ask what a typical day for us is like. Here is a diary of a recent, rainy Monday.

4 a.m. Time to start off the day. Ben heads for the barn to do the chores. We start breakfast and pack lunch for Ben for his noon meal at the dairy farm.

4:45 a.m. Seated at the table to eat breakfast of fried eggs and potatoes, bacon, toast, cheese, rhubarb jam, margarine, bananas, and naturally, coffee and tea. Some take coffee, others like their morning tea.

5:10 a.m. We're starting to wash dishes and my husband is ready to go to work. Floors are being swept and the beds being made.

5:15 a.m. My husband is on his way to the dairy farm with a van. Son Amos is in the van already with one who works at the same place and hauls them to and from. Son Albert gets on next. So I like to once in a while prepare a huge sandwich which I consider a breakfast sandwich. Ha! They usually enjoy the huge sandwich. Mother, naturally, enjoys giving them a treat - they used to be my little boys, but now they are all grown-up and have families of their own. My husband seems to take working at the dairy farm well, healthwise. Last winter he was laid-up a lot with illness.

6 a.m. Daughter Verena is doing the huge ironing which didn't get done last week. Having such a busy week it just patiently waited for it to be ironed. It just waited. It never runs off. I'm starting to make a batch of sandwich spread as I have plenty of sweet peppers and green

tomatoes leftover from the garden - why let them go to waste? It is always good to fill those jars for later use. It's one spread to serve when church services are held in our home.

Noon. Daughters and I are seated to eat lunch. The ironing is completed. What a relief. I got 13 points of sandwich spread made. Glad they all sealed. Daughter Susan grinded the sweet peppers, tomatoes, and onions. So the job was soon completed. The laundry is hanging on the clothesline out in the rainy-like weather. I dread these laundry days like this, but good thing we can't judge the weather so we should be thankful. Right?

5 p.m. Verena goes out to do the barn chores. We were started to clean the cellar this afternoon. The cellar is where we keep those many well-filled jars. The jars look clear once more. We got the laundry in. Most of it wet! Out comes those winter-clothes racks set up by the warm stoves. Ugh! Winter is on its way. So we can expect any kind of weather this time of year.

7:30 p.m. The day's work has ended after having the evening meal and dishes washed and ready for bed. Still rearranging the laundry on the clothes racks as it dries.

8:30 - 9:30 p.m. Ben sits in his rocker and reads. Some of the grandchildren who are over visiting sing songs. Myself and my daughters relax for the evening. I will share some recipes with you great readers.

NO-COOK PEANUT BUTTER FUDGE

1/3 cup margarine, softened
1/2 cup Karo
3/4 cup peanut butter
1/2 tsp. salt
1/2 tsp. vanilla
4 1/2 cups powdered sugar

Blend margarine, Karo, peanut butter, salt and vanilla in a large bowl. Gradually stir in 4 1/2 cups powdered sugar. Knead until well-blended. Roll out on surface that you've lightly dusted with powdered sugar and cut into small pieces.

GRAHAM CRACKER COOKIES

24 graham crackers
1 cup margarine
1 cup brown sugar
1 cup chopped nuts, walnuts or pecans

Preheat oven to 350 degrees. Arrange graham crackers in a single layer on a cookie sheet. Place margarine and brown sugar in a saucepan. Boil for 2 minutes, stirring constantly. Add nuts. Pour hot caramel mixture over crackers. and bake in preheated oven for 10 minutes. Cool before breaking apart into cookie-sized pieces.
DECEMBER 1997

We had an enjoyable Saturday evening meal at a local restaurant. My sister at the benefit auction for Paul's (daughter Leah) gave a supper for 12 people to be bid off to help raise money for Paul Jr's hospital bills. So daughter Verena bid it off at the auction. It was good food!

We were assisting Jacob's (daughter Emma) lately in getting ready for church services to be held in their home. So it was held yesterday in their home. Daughter Verena is over there this morning helping her clean up and get her house back in order. Daughter Leah and Paul were not able to attend as Paul Jr. wasn't feeling his best. They are still giving him daily "mist treatments" prescribed by the doctor. It seems to loosen up his cold. Just hope winter won't be too hard on him. Otherwise, he seems to
be doing great.

It was 15 degrees this morning and snow-covered ground. Our coldest for the season. Looks like a nice winter scene, but cold to hang laundry!

I should get the rest of the garden goodies in anyways if they aren't frozen. Those pumpkins are waiting to be cut-up and cooked and put into jars. Such a busy time, it always seems. But do we appreciate good health enough?

Well, this is all for now. I hope you readers are healthy and happy

DECEMBER 1997

On Wednesday, December 10, another little one joined our family. My daughter Lovina Eicher (husband Joe) became the proud parents of a daughter named Verena J. at 6:32 a.m, weighing 7 pounds, 1 ounce. She joins two sisters, Elizabeth, 3; and Susan, one. This put a great smile on my daughter Verena to hear it was named after her. We're helping with the household duties at present. Verena has been there mostly, in addition to working at her regular job.

Brrrr. It is cold this morning with temperatures of 23 degrees. Ben is at the dairy farm, Verena is at Joe and Lovina's, and Susan is washing off the kitchen wells. It needed a thorough cleaning before the holidays arrive.

Our family gathers during the holidays each year, all our children, and their children come for a day of visiting. This year it will be on Jan. 1. So I will have more to say about our holiday preparations and plans in a later column.
A reader from South Bend, Indiana recently wrote asking about a sandwich called "Hot Brown." Our local banker's wife saw the column where I mentioned the hot brown request earlier, and she was nice enough to send me this. Hopefully it is what you are looking for.

She wrote that her uncle (by marriage) was William Brown and his family owned the Brown Hotel in Louisville, Kentucky where this sandwich is famous. On a piece of toast, place a slice of roast turkey or ham. If desired, place a slice of tomato or a little mayonnaise. Cover the sandwich with a rich cheese white sauce. You can also place the tomato on top of the white sauce. Top the whole thing with two slices of crisp bacon.

Are you readers out there in the holiday spirit of shopping, baking, and candy-making? So much took place this year for us, but much to be thankful for. Do we appreciate it enough. God makes no mistakes.

Will share some holiday recipes, although I am not in the mood to write. What will 1998 have in store for us? Only our Heavenly Father knows. Right?

Wishing all of you a Merry Christmas and a Happy New Year in 1998!

PARTY MIX

2 1/2 cups Cheerios
2 1/2 cups Corn Chex
1/2 package of pretzel sticks
3/4 cup salad oil
a little garlic salt

2 1/2 cups Rice Chex
2 1/2 cups of Wheat Chex
1 teaspoon onion salt
1 teaspoon celery salt
2 tablespoons Worcestershire sauce.

Mix cereals, pretzels, and nuts in big bowl. Add spices and sauces. Pour salad oil over mixture. Heat oven to 250. Put on cookie sheet and bake until good and hot.

BABY RUTH BARS

1 cup Karo
1 cup brown sugar
1 cup chunky peanut butter
2 cups Rice Krispies
2 cups Corn Flakes
melted semi-sweet or milk chocolate (what you prefer)

Bring to a boil Karo, sugar, and chunky peanut butter. Add Rice Krispies and Corn Flakes. Drop with tablespoon on waxed paper. Cool. Form into logs. Dip into melted chocolate.

1998

This was a more tranquil year for the United States and the world than preceding years. Although the residents of Central America, who were battered by Hurricane Mitch during the summer, might disagree. By the time Mitch finished its week-long rampage, 10,000 people, primarily in Honduras, lay dead, with 100,000 homeless.

While storms raged in the tropics, a political storm was brewing in Washington D.C., with the emergence of Monica Lewinsky. It was revealed that President Clinton had an affair with the young intern, beginning only the third time in United States history that impeachment proceedings have occurred against a sitting President.

The Coblentzes also enjoyed a more quiet year. Elizabeth's husband Ben turned 67-years-old in February, and more grandchildren populated the Coblentz household. Emma was born in March to Jacob and Emma, joining her sister, Elizabeth. The summer garden was bountiful and the autumn brought lots of canning duties. In November, Elizabeth made her first public appearance, greeting readers at a Women's Conference in Indiana.

JANUARY 1998

$\mathfrak{B}$eing such a beautiful week, we took advantage to clean all the windows today. Daughters Emma and Susan cleaned all the windows, taking the screens out and putting in the storm windows. What a relief to have that done.

Daughter Verena is still at Lovina's taking care of household duties. Lovina just had a new baby, named Verena. Little Verena joins two sisters, Elizabeth and Susan. They really love their new sister.

My daughter Liz also had a baby recetly, Rosa. Rosa seems to be doing good thus far.

Both new babies are such cute dolls, naturally Grandma would say that.
After a hard day's work today some friends of ours drove in from a distance and brought three big pizzas to eat here as a Christmas visit. The pizzas were so good.

I must get this written today and on its way. Ben is at the dairy farm and the girls at the motel where they work cleaning rooms. Often Amish women will take cleaning jobs at houses or hotels. I need to get things accomplished around here. So much to do. Verena, Susan, and I helped daughter Leah yesterday in getting ready for their church services, which will be held in their home Sunday. Paul Jr. seems to be doing well, but they have to watch out that he doesn't catch a cold during these winter months.

I had to admire our Christmas cactus. The plant is sitting here in our living room and starting to bloom - dozens of blooms. I never seen it bloom as it is now. I've had this Christmas cactus for years, and I have only seen it bloom several times, and then it only had a couple blooms at a time. The buds would sometimes fall off before they would bloom.

Yesterday, while I was at Paul's our daughters, Verena and Susan, went to a local Amish store to do some shopping. While on their way, some people stopped them asking directions how to get to our place. It took them a second to realize who it was. It was our Amish niece, husband, and family from Wisconsin. Verena and Susan directed them to where I was at Paul's. So we all visited awhile at Paul's. They were on their way farther south to his family gathering. Was good to see them.

I will share some recipes for some delicious dishes we have had around our house lately:

LONG JOHN ROLLS

2 packages of dry yeast
2 eggs
1 cup of lukewarm water
1/2 teaspoon of salt
1 cup of lukewarm milk
1/8 teaspoon of nutmeg
1/2 cup of margarine

6 or 7 cups of flour
2/3 cup of sugar

Dissolve yeast into lukewarm water. Scald milk and let stand to cool, then blend together margarine, sugar, and well-beaten eggs. Put in nutmeg. Put the milk in the yeast and water and add 3 cups of flour (until it is easy to handle).
Put in warm place; let rise till double. Roll out and cut into oblong pieces. Let rise again. Fry in deep fat. Frosting may be added if desired. Makes 3 dozen.

BACON AND EGG BAKE

6 slices of bacon	3 hard boiled eggs, diced
1/2 medium onion	2 cups of shredded cheese
salt and pepper	1/4 cup of milk
1 can of cream of mushroom soup	

Heat oven to 350. Fry bacon until crisp. Remove from skillet, drain fat, reserving 2 tablespoons. Fry onions in the tablespoons of fat. Stir in soup, milk, cheese, eggs, and seasonings. Pour into baking dish, top with crumbled bac
on. Bake 20 minutes. Serve over biscuits. Serves 5.

JANUARY 1998

As we take another step into the unknown future of "98", what has our Heavenly Father in store for all of us? Only God knows. So many happenings took place in "97" which were sad ones on our part. God makes no mistakes. Only "He" knows the purpose of it all.

We had our family Christmas gathering on New Year's Day of '98. They all were here for breakfast which our count to 40 people now. We sure did miss our grandchild, Mary not being with the family. Paul Jr. was happy and lively to be with us this year as sick as he was and then God took Mary in "His" care. A healthy, sweet little girl. Death is so final.

We all seated to all eat together for breakfast which everyone enjoys spending the morning together. Gifts were exchanged, that's when the grandchildren are ready to open their gifts. It sounds a hustle and bustle. Everyone is excited! Dinner is served with everyone seated at the table. Stuffed turkey and ham was on the menu, plus a lot of leftovers after dinner. The afternoon was spent with a variety of goodies with ham sandwiches also. It's always good to have them all together, but they all look forward to mother's breakfast. Ha!

Paul's have church services tomorrow, Sunday, and we will have them here on January 11. Son-in-laws Joe and Jacob's are here this Saturday to help clean manure out of the barn. What a relief to Ben to have help to get everything clean to hold church services.

Also, daughter Emma is here today, so we're doing some preparing for next Sunday. Lots of preparation takes place for church. Paul's were to have church services at their place last Sunday, but due to the death of my uncle, it was postponed for this Sunday.

Verena and Emma are preparing pizza for dinner tonight, plus soup and I reckon leftovers from our New Year's feast. Daughter Lovina didn't come today as she was here yesterday and helped clean up from New Year's Day. Daughters Verena and Susan had to go on their job of cleaning.

Paul's took us along on Christmas Day to reveal their "secret pal" of 1997, which was his folks (two hour drive). They were so surprised to see us come. Had enjoyable day. We also have a secret pail for 1997, but they have not revealed themselves to us yet. We can guess and guess and we miss it every year!

Levi's and Joe's both had a daughter in 1997. Such sweet little dolls! Both looked so cute on the bed beside each other on New Year's Day. Levi's had a Rosa and Joe's had a Verena. Amo's little Lovina was walking around the house and Lovin'a little Elizabeth was trying her best. Albert's little Emma was here also. All the grandchildren seem so precious. Naturally, Grandma would say that. Happy New Year to all you great readers out there. I am wishing you a happy, healthy year as we enter our unknown future of 1998. You all take care, thank you for your encouraging letters, cards, etc.

A reader from Victoria, Kansas and from West Jefferson, Ohio each wrote to request some recipes for diabetics, so I reckon there is a need for such things. Following are two that we use in our community.

DEVILED EGGS

5 hard-cooked eggs
1/4 teaspoon salt
dash of pepper
1 teaspoon vinegar

1/2 teaspoon dry mustard
dash of onion powder
2 teaspoons mayonnaise

Halve eggs, remove yolks, and mash them. Cook other ingredients and beat well. Refill egg whites with yolk mixture. Refrigerate until ready to serve.

TUNA SALAD

6 1/2 ounce can water-packed tuna
3 hard boiled eggs, chopped
1/4 cup celery, chopped
3 tablespoons reduced calorie mayonnaise

Combine all ingredients. Refrigerate until served. Serve on a lettuce leaf.

JANUARY 1998

We have a lot of new readers as several new newspapers have added the column in recent months. So some of you out there may not know a lot about our church services. which we have had at our house recently. I have described them in past columns.

Lots of cleaning took place this past week as church services will be held in our home for daughter Lovia and her husband Joe. With their new baby, I thought it would be easier on them if we held their church service in our home instead. Each church member takes turns holding the services in their homes. The bench wagon which holds the church benches is now here. It goes from place to place.

Saturday evening, the benches were set-up in our home for Sunday morning services. After the services, a big lunch is served at noon to all those who attended. Some may wonder what is served at a noon lunch. From one place to another it varies. We served coffee, ham, bologna, cheese, red beets, pickles, lettuce, margarine, sandwich spread, cheese whiz, rhubarb jam, homemade peanut butter mixture (which consists of peanut butter, Karo corn syrup, and marshmallow creme) and bread, which includes home-baked
white and brown. A milk soup or any other kind of soup (varies from place to place) is prepared for the younger children.

Two folding tables were set-up for the men and two folding tables for the women. We could seat 44 at one time for the noon lunch. You usually have to reset the tables for the rest to eat. A tables is set up for the smaller children or whoever wants to eat from it. A "help yourself" deal, I guess. The Monday after church is a clean-up day. Good to have laundry done and the house clean again from Sunday.

Well, now let's answer some reader mail.

To the Burnt Hills, New York reader about what kind of canning we do. There's a lot of canning such as a homemade sandwich spread and hot pepper butter. After we cook it, it's put into jars hot and sealed. Some don't need the water bath or pressure cookers. But I process all meats in pressure cookers.

To the Harrisonburg, Virginia reader: sorry, I don't have the recipe of "hominy flakes" or "pumpkin butter."

To the Bridgeport, Illinois reader here is a Gooseberry Pie recipe from a Kokomo, Indiana reader (thanks for sending it to me, its great!):

GOOSEBERRY PIE

2 cups sugar
2 cups gooseberries

1 tablespoon flour
walnut-sized pat of butter
2 unbaked pie crusts.

Put sugar, berries, flour, and butter into a bowl to mix. Then pour into pie shell and cover with top crust. Bake 35 minutes at 425. Another gooseberry pie recipe came in from a Tiffin, Ohio reader:

3 cups gooseberries
1 1/2 cup sugar
3 tablespoons quick-cook tapioca
1/4 teaspoon salt
2 tablespoon butter

Crush gooseberries. Combine sugar, tapioca, salt with crushed berries and cook until mixture thickens. Stir often. Pour into unbaked 9 inch pie shell. Dot with butter. Adjust top crust. Flute edges and slash top to release steam. Brush top with milk and sprinkle with sugar. Bake in a hot oven, 450 for 10 minutes and reduce temperature to 350 and bake for 30 minutes or until crust is done. Also received recipes similar to the above from Dodge City, Kansas and Payne, Ohio readers, only they add 1 teaspoon grated orange rinds to it. Thank you readers for all the recipes. Greatly appreciated for your help.

To the Greenville, Michigan reader: I don't have a recipe for a candy called "cashew crunch." Sorry.

FEBRUARY 1998

𝔄 nice winter scene out there with a 14 degree temperature. That keeps the home fires burning. More work now to keep those stoves in working order and to keep those chimneys and pipes clean. Our kitchen stove needs a good cleaning out every six weeks. Those wood-boxes need to be kept full with wood and the buckets filled with hard coal to burn. It is a fine heat. Then ash-pans have to be emptied. With the days being shorter, it takes more kerosene for the lamps and lanterns. But, I guess all four seasons have their kind of duties. If everyone is healthy we shouldn't complain. Right?

It is good to open those jars of canned goods which were processed last fall. When we have a taco supper - a family favorite - we use the tomato chunks that were canned last fall instead of buying fresh tomatoes from the store. I haven't bought celery thus far as we raised our own, it has that true celery taste. Also the carrots we eat are what we had in the garden. Lots of work in the summer-time with a garden if you keep it weed-free. Cole slaw goes good from the garden also. Had made some sauerkraut
from our cabbage and it is on the menu at times during the winter. Sounds like sauerkraut is so good for our health as I've read in books.

The highlight of Saturday evening was when we received a "Secret Pal" card, saying to be ready by 5 p.m. as someone will get us, to go eat somewhere which included Ben, Verena, Susan, and I.

So our guessing has ended for our `97 "Secret Pal". It turned out to be Emma and Jacob and their newborn daughter, Elizabeth. At 5 p.m. a van drove in with Emma and Jacob's in it. They had arranged to take us out to dinner. It was a place the girls and I never ate. The van driver and wife got included. It was good food! We enjoyed the evening, also going to and from the restaurant as the van driver and wife and us sang and yodeled together. It seemed a relaxing evening.

Now we have received a "98" secret pal card. So that'll keep us guessing all year. It'll be guess, guess, guess again. Kinda neat! The "secret pal" leaves all kinds of gifts during the year that appears somewhere for all kinds of occasions A reader from Lawrenceville, Illinois requested a quick cheesecake recipe:

INSTANT LEMON CHEESECAKE

In small bowl, beat 8 ounces of cream cheese until smooth. Gradually add 2 cups milk. Beat until well blended. Add instant lemon pudding mix (smallest box) and continue beating about 1 minute. Pour into 9 inch baked and cooled graham cracker crust pan. Top with a few cracker crumbs. Chill.

FEBRUARY 1998

$\mathcal{F}$ebruary is half over. What is becoming of our winter? It's a nice, quiet winter morning at 8 a.m. with the temperature at 27 degrees. The ground looks a bare, brown color with no snow. Thus far, we've' had a mild winter and not much of the white stuff on the ground. Our new sleighs are patiently waiting for the snow and so are we.

Twenty years ago, in `78, we could've used the sleighs most of the winter. Being snow-bound was okay for several days after the big blizzard, but we were glad when the roads could be plowed open again. Was good to be snowbound together with the family. The snow was so deep, we could walk over the fences and we had a 10 foot drift in front of our shed. We could write our names on the shed roof. Was good to have plenty of fuel and those well-filled jars of food in the cellar. We were lucky that no sickness struck then. We had containers of all kinds filled with milk as the milk hauler couldn't make it to our house with the snow-covered roads. 1978 is a winter we'll never forget.

1988 brought a drought on us There wasn't that much from the garden to fill jars with, but we had plenty leftover from the year before. But for some it wasn't much to be thankful for.

Verena and Susan went on their cleaning jobs today. Ben is at the dairy farm working. Well, we plan to help daughter Liz get ready for church today and we're ready now to go. Liz will hold services in her home this Sunday. I will finish this later.

Back in the saddle again. Want to finish this letter. We had an enjoyable day at daughter Liz's cleaning. My daughters, Emma and Lovina (with their children along) joined me at Liz's to help clean. My daughter Leah wanted to come, but she hated to take Paul Jr. out in the cold. Paul Jr. now takes a couple of steps. He seems such a happy little boy. Remarkable, considering what he went through last summer. (Editor's note: For readers new to this column, Elizabeth's 2 1/2 year-old grandson, Paul Jr., underwent open heart surgery last summer)

Butchering beef and pork is on the usual go at this time of year. I am done for now. After a long day, I'm ready to hit the sack!

I will share a recipe.

CREAMY CHEESECAKE

2-8 ounce packages of cream cheese
1/2 cup powdered sugar
1 egg yolk
1/2 teaspoon vanilla
1 can of cherry pie filling (small can)
2-8 ounce packages of crescent rolls

Beat cream cheese, sugar, egg yolk, and vanilla until smooth. Arrange 12 crescent rolls on a round pan or small cookie sheet, pinching together to cover completely. Spread cream cheese mixture over dough. Top with pie filling. Take 4 crescent rolls and cut into 8 strips. Twist each strip and lay over filling and secure ends to bottom rolls. Brush dough with beaten egg white. Bake at 350 for 20 minutes. When cool, drizzle with 2 cups powdered sugar mixed with 3/4 cup water.

MARCH 1998

The highlights of this past Sunday was when Jacob and Emma had a baby girl, named Emma. She was born at 3:34 p.m. She joins her sister Elizabeth. Emma weighed six pounds, one ounce. This makes 26 grandchildren: 18 granddaughters and 8 grandsons. But sad to think that one granddaughter: Mary Shetler isn't with us. But she is in such a nice place, where there is no pain or worry, only peace. We miss her lovely, smiling face more and more. I often think how I had her in a tub of water, taking an early Sunday morning bath last summer. Oh! Was so relaxing to her. That was my last chance to do it for her. Little did we all realize that death was so near, only by early Wednesday morning hours she was in God's care. God makes no mistakes and I guess we shouldn't question it. Mary, who was only 6-years-old, I must say, was an easy grandchild to handle. In some ways she was too good to stay in this wicked world which can be so full of hate. God has a purpose for it all.

For readers new to this column, Mary was in our care for 5 weeks and four days last summer while her 2 year-old brother, Paul Jr, underwent heart surgery in Indiana. Mary died of a sudden illness only days after Paul Jr. returned home from the hospital.

We are so glad that Paul Jr. continues his recovery and can take a few steps at a time now, which he never could do before.

My husband Ben had his 67th birthday Sunday. It was a rainy day. Again, today it is rainy. Our cisterns must've surely filled up from this rainy weather. Some cisterns around here were dry and some almost. Our supply was still good.

Susan went out to do the evening chores. Verena is taking care of the household duties at Jacob's while Emma cares for their newborn. I will assist tomorrow as Verena and Susan are working.

We had quite a scare last week when we had a kitchen stove chimney fire. First time it has happened in that stove. We had plans to bake cookies but that put an end to it. We put the fire under control using a stick called "Chimfex." It did the trick. Later in the day, son-in-law Jacob came here and cleaned out both chimneys (living room and dining room) with a chimney cleaner of our neighbors. Try this favorite pie recipe.

CORN MEAL PIE

2 eggs, beaten
1 1/2 cups brown sugar
3 Tablespoons butter or margarine
4 Tablespoons cream
2 Tablespoons Corn Meal
1/2 cups nuts

Mix all together, bake in a 300 degree oven for 35 to 40 minutes.

MARCH 1998

We had nice weather to butcher seven hogs at son Amos's on Saturday. It was actually for son Amos's and Albert's. It was our annual "butchering day."

The hogs were skinned instead of being scalded as some do it. The hogs were hung on a scaffold and cut wide open and the stomach was removed. If cut in the intestines it is a messy job. The women like to see clean intestines come in as they usually take care of cleaning the stomach, intestines, etc. The intestines are scraped clean twice, which will be stuffed with sausage, which some parts of the meat was ground through the grinder. The women took care of the intestines, cleaned the stomachs, brains, and tongues, and the girls cut up the fat for the rendering of lard.

So many people are fond of the rendering of lard for those delicious "cracklings."

Liver pudding was fried a little in the iron kettle and put in jars to process. The liver pudding is made from the head meat and bones which were cooked in the iron kettle and the meat taken from the bones and grinded. The juice is made into what you'd call "pon hoss."

The juice is cooked with flour, salt, and pepper to thicken. After its cooled it can be sliced and fried. This is "Pon Hoss." Some living pudding is added to it when it is cooking.

The hams and side-meat is usually sugar-cured. Some process or fry down some of the meat.

My folks would usually fry down stuffed sausage, ribs, and pork chops in an iron kettle the next day and put it in a crock and pour lard over it till covered. When used we'd get the lard covered meat. Heat it and what we didn't use pour it into the covered crock. Just so the meat was covered with lard. Sugar cured hams and side-meat.

The morning is spent butchering.. A noon meal is had and it is usually a good feast for all, with people bringing in a cooked meal for butchering day.

To think seven hogs being butchered on Saturday and really they didn't have that much help there. I must say we were done early, but our sons had an early start on it. If I have it right they started at 3:30 a.m. The rendering of lard always has such a good smell when putting through the lard press.

DELICIOUS PORK CHOPS

5 pork chops	1 cup of bread crumbs
dash of pepper	salt to taste
1 egg, beaten	1/4 cup milk
1/4 cup of boiling water	3 tablespoons of fat

Add seasonings to bread crumbs. Beat egg and stir in milk. Dip chops in liquid and coat in crumbs. Brown chops in fat in skillet. Place chops in a baking dish and add boiling water, enough to cover the bottom of the pan. Cover pan and bake at 400 for a little less than an hour.

HAM SANDWICHES

1 cup of catsup	1/2 cup of mustard
1/2 cup of water	2 tablespoons of vinegar
1 1/2 pounds of ground or sliced ham	
1/3 cup of brown sugar	

Stir all of the above in a casserole dish and bake at 250 for one hour. Spoon onto bread and serve on a sandwich. Very good!

MARCH 1998

We are now well into March. It has been nothing but rain, rain, rain lately. The lowlands are flooded. Everything looks muddy. We need the rain, though. The cisterns should be overflowing by now. We just can't judge the weather. Good thing we can't, I guess.

Four of our married children and families arrived here for the Sunday evening meal. The girls suggested a "baked supper." So they had baked beans, baked potatoes, and baked chicken in our wood-burning stove.

They fixed baked chicken by having a pan of melted margarine melted and a pan of Rice Krispies. They dipped the chicken into the margarine and then rolled it in the Rice Krispies to coat it. Then they laid the pieces of chicken on cookie sheets and bake until golden and crispy. That's how they like it when they bake the chicken. It just seemed a different Sunday evening meal for the families, but very enjoyable. We also had buttered corn, peas, lettuce salad, cheese, peaches, apple sauce, cake, pie, cookies, and also there was a homemade cheese ball and crackers and brownies.

I don't know what else they ate but reckon they all got enough as I wasn't feeling my best. I hurt my leg sometime ago, and it has taken a turn for the worse, so I remained seated. Good I have girls yet at such a time especially.

The three last little babies born to daughters Liz, Lovina, and Emma are doing great so far (Liz has baby Rosa, Lovina baby Verena, and Emma with baby Emma).

Paul Jr. is doing well so far. He had a check-up on March 12 and the doctors said he is doing great. Paul's a happy little boy. He can finally walk, just starting to take his first steady steps for the first time in his young life. Paul Jr. is 2 1/2 years old. Who would have thought that he would have pulled through his open heart surgery last summer at Riley's Children's Hospital in Indianapolis? God was above all.

Let me share a recipe with you readers.

A reader in Inverness, Florida sent me this recipe. Thank you for sending it! I will share it.

POTATO CASSEROLE

12 potatoes, peeled, cubed, cooked and cooled
2 pints sour cream
2 cans of cream of chicken soup or one can each of mushroom and chicken
1 cup shredded Cheddar cheese
1 cup butter or margarine
1/2 cup minced onion
2 cups croutons or 1 cup dried bread crumbs

Mix all ingredients except potatoes and croutons. Heat until warm, not boiling. Place potatoes in a large baking buttered dish and sprinkle croutons over the top. Melt another stick of butter and pour on top. Bake at 350 for 45 minutes.

MARCH 1998

It is a cold morning at 13 degrees and a thin blanket of snow is on the ground. The crocuses are peeping through the snow. The yellow color looks beautiful. They've been showing their color for awhile now. The Easter Lilies are ready to bloom, but wonder if it'll be a setback after those cold days recently. Had 16 degrees yesterday morning. It's been cold, snowy and windy this March, but today the sun is shining. We had what you'd call a mild winter but as we entered the month of March, it feels like winter has finally arrived. Winter fun activities around here couldn't be done because it was so warm. We have a brand new horse-drawn sleigh that didn't get any use this winter, and the skaters on those frozen ponds couldn't skate too much.

I can't believe how my Christmas cactus keeps blooming since Christmas. Quite a few blooms are ready to open again. First year it has been blooming like this.

Today, 40 years ago, my husband and I started our own home. Lots of memories through these gone-by years. It was something to get adjusted as all you readers out there know how it was or is. We were blessed through the years with six daughters and two sons. We have 26 grandchildren, although one has left us. We miss granddaughter Mary as the days roll on, but she is in a place where there is no pain - only peace.

The flu bug has been in the area. We thus far are lucky, but daughter Verena had a bad case of poison oak. She has it under control now. Poison oak in the winter? Yes, very possible! Verena carried in cut wood from our woods all winter and it finally took hold. Very miserable!

Talking about this cold weather, the last couple of days we have our kerosene heater in gear which was at a standstill all winter. Makes good heat with our coal and wood-burning stoves. Winter has its duties, but all the seasons do. Right? Only the stoves need great care at all times.

My husband and two sons with their dairy farmer boss enjoyed the day at Middlebury, Indiana to a cattle meeting. Quite a few attended. They were served a good noon meal.

SQUASH COOKIES

1 cup lard
2 cups sugar
2 teaspoons soda
2 teaspoons cinnamon

2 cups squash or pumpkin
4 1/2 cups flour
2 teaspoons baking powder

Cream together lard, squash, sugar, and add dry ingredients. You can also add 1 cup of nuts or dates, if you like. Mix everything well. Drop by teaspoon on cookie sheet at bake at 350.

PINEAPPLE-RHUBARB PIE

1 cup sugar
2 tablespoons corn starch

2 tablespoon flour
1 1/2 cups chopped rhubarb
1 small can crushed pineapple, with juice

Mix all the above well. Pour into unbaked pie shell. Dot with margarine, adjust top crust. Bake at 450 for 10 minutes, then 375 for 25 minutes till done,

APRIL 1998

This was an enjoyable evening with son Amos and family. We decided to take supper in at Amos' since he is laid up with two breaks in his ankle and one break in his leg. Joe's (daughter Lovina) and son Albert and family wanted to go along. So we took potatoes, barbecued pork steak, ham, cottage cheese, and dandelion greens with sour cream and hard-boiled eggs. Joe's took buttered corn, hot peppers, cake, ice-cream, and cones. Albert's took macaroni and cheese, deep-fried ham, buttered peas, cole slaw, deviled eggs, and a cherry-covered cake. There was plenty of food!

Amos was to the doctor Monday. They took X-rays of his foot and seen the ankle bones weren't in correct place so two doctors had to twist the foot to get it in place, which I guess was a painful ordeal. They put another cast on. The break in the leg seems
to be healing good. They have to go again, Wednesday. Just hope for good results. They have six children. A grocery shower was brought to them the evening before from friends of their church. So the people have been very good to them to help them along.
They feel so unworthy of it all.

Saturday was our annual family reunion at the home of my sister Lovina. Around 330 present with a carry-in supper. Had plenty of food and a beautiful day. Singing took place in the afternoon. Sister had also invited mother's (she passed away last year at age 91) remaining family and their live-ins: they're still five sisters and two brothers. So five they were present. Most are in their 80s. Lots of work to undertake a huge gathering. They barbecued 200 pounds of chicken. Was real plenty.

Levi Jr., son of daughter Liz and Levi, is now home from the hospital after pneumonia. He seems his jolly self again. Lots of sickness around it seems. Good when the warm weather arrives once more.

Talking about dandelion greens, they have been on our menu the last week. We're always glad to see the first sign of the rebirth of the dandelion. They're nestled in lawns, gardens, roadways, and pastures. It always delights us to see them grow to have on the menu. We use it as a salad and some wilt them. Must say it is good, healthy green salad. We make a sour cream to it and add hard-boiled eggs to it. Yum, it is good with potatoes and back or ham. Makes a good, cheap evening meal. We always feel that when we eat the dandelion greens, they relax us for a good night's rest. Well, I will share some recipes. You all take care.

AMISH OATMEAL BREAD

4 cups boiling water
1 cup whole-wheat flour
2 cups quick-cooking oats
1/2 cup brown sugar
2 tablespoons salt
4 tablespoons butter

2 packages active dry yeast
1 cup lukewarm water
10 cups bread flour
Yield: 4 loaves
Prep time: 1 hour
Baking: 30 minutes or more

Pour boiling water over the whole-wheat flour, quick oats, brown sugar, salt and butter in a large mixing bowl. Let cool to lukewarm.
Dissolve yeast in lukewarm water, stirring well, and add to the oat mixture. Add enough bread flour to make an elastic dough.

Knead thoroughly until smooth and elastic; place in large greased bowl and turn dough so it's greased lightly on top. Cover with a towel or loose plastic wrap and let rise until double.

Punch dough down. Let rise again until nearly doubled.

Divide dough evenly and shape into four loaves. Place each in a greased loaf pan and let rise until nearly doubled.

Bake in a preheated 350-degree oven for at least 30 minutes or until loaves are nicely browned and sound hollow when tapped.

APRIL 1998

Saturday morning it was decided to go ahead with the butchering of a hog at Paul's (daughter Leah). Jacob's (daughter Emma), who were here at the time, also decided to go over with us and help.

The hog was skinned and all that takes place with it. Removing the intestines, rendering of lard, and cleaning of the stomach was done by the girls and I. Some of the meat was ground into sausage and later put in jars to process. Everything being processed in the big pressure cookers. The juice of the bones was to be tossed, but I said I'll take it and make Pon Hoss with it over at our place. Well that is what daughter Verena and Susan and I took a try at. Made enough so all our married children could have a taste of it, which they all liked for breakfast.

After it is cooked and put it loaf pans to set, then we slice and fry it. Ours like it fried hard. So our breakfasts lately have been Pon Hoss, coffee soup with crackers, fried potatoes and eggs, toast, cheese and, naturally, coffee and tea.

The pork chops were sliced, put into jars and processed. It is a good feeling to fill those jars.

Son Albert was also at Paul's close to the finishing point of butchering. Help was appreciated with this quick plan to butcher the hog. The air was well chilled outside. If they had waited for

Friday, it would've been plenty warm outside. So they hit the weather just right on Saturday, being cold.

It is so good to see Paul Jr. walking around. Such a happy, active little boy.

BUTTERMILK RAISIN PIE

Pie filling:

1 1/2 cups sugar	3 egg yolks
3 cups buttermilk	3 tablespoons lemon juice
1 teaspoon vanilla	6 tablespoons cornstarch
1/4 teaspoon salt	3/4 cup raisins
1 tablespoon butter	1 8 or 9 inch pie shell, baked and cooled

In a saucepan, combine sugar, cornstarch, and salt. Beat egg yolks and buttermilk. Stir into sugar mixture until smooth. Add raisins and lemon juice. Cook and stir over medium heat until mixture comes to a gentle boil. Cook and continue stirring for 2 minutes. Remove from heat. Stir in butter and vanilla. Pour into a pie shell.

Meringue:

3 egg whites
1/4 teaspoon cornstarch
6 tablespoons sugar

1/4 teaspoon cream of tartar

Beat egg whites and cream of tartar in a mixing bowl until soft peaks form. Gradually add sugar and cornstarch. Spread over pie filling. Bake in a 350 oven for 12 to 15 minutes.

PECAN PIE BARS

1 cup corn syrup	2 cups flour
1 cup brown sugar	1/2 cup butter
5 eggs	1/2 cup margarine
3/4 cup sugar	dash of salt
1 teaspoon vanilla	1 cup broken pecans

Preheat oven at 350. In a large bowl, combine flour and brown sugar. Cut in butter and margarine with two knives until mixture resembles coarse crumbs. Press into a 9X13 pan. Bake 10 minutes or until brown. While crust is baking, combine eggs, corn syrup, sugar, salt, and vanilla. Blend well and stir in pecans. Pour filling over hot crust. Reduce oven temperature to 275 and bake 50 minutes or until center is set. Cool in pan or on wire racks before cutting into bars.

APRIL 1998

𝔓aul's, Joe's, and Jacob's were here for supper last night. We were having a taco supper so they all got in on it.

The way we fix a taco supper is to brown flavored seasoned hamburger, diced up tomatoes, green peppers, onions, lettuce, hot and medium sauce, and shredded cheese. Hamburger goes on the bottom, covered with shredded cheese. Then we stack vegetables on top of the hamburger and cheese - lettuce, tomatoes, onions, peppers and top it with the sauce. You soon have a well-filled plate. Paul's had brought ham and beans. And in addition to that, we also had two pizzas, sliced tomatoes, cheese slices, potatoes, celery sticks, Cole slaw, mixed fruit salad, and cookies. So we had plenty to eat.

I am always glad to see the children come home. Told them they could also stay for bed and breakfast. Ha! Joe's and Jacob's took up the offer. We then were all soon asleep only to be awakened by another day. Only three more days left in March at the time of this writing.

We prepared a hearty breakfast for Joe's, Jacob's, and us, which is enjoyable to prepare a bigger amount than usual. We had fried eggs and potatoes. It was an enjoyable morning together. Dishes were washed, and Saturday cleaning was done. Everything back in order.

Daughters Verena and Susan went to assist son Albert's as they have church services coming up to be held in their home. So there's always plenty to clean. It seems that there is always a big clean-up before church , but sometimes the cleaning is worse after holding it.

Paul and his boys came after 100 bales of wheat straw this morning with teams and a wagon.

We were helping daughter Lovina with their beef canning. They butchered a steer lately on Saturday. Probably two weeks a go. The girls and I went to cut up 4 quarters. We processed 67 quarts. We were done by early afternoon. We did chunk beef, 36 quarts of hamburger We also got some huge steaks to be frozen. I then helped her the next day with making beef soup. We cooked the beef bones in 4 large pressure cookers and took meat from bones and processed 42 quarts of soup. So I've been making some beef stew with those bones lately. Here is our simple recipe for beef stew, and a tasty dessert. Hope all you readers are well!

HOMEMADE BEEF STEW

Cook a beef bone in water till done. Then add a couple of diced potatoes and some shredded cabbage. Cook and season with salt and pepper. Diced carrots can also be added. Beef broth will do if a beef bone is not available.

APRIL 1998

𝔈aster Sunday appeared on the calendar recently. Most of the family was here for dinner and supper. Enjoyable day together. The children enjoyed the colored hard-boiled eggs which were brought in by daughter Lovina and family. Cracking eggs was always the thing in our younger years, to see who had an egg who wouldn't crack so easy. Mother always fried eggs on Easter Sunday for breakfast, dinner, and supper for whoever came that day. This food was in addition tos our colored hard boiled and pickled eggs. It seemed it was eggs, eggs, eggs. Horse-radish and catsup went good with it.

It was always great when the Easter Bunny would put his eggs in the yard for an Easter egg hunt. Enjoyable memories!

Wednesday all our daughters and children and the writer spent the day at daughter Leah's. It was a work day. We made noodles with 50 eggs. We also did some sewing and patching. It was an enjoyable day together. One missing spot is not having our sweet, loving granddaughter Mary around. Seems to be missed more and more as time goes on. But Paul Jr. seems so more advanced. He is so happy-go-lucky.

We butchered a hog here on Saturday for daughter Emma and Jacob. So that's done. We processed all the meat by 8:20 p.m. It was a quick deal as the weather turned colder.

Today, our oldest grandchild, Ben, is 15-years-old. Memories go to daughter Leah's and Paul's 17th wedding anniversary tomorrow. So it was a busy time around here. Had a nice day for their wedding, our first time to preparing for a wedding. We fed around 1,000 people that day for dinner and supper.

Now, to answer some mail:

To the Hartford City, Indiana reader: pour boiling water over tomatoes, peel, and put it in jars. Process them 20-25 minutes. Yes, we use them canned tomatoes during winter

To the Ohio reader for a lettuce salad. Here's a good overnight salad: 1 head lettuce, 1 head cauliflower, frozen peas (quantity to your taste), 1 onion, carrots to your taste, 1 onion (chopped fine), shredded cheese. Cut and mix together the above ingredients, except cheese. Stir together 1/2 cup salad dressing and 1 cup sugar and put on top. Then add bacon bits and cheese on top.

To the Ganservoort, New York reader about dumplings:

We use 5 cookspoons (large kitchen spoons) water, 1 egg, pinch salt, and add flour to make a stiff dough to roll out, then cut in squares and drop in brother water. Diced potatoes and an onion can be added to broth. Cook.

To the Belding, Michigan reader: I don't know where you can get gooseberries.
We put two of them in the ground yesterday. Hopefully we'll have luck with it, and our blackberries.

MAY 1998

Spring is always the season that all nature comes to life. There are beautiful, colorful flowers. The rhubarb plants are in use, and they can be used in so many ways. The green winter onions are on the menu. And dandelion greens were so delicious while they lasted. Cheap and healthy! Very good also.

The purple martins are back again in the bird-houses. They are very noisy with their cheery, happy little songs.

The farmers are busy in the fields, and gardens are being planted. This is the season to sow, plant, prune, trim, and paint, or whatever. It's just a desire to work outside.

We saw three deer running across our field and finally went into a nearby woods. What a nice, wild scene.

The laundry hangs on the clothesline now. I just hope they will be dry by evening. We are having frequent rain showers this afternoon.

I have a bread dough rising. So home-baked bread will be on the evening meal menu. Daughter Emma and her two daughters are here today. Always glad to see the family come home. The winter-stoves are still in gear. It's been on the cold side. We had a mild winter and not much snow. Never could use our new horse-drawn sleigh, which we were looking forward to. Probably my next column will be written next month, May, April of 98 is almost history.

Well, it is about time I put the bread dough in pans to rise double and bake it then.

Daughter Verena has dinner ready. Emma is sewing on our treadle sewing machine. Susan is putting snaps on a coat and here I sit to complete this letter. Ben is at the dairy farm working. I hope to beat the mailman to the box. Hope all are well and happy. Here are some rhubarb recipes. Enjoy them!

RHUBARB JAM

Mix 5 cups rhubarb (cut fine) and 4 cups sugar together and set overnight. In morning, boil it for 5 minutes, then add 6 ounces Jello. Whatever flavor you prefer. Stir. Put into jars to seal.

FRENCH RHUBARB PIE

Mix together: 1 egg (beaten), 1 cup sugar, 1 teaspoon vanilla, 2 cups rhubarb (cut fine), 2 tablespoons flour, and dash salt. Put this rhubarb mixture into unbaked pie shell. Cover with the following topping: Mix 3/4 cup flour, 1/2 cup brown sugar, 1/3 cup margarine. Bake at 400 for 10 minutes, then at 350 for 30 minutes or until done.

RHUBARB CAKE

1 1/2 cups brown sugar	1/2 cup shortening
1 egg	1 1/2 cup fresh rhubarb
1/2 teaspoon salt	2 cups flour
1 cup buttermilk	1/2 teaspoon baking soda

Combine shortening, and egg. Beat until light and fluffy. Combine soda, salt, and flour together. Add to shortening mixture. Alternately with buttermilk, fold in rhubarb. Mix well. Pour into greased 9X13 in ch pan and bake at 350 for 30 to 40 minutes. Top with whipped cream afterwards.

MAY 1998

We attended church services at son Amos's yesterday. Was a rainy, dreary day. Their twins Arlene and Marlene were five years old, yesterday. How well I remember when they were born. To this day, I have to ask which is which. Sometimes I just guess it right.

Last Wednesday, we had an enjoyable day.

Our niece had a quilting bee for her mother's (my sister) birthday, April 22, which was a surprise on her to see most all her sisters and nieces arrive to quilt for the day. We were served a lot of baked goodies and coffee in the a.m. and a delicious meal at noon. In the afternoon again we had a lot of snacks and pop. Singing, yodeling, and visiting also took place through the day. Happy Birthday was sung so often during the day to my sister to remind her it was her birthday. We had a good laugh every time it was sung again. Enjoyable day together as us sisters hardly see each other so often.

Our oldest grandson, Ben, (daughter Leah's son) is in the eighth grade and has never missed a day of school in all his years. Leah went seven years without missing a day of school, but in her 8th year she missed with a bad case of hives and kidneys. Probably was too hard on her being mother was in the hospital and afterwards my sister Lydia, who died then. So I had went to the hospital so often at the time of mother being hospitalized, then my sister, and then Leah took over with home duties, being in the summer-time. My oldest sister died in a freak buggy accident.

Daughter Verena made a casserole for our evening meal tonight. It is a simple casserole. She took 1 pound of ground beef, put it in a skillet and covered it with one diced onion, 2 diced potatoes, one can of cream of mushroom soup, and salt and pepper. Simmer for one hour covered. You can add any other vegetable to it.

We also enjoy a nachos snack in the evening. Here is a good recipe for that.

NACHO SNACK

1 can of Campbells Nacho Cheese soup

8 ounce of warmed tortilla chips
1/4 cup milk
1 cup of homemade salsa (we made our own, you can buy it)

In a saucepan, stir soup and milk. Heat thoroughly, stirring often. Pour salsa over layer of warmed chips. Then pour soup over top. You can top with sliced green onions or peppers if you wish.

MAY 1998

We had a busy, busy Wednesday.

Daughters Leah, Liz, Emma, Verena, Susan, and I went to daughter Lovina's to do some spring cleaning. It is always enjoyable to get together for a work-day. In the evening, we went on to Albert's (and wife Sarah Irene) to cut-up four quarters of beef, which had been placed in a cooler. It had been butchered the Saturday before. They had six pressure cookers in gear. The beef was cut-up and some was cut-up into chunks. Other was grinded into hamburger. We ended up with 91 quarts of beef chunks. Steaks were cut out and put into the freezer. It was nice to put meat in a cooler of our neighbor. Beef chunks were put in jars, seasoned, and the lids put on and then processed. All our family took in on the ordeal to help. It was like a family work-gathering in the evening, which is always enjoyable. Barbecued steak was on the evening meal menu for all.

Today, Saturday, Ben and I were putting out the garden. The girls are at work today. Verena and Susan clean rooms at a motel in town, they enjoy the work.

Talking about the garden, so many didn't have their gardens planted. It was so cool and wet, but these recent warm days have allowed for planting. We could use a shower now.

The farmers have been busy in fields and womenfolk in the garden. A busy season, and yet so refreshing. Hay is being made, looks like a good crop this year.

Thanks, readers, who are sending recipes and letters. Greatly appreciated. Personally impossible to thank younce all.

To the Weyers Cave, Virginia reader who requested a sauerkraut recipe:

SAUERKRAUT: Shred cabbage and put into jars. Add 1 teaspoon salt and 1 tablespoon vinegar. Fill with cold water. Put lids on and turn tight. Put in basement for 2 months, then its ready to use.

To the Celina, Ohio reader who requested a recipe for homemade "Miracle Whip."

SALAD DRESSING

3/4 cup cooking oil

1 tablespoon lemon juice
2/3 cup sugar
2 teaspoon dry mustard
1 egg, plus one tablespoon water

Beat water and egg thoroughly with beater. Set aside. Cook the following in a one quart saucepan:

2/3 cup flour, 1 cup water, and 1/2 cup vinegar. Bring to a boil, then blend in the other ingredients. Beat until smooth and refrigerate. Good on sandwiches!

To the Bloomington, Indiana reader, here is the recipe you requested for "corn fritters."

2 cups fresh grated corn

2 eggs, beaten
3/4 cup flour
3/4 teaspoon salt
1/4 teaspoon pepper
1 teaspoon baking powder

Combine corn and eggs. Add flour which has been sifted with remaining ingredients. Drop corn mixture from tablespoon into 1 inch of melted shortening. Fry until golden brown on both sides, turning once. Makes 12 fritters. Good luck!

JULY 1998

July 4th was well spent around here. The evening before, five tents were set up in our yard for our visiting children to camp out. Daughter Liz and husband Levi cooked a ham bone and beans on the open fire in an iron kettle.   Made one think of years ago when we used to cook potatoes (in their jackets) like that. Cooking outside, kept the heat out of the house. Well our fun evening outside ended when a storm came up during the night so everyone took for the house. Twenty-seven in all for lodging for the night was somewhat different, but enjoyable for a holiday. Coming in the kitchen it looked like a lot of dishes. but being stormy outside, and us all together, the women washed all those messy containers until 2 a.m.

The next morning, the morning of July 4, daughter Liz and husband Levi were once again the chief cooks. They made a fire with brick blocks with racks placed on top: eggs, potatoes, toast, bacon and sausage gravy all made for a delicious breakfast. It looked so neat. Folding tables and benches were set up in the yard and all 27 ate out in the open. I baked 40 biscuits and also made a white gravy in the house. There were quite a few other goodies along with the morning meal.

As everyone left we had happy memories of July 4th even with the rain-out of the camp-out. After breakfast, a water battle took place which our children enjoy (splashing, spraying with water). On the Fourth of July evening we enjoyed an evening meal at the dairy farm where my husband works.

Well, I had best get dinner on the table as I have plenty to do, 70 to 80 people here for supper tonight.

Thank you for the birthday cards from you readers.

Must hurry. Made some cottage cheese recently. If you have sour milk, heat it till hot - not boiling. Remove from heat. Let cool. Then strain and add salt and pepper to your taste and add some milk or cream. Surprisingly so many who have tasted this cottage cheese say that they prefer it.

Now, here is a recipe to use your garden tomatoes:

HOMEMADE TOMATO CATSUP

1 gallon of ripe tomatoes
1 large onion
1 tablespoon of pickling spice
2 teaspoons of salt
1 cup sugar
1 cup vinegar

Chop tomatoes, cook with onion and pickling spice until well done. Drain off the juice. Put through sieve, add salt, sugar, and vinegar to tomatoes. Cook until tomato mixture is thick. This mixture is your catsup. The leftover juice can be used in chili or vegetable soup.

JULY 1998

Today, Saturday, July 25, makes this column 7 years old today. Kevin Williams from Ohio drove into our driveway and asked me if I would write the column. We were strangers to one another back then. I took up this task then, and a lot has taken place in these years.

A week ago was my birthday, so we had 74 here for the evening meal. We decided to go with a taco supper. Well, with everyone bringing food the second 8 foot folding table was set up. Lots of food. It was all our married children and families invited. Had such a good turnout. Had a nice evening singing, yodeling, and visiting. People from the dairy farm where Ben works also showed up.

Speaking of stormy and rainy, it has been bad around here. So many flooded areas. Our glass showed almost six inches from Sunday evening until Wednesday morning with high winds. Most of our sweet corn was drowned. Hopefully, most of it will stand up again. But what would we do if we were to have 12 - 18 inches of rain like some areas of the country get? I should've picked some of our garden goodies, but it has been too wet to get them. Worst floods in years in some areas. The road between Lovina and Emma's house is cut off because of high water, so

58

they have to a long way to get to each other's homes. Lots of hay has been made and crops look good. Probably now some have drowned out. Today was such a beautiful day. Not so hot as we've had temperatures in the 90s.

Following is a recipe for zucchini cake, zucchini is a very good summer vegetable to prepare. It is very high in water content, so it makes for good cakes and breads, as well as fried in a skillet. Zucchini goes good around here. The other recipe, peanut butter swirl bars, are good for the kids during these summer vacations from school. The schools around here will be starting up next month.

ZUCCHINI CAKE

3 eggs
1 cup vegetable oil
1 teaspoon salt
1 tablespoon cinnamon
1 cup nuts
2 cups zucchini

2 cups sugar
1 tablespoon vanilla
1/4 teaspoon baking powder
2 teaspoons baking soda
4 tablespoons cocoa
2 cups flour

Mix all ingredients together and pour into lightly greased 9X13" loaf pan, bake at 350 degrees until done, about one hour.

DELICIOUS PEANUT BUTTER SWIRL BARS

1/2 cup peanut butter (crunchy or plain)
1/3 cup butter
3/4 cup brown sugar
3/4 cup sugar
2 eggs
2 teaspoons vanilla
1 cup flour
1 teaspoons baking powder
1/4 teaspoon salt
6 ounce package of chocolate chips

Preheat oven to 325 degrees. Cream first four ingredients. Add eggs and vanilla, mix well. Add dry ingredients and mix. Spread in greased 13X9X2 inch pan. Sprinkle chocolate chips overtop. Place in oven for five minutes. Then swirl chocolate chips through dough with a knife. Return to oven for 25-30 minutes. Makes 24 bars.

AUGUST 1998

My husband is at the dairy farm and the girls are at their jobs, so I thought I would quick take time for this task of writing. It is a nice, sunshiny, Thursday morning here on the Coblentz farm. A nice breeze is coming through the windows. Hopefully, I will do some sewing today.

It sounds quiet around here, because yesterday daughters Liz, Lovina, and Emma and children were here as everything in dining and living rooms were washed off, curtains washed, windows cleaned, and ironed, plus other laundry done. Weeding in the garden also took place as weeds are taking over. Daughter Leah also stopped in on her way to enroll her two children for school which starts soon. So I told them to come back here for dinner when they return which they did. So it was an enjoyable dinner together. Son Albert's wife, Sarah Irene, and their children had also stopped in on her way to school to enroll her four children. Just seems impossible how the grandchildren are getting older and to think having one grandchild out of school already! Life goes on.

Sunday was no dull moment having some here for breakfast, dinner, and supper. You never really know when the married children and families will show up on a Sunday evening meal. It is always good to see them come and a meal can be quickly prepared.

Anyways, barbecued pork steak, hamburgers, and wieners were on the menu with sons Amos and Albert's, Paul's, Joe's, and Jacob's here for supper.

Daughter Verena had our family here Saturday evening for pizza on her birthday. The pizza is also on order for this coming Saturday as it is Albert's, Elizabeth's, and Paul Jr's birthday Saturday. Paul Jr. seems to be enjoying life. He gets around good.

He is 2-years-old (he'll be 3) and had open heart surgery last year. Mary would be enrolled for school now also, but is in a such better place in our Heavenly Home. She would be seven years old today, August 20. We miss her more and more. God makes no mistakes.

Here are two delicious recipes!

GARDEN SKILLET

2 cups diced zucchini squash
1/2 teaspoon basil leaves, crushed
1 can cheddar cheese soup
16 ounce can tomatoes, chopped and drained
1/2 teaspoon prepared mustard
1/2 cup chopped onion
2 tablespoons margarine
3 cups cooked elbow macaroni
2 cups shredded sharp Cheddar cheese

In skillet, cook zucchini and onion with basil in margarine until tender. Add remaining ingredients. Heat until cheese melts. Stir occasionally. Makes about 5 servings.

PICKLE RELISH

5 cups ground, peeled cucumbers
2 green peppers, ground
3 cups celery, ground
2 red peppers, ground
3 cups onion, ground

Mix the above ingredients with 1/2 cup salt. Let set overnight. Drain the next morning. Add:

6 cups vinegar
2 teaspoons mustard seed
2 teaspoons celery seed
3 cups sugar.

Bring to a boil and cook slowly for 10 minutes. Put in sterilized jars and seal.

SEPTEMBER 1998

It was a nice, sunshiny day. We could use some rain.

Filling those glass canning jars is a good feeling for use during the long winter to come. We have processed a lot of homemade V-8 style tomato juice, although I should call it V-??? because we canned 55 quarts one day.   We cook together red and orange tomatoes, onions, sweet peppers, hot banana peppers, jalapeno peppers, cabbage, parsley, celery, and green beans. Daughter Emma also added some green beans and red beets to hers. Ours tastes good and hot. So it'll be good for next winter when there's no garden goodies. The other day we canned 23 quarts. We also canned tomato chunks. We use those with tacos in winter instead of store bought. I want to can our red beets soon. There beginning to go in big sizes. We like to eat them when cooked, sliced, and fried
in butter with salt and pepper. In so many ways, these vegetables can be prepared. Looks like the '98 garden will soon be history.

Daughter Verena had all our family invited for supper on her birthday and served pizza. All were present to enjoy the evening of singing and yodeling. An evening well spent. Elizabeth of son Albert's and Paul Jr. also have a birthday the same day. Yes, there was plenty of food, also on the table.

The grass looks so green to think we're at the end of the days of August and early September.

My husband is at the dairy farm and the girls are at work right now so I am getting this task of writing done.

We assisted daughter Lovina with painting, canning tomato juice, and red beets one day this week. Was an enjoyable work day together.

Was good to see my cousin from Seymour, Missouri here on Saturday morning. I hadn't seen him in years and years. He had come to attend a class reunion which was to take place Saturday evening. In our school days we lived across the road from one another.

Well, I will share some recipes.

CHICKEN CASSEROLE DINNER

1 can cream of chicken soup
1 can of cream of mushroom soup
1 can boned chicken
1 can Pet milk
1 medium can chow mein noodles
potato chips

Mix ingredients, except chips and pour into casserole dish. Crumble potato chips and sprinkle on top. Bake at 350 for 40 minutes.

HOMEMADE PIZZA SAUCE

1 large onion
4 bay leaves
10 cups tomato juice

1/2 cup salad oil
2 teaspoons oregano
4 teaspoons salt
1 1/2 teaspoons garlic powder
4 teaspoons sugar
1/4 teaspoon red pepper
1/2 teaspoon pepper
3/4 cup Clear-Jel thickening
Water

Cook tender onion and bay leaves in tomato juice. Strain. Add salad oil, oregano, garlic powder, sugar, red pepper, and pepper. Bring to a boil and add paste of Clear-Jel and water. Boil 5 minutes. Makes 5 pints.

NO BLANCH SWEET CORN

15 cups corn, cut fresh from the cob
1/3 cup sugar
2 1/2 cup water
1/8 cup salt

Mix well. Seal in plastic containers and freeze.

SEPTEMBER 1998

4 a.m.
Time to get the day started off. Rainy-like outside in these early morning hours. We could use rain. Hope enough rain to lay the dust, especially living along a stone road. Gets quite dusty at times.

4:45 a.m. Breakfast is ready and we're seated at the table. Fried potatoes and eggs, bacon, cheese, toast, peaches, marshmallows, sliced tomatoes, hot peppers, coffee and tea (some prefer coffee and some tea), margarine, etc. are on the table.

5:10 a.m. My husband is off to the dairy farm and Susan and I wash dishes and Verena starts ironing the laundry. Plenty of it. This will just be another laundry morning so I gathered the laundry and Susan completes the cleaning.

7:30 a.m. Girls getting ready now for work. Verena quits ironing. Yesterday, they assisted daughter Leah with her cleaning. Paul Jr. seems such a happy boy. He's 3 years old now. We miss granddaughter Mary not being around. She would have started school this fall, but our Heavenly Father has a purpose for it all.

7:55 a.m. Girls off to work. and I'm about ready to hang the clothes on the clothesline. Looks rainy, but I'll take my try to get it hung out. Little more breezy.

8:50 a.m. The laundry hangs on the clothesline now. The sun is peeping through the clouds Hopefully the wash will dry. Now here I sit to write this task, whether it'll be good or bad, is for you to decide. Ha!

Wednesday, daughters Liz, Lovina, Verena, Emma, Susan, and I assisted daughter Leah with her painting, cleaning, and canned around 26 quarts of tomato juice. It was an enjoyable day together. Levi's was here for supper then and Joe's and Jacob's had joined in the evening before. It is always good to see the marrieds some home. Well this is 12:30 p.m. as I write this and I should get this in the mail today, so I hope to beat the mailman to the box.

I want to can some hot peppers this afternoon. It seems such a busy time. Sometimes it's like are you coming or going? The laundry is waiting to be folded and that puts some more ironing on the list. The day has turned out to be a nice, sunshiny day. Much to be thankful for. Anyways, I am glad the laundry has dried as I write this. Maybe some of you readers out there would enjoy the following recipes as to look out on those calories. You readers out there take good care.

BREAKFAST IN A GLASS

1/2 cup cooked oatmeal
1/2 cup fresh peaches or berries
1 cup skim milk
1/2 teaspoon vanilla

Combine all ingredients (those blenders would come in handy here!) Serve cold. Yield 1 serving.

APPLE PIE

4 cups apples, sliced
2 tablespoons cornstarch
2 tablespoons margarine
9 inch pie shell, unbaked
1 tablespoon sweetener (we use Sweet-10)
1/2 cup orange juice
1/2 teaspoon cinnamon
1/4 teaspoon nutmeg

Mix all ingredients together in a saucepan. Heat until warm. Pour into unbaked pie shell. Put strips over top of pie. Bake 30-35 minutes in 425 degree oven.

OCTOBER 1998

This week I'll answer reader questions that have come in over the past month.

To the Cincinnati, Ohio reader who requested a recipe for a simple Pineapple Pie: Here's a pineapple cream pie recipe. 1 can Eagle Brand Milk, 3 tablespoons lemon juice, 1 large can crushed pineapple (drained), 1 large container of Cool Whip. Beat milk and lemon juice together. Add pineapples and Cool Whip. Stir until well-mixed. Pour into 2-8 inch graham cracker crusts. Chill several hours.

To the Schagticoke, New York reader who requested potato salad: 6 large potatoes, 1 onion, 5 boiled eggs, 1/2 cup sugar, 1 cup salad dressing, 2 teaspoons vinegar, 2 tablespoons mustard, 1/2 cup celery (cut-up) and salt to your taste. Dice or however you want with your potatoes, eggs, and onions and toss together. Add mixed sugar, dressing, vinegar, mustard, and celery. Blend well.

To the Mitchell, Indiana reader: When canning hot peppers, put hot peppers into jars. Boil together 3 cups vinegar, 3 cups water, 1 cup sugar, and 1/4 cup salt. Pour over hot peppers in jars and seal.

To the Mishawka, Indiana reader: Here is the recipe for potato rivvel soup that you requested: 1 medium-sized onion, 5 medium potatoes (diced), salt and pepper. Cook potatoes in a little water till soft. To make rivvels, take 2 beaten eggs and 1 teaspoon salt and add flour and toss and stir until lumpy and rather dry. Sift excess flour out of rivvels, then dump rivvels into the potato mixture and boil 5 minutes. Add 1/2 cup butter, 1/2 teaspoon celery, 1 to 1 1/2 quarts of milk, a pinch of parsley. Heat and serve.

To the Kokomo, Indiana reader: Yes, I will reprint my recipe for hot pepper butter for younce. It is: 42 hot peppers, 1 pint yellow mustard, 1 quart vinegar, 6 cups sugar, 1 tablespoon salt, 1 cup flour, 1 1/2 cup water. Grind hot peppers. Add mustard, vinegar, sugar, and salt and bring to a boil. Make a paste with the flour and water and add to boiling mixture and cook 5 minutes. Pour into pint jars and seal. Makes 7 pints.

To the Muncie, Indiana reader for Coney Sauce: Brown 2 pounds ground beef with 1 large onion. Then add 2 sticks celery, chopped; 1 tablespoon chili powder, 1/2 tablespoon cloves, 1 cup catsup, 1 quart tomato juice, 1 1/2 tablespoons salt, 1/2 cup sugar. Boil or simmer slowly for 1 hour. This you can freeze or it keeps in the refrigerator for weeks.

To the Winchester, Indiana reader: Here is the recipe for "End of the garden relish" you requested: 1 cup chopped cabbage, 1 cup sliced onion, 1 cup chopped green tomatoes, 1 cup chopped carrots, 1 cup lima beans, 1 cup green beans, 1 cup chopped celery, 1 tablespoon celery seed, 2 tablespoons mustard seed, 2 cups sugar, 2 tablespoons turmeric powder, 2 cups vinegar, and 2 cups of water. Soak pickles, pepper, cabbage, onion, and tomatoes in salt water overnight in the following proportions: 1/2 cup salt and 2 quarts water. Drain. Cook carrots and beans in boiling waster until tender. Drain well. Mix ingredients and boil 10 minutes. Seal at once.

Well, I hope you all out there get good results from the above recipes. Must get busy as we're prepare for church services to be held in our home and daughter Liz and husband Levi have it Sunday. Leah's had it last Sunday in their home. So lots of cleaning got done lately. Will write more later. Have more reader mail to answer yet.

To people who asked about clear-gel. I would think the clear-gel thickening could be bought in stores. A local Super Valu grocery store has it near us. But for those of you who can't find it, you could probably use cornstarch instead.

OCTOBER 1998

It is Tuesday evening and I should hike to bed, but I must get this column written. How would it be like to have to write this by candlelight? Reckon our forefathers did and probably were satisfied with it. We don't have electricity in our home, but we can keep our kerosene lamps and lanterns well-lighted if we keep them cleaned.

Our son-in-laws, Joe and Jacob, just took my aged uncle from New York to his daughter's for the night. They have returned and it is raining. We are having dreary, fall weather now. We can expect these days, but we still have a plentiful garden that we are sharing with our married children. It makes a meal with so many garden eats. Like tonight, on the menu were different salads that we made: cucumber, Cole slaw, and lettuce salads. Also, sweet and hot peppers, winter radishes, sliced tomatoes, horseradish pickles hot pepper butter, and then I used tomatoes for a fresh vegetable soup. We also had fresh green beans and zucchini bread made from zucchini from the garden. We haven't bought any lettuce from the store since the spring. Also on the menu were cooked potatoes, beef, Swiss cheese, fruit salad, and cookies. I never raised lettuce this long, but all summer I kept planting. The conditions were ideal for lettuce this summer.

Other usable vegetables from the garden right now include: red beets, celery, carrots, endive, Chinese cabbage, and turnips. Hopefully, we'll have nice days ahead without a killing frost. The trees are a beautiful color with those shades of yellow, red, and orange. It will soon be history.

Jacob and Emma's daughter, Elizabeth, is doing fine. Also our son Amos and his wife, Nancy, are doing well with their new baby named Lovina. Son Amos's were here for Sunday supper to see Jacob's baby. We've had a lot of visitors since the baby.

October always brings back happy and sad memories. It will be our wedding anniversary on October 17 - thirty-nine years for Ben and I. Anyone out there married on October 17, 1957? Levi and daughter Liz had their fourth wedding anniversary on October 4.

Son Albert's had their tenth wedding anniversary on October 2. It will be 33 years that Ben and I moved onto this farm on October 29. We just had two children at that time (Leah and Amos). Amos became two years old the next day. It was a nice warm, fall day when we moved here.

On the sad side, my grandma died the year before we were married which is easy for me to remember. How these years have taken place. The Asian flu struck the area which some of our family caught after our wedding day was announced in 1957. It was a severe epidemic of influenza caused by a virus strain. Believe me, my fever went up to 105 the week before my wedding. I can still recall the feeling I had.

Well, the years have blessed Ben and I with six daughters and two sons All wonderful children. We have 22 grandchildren (14 girls and boys). The oldest grandchild is 15 and the youngest, 3 1/2 weeks.

Here is a nice recipe to use some of your garden goodies.

ZUCCHINI DISH

8 small zucchini, thinly sliced
3 tablespoons margarine
3 medium tomatoes, cut into wedges
2 teaspoons of salt
1/2 teaspoon of pepper

Heat zucchini in margarine in 10 inch skillet over medium heat. Add rest of ingredients. Stir constantly until tomatoes are hot - about five minutes. Do not overcook. Serves 8.

OCTOBER 1998

𝕿oday, October 17, marked our 41st wedding anniversary with such a beautiful autumn day. We, with our friends (my editor and his parents), motored to Ft. Wayne. (Editor's note: Elizabeth was invited to meet readers at The Midwestern Women's Conference, the first time she's ever made a public appearance). We met a lot of great readers there. Such a nice group. While driving along, the trees were in their beautiful colors of red, green, brown, and orange. We really admired them all the way to Ft. Wayne.

These friends also took us out for dinner in honor of our anniversary at a restaurant called Ruby Tuesday's. It was an enjoyable day together, a day to be long remembered. The weather 41 years ago was like now. We didn't have a frost as yet, but one of these days the snow will be flying. Dread to see those Brrrr cold, winter days approach.

We were helping daughter Lovina and Joe's in cleaning and preparing for their church service which will be held tomorrow in their cleaned out buggy garage, attached to their house. A noon lunch will be held in there after services with tables and benches set up. It is so good when services can be held outsides, as the furniture in the house would have to be rearranged to set up those church benches for the services. Afterwards, the benches will be carried out and stored in the church bench wagon which goes from one place to another, wherever the services are going to be held.

Son Albert and his wife, Sarah Irene, will take their turn for services in two weeks. We had it two weeks ago. Levi and daughter Liz had it the week before us. Jacob and daughter Emma six weeks before Paul's. So we have been helping each other with assisting with the cleaning, etc. Son Amos and his wife, Nancy Jean, have also been helping out.

Albert's are putting up an addition to their home, so they'll be plenty of work to get it done and you can imagine they'll be plenty of cleaning up then. Glad I have 2 daughters still living at home, Verena and Susan, to help everyone.

OCTOBER 1998

𝕿he morning of Thursday, October 22 was our first frost of the season. The temperature dropped to 33 degrees. So the leaves keep falling from the trees as I look out the window. I'm admiring those trees in our woods. Colors of all kinds. No artist's paintbrush could quite reproduce the scene produced by our Master Artist, Our Creator.

Yesterday afternoon, in anticipation of the frost, we dug out the carrots, celery, red beets, and picked the tomatoes, mangoes, and hot peppers. So the garden will have a rest till spring. It needs to be plowed now. So many meals that came from the garden. We'll miss those goodies once we run out. Nothing better in taste as when we get it from the garden.

The area farmers are having nice weather which is letting corn and bean harvesting progress so well. Our crops are all harvested now.

My husband is at the dairy farm and the girls at their jobs. Here I sit to do this task of writing.

The girls were home yesterday to help and visit. It always is a good feeling to see them come home. Without the family, life would seem dull. Son-in-law Jacob (daughter Emma) took ladders to the roof and cleaned out both chimneys last night. So glad that's done. Hopefully for most of winter. I'm always afraid of those chimney fires. Good we don't know our future. It seems when in need of help, it usually gets done. So we are thankful for our children of their help.

Daughter Liz and Lovina each came with their horse and buggy for breakfast. Was a chilly drive for them. Emma and her daughters also came for breakfast. We are all going to enjoy breakfast together.

What kind of a winter will we have in store? Cold, snowy? If we have plenty of snow we can go sleighing as the sleighs never were used last winter, not enough snow.

PLAIN CAKE

4 cups graham crackers, 1 1/2 teaspoons baking powder, 1/4 cup melted oleo, 3/4 teaspoon cinnamon, 1/8 teaspoon Allspice, 3 eggs, beaten, 1 1/2 teaspoons liquid sweetener, 1 cup skim milk. Mix ingredients in a bowl. Add a beaten egg, sweetener, and milk. Mix well. Bake 15 - 20 minutes in a 9X13 pan at 375.

BANANA MUFFINS

2 cups flour, sifted	2 teaspoons baking powder
1 teaspoon salt	1/2 teaspoon baking soda
1/4 cup cooking oil	1/2 teaspoon nutmeg
1 egg (slightly beaten)	1 cup ripe bananas (mashed)
1/3 cup skim milk	2 teaspoons Sweet-10

Grease and flour baking dish or use paper baking cups. Sift flour with baking powder, salt, soda, and nutmeg into a mixing bowl. Combine remaining ingredients. Mix with dry ingredients only until dry particles are moistened. Fill muffin cups 2/3 full and bake at 375 for 20-25 minutes.

To a reader who requested a recipe of haystack, a family favorite around here:

HAY STACK

Crushed Saltine crackers
diced onions
spaghetti cooked
tomatoes, catsup
hamburger, browned

rice, cooked

You can add anything more such as: celery, peppers, raisins, cashews, cauliflower, etc.

Sauce: Velveeta cheese and milk (as much as you like)

Melt cheese and milk together to make a sauce. Put hamburger on a plate and stack rest on top of each other on your plate and top it off with the cheese sauce.

NOVEMBER 1998

The harvest has been completed for the year on this farm. The farmers had such beautiful harvest weather. It just seems springtime had arrived and the seeds were put in the ground and we were watching for the sprouts to pop through. This was a good year for hay. Had plenty of pasture for the animals.

The trees look so beautiful, although they are losing most of their colorful leaves now. The trees are beginning to look bare and the fields are taking on that dirty brown tinge that will be there until the warmth of spring. The flowers are looking droopy and their colorful looks are gone. The bulbs have been taken from the ground and stored until next spring.

My husband left for the dairy farm at 5 a.m. So breakfast was over with and I started to do the dishes. Verena started to make "Toll House cookies" and Susan was doing our weekly cleaning which has such a good smell when cleaning.

It is now late in the morning. We have three grandchildren here now as mothers went grocery shopping this a.m. It is so good to watch them as we do our daily work. Verena and Susan are home helping me today. What a relief when they're home to help. Verena baked 80 cookies. They were baked by 7:30 a.m. and Susan now has all the cleaning completed.

Sunday evening our family all got together at son Amos and Nancy Jean's and family for a good evening meal. He had the chicken marinated and grilled. Was so delicious. It was in honor of his birthday. A delicious meal! After supper, dishes were washed and singing and yodeling took place. It always seems so relaxing being together and when singing takes place. The evenings are too short at such a time. We always sing "the parting song" before everyone leaves. It is almost heart-breaking to have those warm, together family evenings end.

Here is the recipe Verena used for her toll-house cookies, they were a hit!

HOMEMADE TOLLHOUSE COOKIES

1 cup of shortening
3/4 cup of brown sugar
3/4 cup of white sugar
2 beaten eggs

1 teaspoon of hot water
1 teaspoon of vanilla

Sift the above ingredients together and add:

1 1/2 cups of sifted flour
1 teaspoon of salt
1 teaspoon of soda

Stir well. Add the following ingredients:

2 cups of oatmeal
1 cup of chopped nuts (Optional)
1 package of chocolate chips

Stir well. Drop by teaspoon onto a cookie sheet. Bake at 350 for 10-15 minutes.

NOVEMBER 1998

𝕴 will recopy part of my first Thanksgiving column from November of 1991, as most newspapers didn't receive the column at that time. How these years slipped by. At that time we had our five youngest daughters with us and the one daughter and two sons married. Had five grandsons and five granddaughters which now totals 18 granddaughters and eight grandsons. Seven granddaughters are living as Mary is in such a better home with our Heavenly Father. She is so greatly missed but God has a purpose for it although we don't understand. The "One" who never makes a mistake and who will do the judging someday.

Here is what I wrote in November of 1991:

"Over the river and through the woods to grandfather's house we go.
The horse knows the way to carry the sleigh,
Over the white and drifted snow."
Poems such as this sound as if the "good old days" were happier, easier times. But would we really want to go back to them? Were they really so good? Let us be thankful this Thanksgiving Day to think of those struggles the Pilgrims must've had long, long ago. We shall never know the terrors that the Pilgrims braved years and years ago. We should be thankful for the bounteous harvest. In so many ways we should be thankful. But too often we forget.

Those words are just as true now as when written in 1991.

Lots of gatherings and weddings occur on Thanksgiving Day. Thinking of that day, we usually have a full menu at our house. A stuffed turkey, chicken, ham, sweet potatoes, cranberry salad, pumpkin pie, and pumpkin bread, and the list can go on and on is served. I guess if plans hold out this year we plan to attend a wedding on Thanksgiving Day in La Grange County, Indiana. A daughter of my niece is getting married and I'm to help cook. Also, if plans hold out I'll go the Tuesday before to help bake pies.

There will be no turkey in the oven this year because of our out of town plans. Usually, though, I like to have a stuffed turkey in the oven on Thanksgiving Day. I stuff it with a mixture of bread crumbs, cut-up onions and celery, adding water, salt and pepper to taste. Also diced potatoes at times. Yummy!

Then we have mashed potatoes, gravy, mixed vegetables, sweet potatoes, macaroni and cheese, pumpkin pie, lettuce salad, a pudding of some king, and celery and carrot sticks on the side. There is always plenty of food when the children come home on Thanksgiving Day. We also have home-baked cookies and a Jell-O cake on the menu too.

PUMPKIN BARS

2 cups flour	2 teaspoons of baking powder
1/2 teaspoon of salt	2 teaspoons of cinnamon
4 eggs	1 cup walnuts
2 cups pumpkin	1 teaspoon of baking soda
2 cups of sugar	1 cup of oil

Mix all of the above ingredients very well. Shape into bars. Put on a large cookie sheet that has been greased and floured. Bake at 350 for 25-30 minutes. Ice with cream cheese icing:

CREAM CHEESE ICING

1/2 stick of oleo
8 ounces of cream cheese
1 box of powdered sugar
1 teaspoon vanilla.

Mix very well. Ice bars after they are cool.

THANKSGIVING SWEET POTATO CASSEROLE

6 red sweet potatoes
1 cup of sugar
3 eggs
1/4 cup butter
1 cup of milk
1 cup of raisins
1 teaspoon of cinnamon
mini-marshallows

Boil potatoes until tender. Drain. Mash until creamy. Add eggs, butter, milk, cinnamon, raisins, and nuts. Pour into baking dish and place marshallows on top. Bake 30 minutes at 350. Serve hot.

This is Christmas week, and it brings back memories of when all eight of our children were still in our care. Life was very busy then with washing, ironing, sewing, and cleaning. It was definitely a hustle and bustle at that time. I recall sewing at the sewing machine till late at night while our little peaceful sleepers were in bed. That's the quiet time when I made headway with finishing their new clothes to be given to them as Christmas gifts. My eyes couldn't take it now to sew by the light of the kerosene lamp. Now we have six children married and 25 grandchildren to think of (we had 26 but the good Lord took Mary into "His" care). Glad I have two hard-working girls -Susan and Verena - at home yet to help out.

When the children were in our care, on Christmas Eve we put eight plates on our dining room table later in the evening when the little ones had fallen asleep. We filled the plates with candy and peanuts and put their gifts beside each plate. We always put a glass dish with each plate as a remembrance in years to come. All kinds of games and toys were always enjoyed the next morning when Santa had come down the chimney. Ha! Those were the good old days.

I feel the children all took good care of what they got at Christmas. I'd always liked to sew new clothes for all the family: same color and material. I hardly do much baking and candy-making like I did back then. I always baked a lot of cookies, made various kinds of candy (peanut butter cups were a favorite) and they didn't last long around here then. Fruit cakes were also made.

Breakfast was had in the morning, and some candy, but eating candy in the morning isn't the best idea. We also peeled oranges and ate them. We never decorate for Christmas as our electricity always runs out. Ha!

There weren't as big of gifts years ago, there just wasn't the money. But the children were just as happy. Money wasn't as plentiful, but what is the true meaning of Christmas? It's not money.

We always took the young ones to town before Christmas to see Santa. They were so glad for their sack of candy from Santa and telling him what they want for Christmas.

It's good to see our grandchildren today wear the clothes I made as our youngest daughter out-grew them. It is a real help to these young mothers. It's good to have plenty of good Sunday clothes and school clothes.

We are having our Christmas gathering on New Year's Day of 1999 with our six married children and families all over for the day. There will be 41 in all They'll come for breakfast, they look forward to mother and grandmother's breakfast. Everyone will also be seated to eat at dinnertime (lunch). There will also be plenty of snacks in the P.M., and whoever is still hungry, there will be an evening meal. Gifts are passed out to everyone. We've started this New Year's Day tradition going since the children started to be married. The New Year's Song is sung in German along with Christmas carols several times during the day. This is a tradition passed down from my grandparents to my parents.

Our first snow of the season appeared here on Dec. 16. This is the first time in all my years that I can recall a first snow this late. Good thing we can't rule the weather. God is above all, regardless.

Here is a recipe for the peanut butter cup candy I used to make:

PEANUT BUTTER CUPS

1 pound of margarine
2 pounds of peanut butter
3 pounds of powdered sugar
Melted semi-sweet chocolate

Mix peanut butter and margarine, then work in powdered sugar. Shape into balls the size of big marbles. Dip in melted chocolate and let set. Delicious!

Here is another family favorite.

CHURCH WINDOWS FOR CHRISTMAS

12 ounces of semi-sweet chocolate
1 stick of oleo
1 package of colored marshmallows
1 cup of coconut (optional)
1 cup of nut meats

Melt chocolate together until creamy. Fold in one package of colored marshmallows. Spread one cup of coconut and one cup of nut meats on wax paper. Cover with marshmallow--chocolate mixture. Roll up like jelly roll. Refrigerate until solid. Slice and serve.

DECEMBER 1998

It is Sunday afternoon and I just got up from a nap and thought I would tackle this task of writing. A nap on a Sunday afternoon always seems good. The girls are gone for the day so it leaves just my husband and I in this household. The marrieds probably had other plans for the day as none showed up.

New Year's Day is coming. The children and grandchildren will all arrive here on New Year's Day for breakfast, dinner- all day till they leave for their homes in the evening. They always enjoy Mom's breakfast. Ha!

Years ago, we gathered at Grandpa's on my mom's side for New Year's Day. Memories still linger of those by-gone days. They had 14 children living (one had passed to that Great Beyond), over 100 grandchildren, and some great-grandchildren. Some went to their house for breakfast, some for dinner. I remember we went once to be there by 4 a.m. to sing the New Year's Song to Grandpa. Grandma and Grandpa must have been very tired by evening. The New Year's song was sung in various ways.

The New Year's Song was brought over from Switzerland and has been sung in my family ever since. My grandparents and parents sang it. On New Year's Day the young people, sometimes up to 20 horse-drawn buggies, will stop from house to house and sing the New Year's Song. It is sung in German: "Die Zeit Ist Ankummen das fried" are the first words, the song roughly translates into: "The time has come for the New Year, God will give us a good New Year." There are several variations of the song.

We used to stay up until midnight as my father would blow his big seashell which could be heard for miles away. Guns were also shot to shoot the old year out and shoot the new year in, which is still being done.

At Grandpa's the grandchildren would all receive a sack of candy and sometimes a hanky or a dish of some kind in the afternoon. Their children received some nice, useful gifts. Now today we give more gifts. Probably we were more satisfied then.

It was a sad New Year's Day when all had gathered at Grandma's when Grandpa left this world. I can remember they used to have one long folding table set to eat, so it had to be set and reset so all could eat. The small children ate help-yourself style. As time went on my parents had us children home on New Year's Day, having the same traditions Grandpa's had. Now, my parents have passed on and we are taking their place to have our children home on New Year's. It's nice to have it on New Year's Day. The day just doesn't' seem long enough when we are all together. We eat snacks, sing, yodel, and play games. It is very enjoyable.

CUP OF COOKIES

1 cup margarine	1 cup Rice Krispies
1 cup sugar	1/2 cup nuts
1 cup brown sugar	1 cup coconut
1 cup oatmeal	3 1/2 cups flour
1 cup cooking oil	2 eggs
1 teaspoon baking soda	1 teaspoon cream of tartar

Mix all together very well and drop on ungreased cookie sheet and bake at 350 for one hour and 10 minutes.

1999

This year brought the hype of the approaching millennium. The phrase "Y2K Compliant" entered everyone's vocabulary. Fear reigned that computers wouldn't recognize the year 2000 when the next century was ushered in. People stocked up on canned goods and prepared for Armeggedon, while computer programmers worked feverishly to rewrite old programs.

The year was not without its tragedies. Student gunmen killed 13 of their own in a brutal rampage at Columbine High School in April. August brought the tragic death of John F. Kennedy Jr., the only male heir to the Camelot legacy of his father. Meanwhile, President Clinton was acquitted after a lengthy soap-opera trail that linked him romantically with a former intern. The United States economy sizzled, with the Internet and dot.com companies becoming the darlings of modern-day gold rush.

The New Year brought a big snowstorm to the Coblentz farm, which closed roads and schools with wind-whipped drifts. Elizabeth's daughter, Susan, endured a year of injuries. In February she cut a big gash on her hand on a broken canning jar. No sooner had she recovered from that then she broke her ankle in three places while slipping near the well. So Susan spent most of the summer laid up. August saw Elizabeth's oldest daughter, Leah, turn 40. A new grandson entered the Coblentz home with the birth of Benjamin, to Lovina and Joe.

A cold rainy December brought out the puzzles at the Coblentz home, to wile away the chilly early winter nights. Meanwhile, while the rest of the world held it's collective breath, the Coblentzes looked to the approaching millennium without much fanfare.

$\mathfrak{L}$ast night, five of our married children and their families showed up for dinner. It didn't take long to get that evening meal prepared. Soup is good on a cold night, so that is what was prepared. Today, I made a chili soup taking hamburger and browned it with a couple chopped onions. Then I added homemade V-8 hot tomato juice to it. I also made a thickening of several tablespoons of flour with water, adding it to the above in a four quart kettle, poured it in the boiling mixture, added a can of red kidney beans, and also seasoned it with 2 tablespoons of brown sugar and salt and pepper to your taste. I didn't add chili powder as the V-8 made it hot enough.

The girls also like their potato soup. I make it by peeling potatoes and an onion in a small amount of water. Cook till soft, mash it up and add milk, salt, and pepper and also add a teaspoon of margarine and heat. Don't boil after adding the milk. Just so its hot.

My mother didn't have to use a recipe book for her cooking. We had more of all kinds of soups when we were smaller. There were soups like bean soup, rivvel soup, potato soup, vegetable soups, brown flour soup, coffee soup, beef and homemade noodle soup and pot pie soup. Mother didn't have recipes for any of these, she just knew how much of this and that to put in.

Corn mush was a favorite of mother's for supper, especially in the cold winter months. She would have her cup of milk with it. I never was too fond of it. Fried mush was usually on the breakfast table the next morning. Corn mush, soups, potatoes (jackets) and sour cream were the main items on the supper table at that time. For good homemade mush bring three cups of water to a boil. In a bowl, make a thickening with one cup of corn meal, one teaspoon salt, and one cup of water. Add this mix to the boiling water. Stir mixture until it has reached the boiling point then stir occasionally. Cook for 15-20 minutes. Then pour into a deep baking dish. Cool then slice and fry until brown. We spread some apple butter, honey, molasses, or whatever which tastes
best to top it.

Tomato soup was a simple soup mother used to make. Heat tomato juice, salt, and pepper adding milk to it then and heat. Mother often would make a tomato gravy for us children for dinner. Now I hardly cook it as when my children were young. It was like taking one quart of tomato juice and made a milk thickening of 2 tablespoons flour. Add the thickening to the boiling juice. Season with salt and pepper.

When you think to back then, meals were much simpler and probably better for health. In the summer months, when it was hot a cold milk soup was on the menu for supper. Sweetened cold milk was poured over crumbled bread, strawberries, mulberries, raspberries, or bananas. We could change the cold soup as different fruit came in and out of season.

Now, a summer favorite is a homemade cheese soup. It's made of 1/ 2 cup finely chopped onion, 4 tablespoons margarine, 1/2 cup flour, 4 cups milk, 4 cups chicken broth, 1/2 cup finely diced carrots, 1/2 cup finely diced celery, dash of salt and pepper, 1 cup diced sharp processed American cheese. In a 4 1/2 - 5 quart kettle, cook margarine and onion until tender. Blend in flour. Add remaining ingredients except cheese. Cook and stir until thickened and bubbly. Reduce heat. Add cheese. Stir until it melts. Simmer for 15 minutes. Serves 8.

Let me answer some quick pieces of mail.

To the Muncie, Indiana reader who requested a recipe for tomato butter. The best I can offer is a recipe for tomato jam. Is this what you are wanting? Does anyone out there have a recipe for tomato butter?

TOMATO JAM

5 pounds ripe tomatoes (quartered), 11 cups
5 cups brown sugar
1 tablespoon whole cloves
1 tablespoon Allspice
1 tablespoon stick cinnamon
2 1/2 cups of vinegar
3 cups seedless raisins

Cut tomatoes into pieces after peeling. Add the sugar and the spices (tied in cheesecloth) Boil slowly for two hours, add raisins. Boil one more hour. Take out and discard spices. Pour into sterilized jars and seal while hot.

Also, to another Muncie reader inquiring about why canning jars are on "homemade trees" out in yards. Years ago more of them were seen that way. It was a way to put the canning jars on. It saved space instead of boxes, etc. A good way to keep jars in order also.

I hope everyone had a very merry Christmas and a happy new year!

JANUARY 1999

On the second day of 1999 a snowstorm hit us. It came with big winds, freezing rain, and drifting snow. Walking was hard out there.

Last night, our son-in-law Jacob noticed his neighbor down the road, old and not in good health, had not been stirring in awhile. So he told his wife, my daughter, Emma: "I'm going to go over to see if he's in need."

When Jacob arrived, he discovered the neighbor was okay, but door to his house was frozen shut and he couldn't open it. So Jacob went back home and got some tools to open his door, he also brought some groceries along in case the man needed some. Emma gave Jacob some home-canned pork chops to take along. During times like this, bad, snowy weather, neighbors need to stay in touch with one another. The man was very grateful to Jacob for freeing the door. He was worried if there had been a fire he wouldn't be able to get out.

My daughter Verena, who still lives with us, tried out our new sleigh. Last year we couldn't use it as there was never enough lasting snow. Well I just didn't go outside today as it looked too slippery. I can hear the wind blowing now. Probably some huge drifts by tomorrow. We've experienced some bitter cold days this week so far. I will share a little bit about our family's New Year's Eve and Day.

My daughter Liz, her husband Levi, and their children came on New Year's Eve and stayed overnight . As a way to celebrate the New Year, a few menfolk will safely shoot off guns. Guns were shot off in every direction at midnight to shoot in the New Year as a safe, fun form of fireworks. It sounded "boom - boom" every which way. Levi and Liz's five-year-old daughter, Elizabeth, had such an expression on her face. She said: "I never heard such." She was staying safely inside with the girls listening to the "fireworks." The rest of us were fast asleep, too tired to hear the old year shot out and the new year shot in.

We had our family here for breakfast and dinner on New Year's Day. All 41 were present. We were all seated at the folding tables and benches to eat together all at one time in our dining room for breakfast and dinner. Snacks - including a homemade cheese-ball - were served in the afternoon. Games are played and so is the singing of the New Year's song in German. A tradition to have the family over when we went to my grandpa's and then at my parents. Now we are next in line to continue the family gathering tradition on New Year's with our children and grandchildren It's always exciting to see the grandchildren open their gifts, it always is good to have them all come over for the day.

This past New Year's Day we prepared a breakfast that we had never had before. We had homemade breakfast burritos. I made 50 big ones and we had 18 leftover. That was a lot to have leftover but I would always rather prepare too much than run out of food.

The tortillas were filled with fried eggs and ham. We had potatoes also. Cottage cheese and bacon were also served. The children all brought food for our New Year's Day also, when they come the tables are more than full. A day like that just isn't long enough.

On January 2, some of the family wanted to come back to help my husband Ben cut-up wood, but the snowstorm was coming already. Amo's and family came over early in the day for a breakfast, but then they returned home as the snow started up. Wood-cutting was canceled. Good we can't rule the weather.

The New Year holiday is now behind us as we settle in for the long winter. Chicken and dumplings is a popular meal around here, so I will share a recipe for that. I will also a share a good,quick tuna recipe.

HOMEMADE CHICKEN & DUMPLINGS

1 whole chicken

1 small onion
1 teaspoon of parsley
1/4 teaspoon of sage
1 teaspoon of salt
3 medium potatoes, diced
1 pint of peas

Boil chicken in 8 to 10 cups of water until tender Pick chicken from the bones. Remove skin. Put back in pot and add other ingredients and bring to a boil. Prepare dumplings as follows:

Dumplings

1 1/2 cups of flour
1/2 teaspoon of salt
2 teaspoons of baking powder
1 egg
1/3 cup of melted oleo
3 tablespoons of milk

Mix all dry ingredients and then add egg and milk and stir just until moistened. Drop dough from teaspoon until boiling broth. Cover tightly for 15 minutes. Do not uncover until ready to serve.

TUNA PATTIES

6 ounce can of chunk tuna
1/2 cup ketchup
3/4 cup graham cracker crumbs
1 egg

Combine all ingredients. Mix well. Shape into patties. Fry in skillet until golden brown. Serves 6-8.

FEBRUARY 1999

We got our pork and beef put up on Saturday. All our children and their families were here to help us, so it was a very enjoyable day of working together on our farm. Three quarters of beef were cut-up and chunked and put into jars. Beef was also grinded up into hamburger and put in jars to process. With the pork, we processed sausage, liver pudding, and pork chops. By the time we were done, we had everything in pints and quarts: 75 quarts of chunk beef, 39 quarts of hamburger, 53 quarts of sausage, 2 quarts of pork chops and 23 quarts of liver pudding. We canned 180 quarts in all. Seven pressure cookers were in gear, so it made for a busy Saturday.

Our children were all willing workers. I can hardly believe our grandchildren have grown and have turned into such helpful workers also We enjoy them all. We have never, in all these years, done our pork and beef processing in the same day. But at least it is out of the way, it is a hard day's work. All the jars of food are marked on the lids the month and year they were filled. The jars are then stored in the cool cellar and will make great meals in the future.

Also today, the pork stomaches (3 of them) were cleaned, cooked, and cut into slices When cool, salt, vinegar, salad dressing is added to it, along with plenty of diced onions. The steer stomach wasn't cleaned, but we unusually do use that - lots of people like that. So now we are done with the day's work. Hard to believe the day is done. The day is so short when the family is together.

At home, when I was single, my parents would fry down meat in the winter and use it later in the spring. They'd fry down the meat in an iron kettle or in pans in the oven and afterwards put it in a crock and pour melted lard over it to cover the meat (usually, stuffed sausage in casings or back bones). But I'm not fond of that. For us, it's usually processed meat, sugar-cured, or frozen as ways to preserve our meat.

After it was all over, we cooked the beef bones with the pork bones in the big iron kettle. The ribs leftover I will barbecue as the family likes that. I also made some liver and onions today, which some prefer. Have plenty of liver and onions, in our family it seems like one meal for us and that does it for awhile.

Some readers have had requests recently in the mail, so I will try to answer some in this column.

A letter from Beeler, Kansas inquired about home-cure meats. We usually buy ours in stores, but we have used this home-made sugar-cure for our hams. For 12 hams, take 12 pints of salt, 1 pint of brown sugar, 1/4 pound pepper, and 1/4 pound of salt peter.
Mix all together. Rub mixture good on hams, let lay to cure.

To the Manasota, Florida reader and all the rest who have requested the starter for Amish friendship bread. Here it is - again:

3 1/2 C. bread flour

1 T. sugar
1 pkg. dry, active yeast
2 C. warm water

Combine flour, sugar, and undissolved yeast into a large bowl. Gradually add warm water to dry ingredients. Beat until smooth. Cover with transparent wrap and let stand in a warm place for two days.

A request from a Washington C.H., Ohio reader on what coffee soup is? It is a simple soup we make by crumbling bread or toast in a bowl. You then mix coffee, milk, and sugar (all amounts according to your taste) and pour over bread.

Speaking of bread, a Harrisonburg, Virginia reader requested I repeat the recipe for Poor Man's Bread pie. All you do is crumble bread into an unbaked 9-inch pie shell till its full. Then add 6 tablespoons sugar, 1 tablespoon flour, and 2 teaspoons cinnamon. Fill pie crust with milk. Bake at 350 to 400 until done. You can tell when it is done by when its thickened together.

Both the coffee soup and poor man's bread pie are cheap, economical dishes that were used a lot during the Great Depression.

To the Greenville, Ohio reader, is this the bread pudding you were wanting?

BREAD PUDDING

4 C. bread cubes
1 qt. hot milk
3 T. margarine
4 eggs, separated
dash of salt
1 C. sugar
1/2 tsp. vanilla

Boil milk. After it has been boiled, combine it with bread cubes and butter. Then allow to stand 10 minutes. In a separate bowl, beat egg yolks and salt until fluffy. Add sugar and vanilla to the yolks. Beat until lemon-colored. Add bread mixture. Pour into a greased 2 quart baking dish and bake at 350 for 50 minutes.

MARCH 1999

Some of my daughters are here today to clean for our upcoming church services. For those new to the column, we hold church services in our home instead of a church building. The cellar and steps were cleaned this morning, plus we washed out the sink, cleaned the cabinets, and did a lot of odds-and-ends type jobs. Was a busy morning. So good to get everything done and cleaned in the house. Some of the family are coming Saturday to clean out our barn and do those outdoor cleaning tasks.

My husband Ben has been home from work the last two weeks. He has pneumonia, so he's been housebound. He seems a lot better this morning, although he is still not going outside. Ben did a little repair work around the house today, so that sounds like a little more strength to me. What would we do without a helping family? Daughter Verena has been doing most of the barn chores while Ben has been recovering. Daughter Susan has been recovering from a deep gash in her hand, which she cut on a broken glass canning jar. Glad it is healing. I'll be glad when everyone is back in good health around here.

There has been so much going on that the sewing machines are at a standstill right now. One of the girls plans to sew a dress and apron this evening. I should cut out another dress and apron so they can sew it. The sewing machine was new when it was a gift to me probably 45 years ago, a gift from my husband. At that time, he was my husband-to-be. Ha! The "new home" - the house we live in now - we bought at a public auction years ago. There was lots of sewing on the machines in those by-gone years I often think when the children were small of all the sewing I had to get done. Evenings, after they were fast asleep, is when I could make headways finishing up their clothes. Now the grandchildren are wearing those same clothes since ours outgrew them. It is good to help those young mothers to give them the gift of sewing.

To the Noblesville, Indiana reader about sausage: Grind the sausage from the different parts of the pork. And for every one gallon of sausage we add 2 tablespoons of salt and 1 tablespoon of pepper.

I'll answer some more reader mail now. A Quincy, Illinois reader wrote asking me for some homemade icing recipes. I hope this will do.

FROSTING

5 C. powdered sugar
1 1/2 C. shortening
6 T. milk
1 t. vanilla

Mix well the powdered sugar and shortening. Then add the milk. Beat hard and then add vanilla. Beat until soft enough to spread easily.

To the Olney, Illinois reader who requested a vinegar dumpling recipe. Readers sent in some recipes for it. Here is one:

VINEGAR DUMPLINGS

Dumplings:

3 C. flour

pinch of salt
2 t. baking powder
2 t. shortening
enough water to make a soft dough

Method: Combine ingredients and knead to make a smooth dough. Roll-out and cut into 1-inch squares or strips. Then prepare syrup as below:

Syrup:

1 C. vinegar
3 C. water
2 C. sugar

1/2 t. butter
1 t. vanilla
1 1/2 t. allspice

In a saucepan mix syrup ingredients and bring to a boil. Drop in dumplings and boil for 12 minutes.

MARCH 1999

𝕴 am writing this on March 10 and I see huge snow drifts outside of my window. The snowstorm started Monday evening So glad it didn't strike Sunday when we held church services here at this household. We had a small enough attendance as it was. There is so much sickness around here at the present time, including my husband Ben. He has been housebound for over three weeks now from pneumonia. He was to the doctor on Monday and if he isn't better by next week, he has to go back. At least I have a pair of extra hands around to help wash and dry dishes. Ha!

Daughter Verena has been doing the barn chores and everything else that takes place on a farm. Glad for all the help the family has given during these weeks leading up to church services.

Meanwhile, daughter Susan's hand has really mended. She cut a gash in her hand after falling down the cellar steps with a 32 gallon tub full of glass jars. What a glass mess it was to clean up, but glad she didn't have a break on her. Only cuts and bruises. She showed the Doctor her hand on Monday and he complimented her on taking care of it the right way. She had been in the hospital right before her fall from being badly dehydrated, so she probably was still weak.

A piece of siding blew off our house during the snowstorm. So Verena and Susan got the ladder and put it back on this morning. I had to laugh when they came back in to the house announcing that they were now the Coblentz carpenter crew.

Back about church services. I am glad our house is now all clean and back in order. Daughter Lovina and Emma and their daughters are here today. Lovina is ironing and Emma is sewing caps (head-coverings worn by women). So I got dinner, a taco dinner, ready for all of us to eat. We like to top our tacos with a homemade mild or hot sauce. So nice to be together on a snowy day like this. A lunch like this also consists of leftovers from the meal served after Sunday's services: homemade potato soup, fresh fruits, cherry and pumpkin pie, potato salad, and other baked goodies.

Grandson Paul Shetler Jr, 3, who had open heart surgery a year and a half ago, was unable to attend church services due to not being well lately. We can't take the cold weather.

We use a mild or hot sauce on taco meats and other meats. Here is a good, homemade sweet and sour mild sauce recipe we use for meats:

SWEET AND SOUR SAUCE FOR MEATS

8. oz. of cream cheese
1/2 c. of sour cream
1/4 c. of milk
2 T. of sugar
1 T. of vinegar
dash of salt

Combine ingredients, mixing until blended. Serve over meats.

ONE DISH MEAL

3 C. cooked, fluffy rice
1/2 lb. browned hamburger
1 pint green beans, undrained
1 10 oz. can cream of mushroom soup
Buttered bread crumbs

Mix ingredients together. Top with buttered crumbs. Bake at 350 until thoroughly heated and crumbs are browned.

MARCH 1999

It is 5 a.m. as I write this. I meant to sit down and write this letter to you readers last night but we had supper guests and this got neglected. Today, I'm going to my sister's for an all-day "quilting bee." So I want to get this written and in the mail before I go. She has three quilts in frame right now. It is a lot of work to stitch those quilts, so when many people can pitch in and help at a "quilting bee" the work goes quicker. I often wonder how many stitches are on a quilt.

To do a quilt is expensive. You have to buy the material , thread, needles, and prepare those good noon meals that are part of a quilting bee, plus refreshments that are served in the morning and the afternoon. The work goes quicker as there is lots of singing, yodeling, and, naturally, gossip at a day like that. It always seems enjoyable.

I am glad we have all our quilts done for our children. I wanted each of our daughters to have their own quilt before moving out on their own. We completed all of the quilts seven years ago when five of our daughters were still in our care. We had to buy the material, sew it together, and then put it into a quilting frame. Then the pattern is marked off with whatever design. At that point, it is ready for those stitches.

It is still a pleasant memory of when we all worked on those quilts together one winter. The girls would help sew before going to work in the morning and when they got back in the evening. Our older daughter, Leah, who was out on her own would come over to help. Every stitch helped. That winter we did five quilts and some bed comforters. What a relief when all the children had their quilts. Those are happy memories.

My husband went out to do the chores this morning. It's been four and a half weeks now since he has felt well enough to do them. So it is good to see the results from rest. Although he still seems weak.

Ben appreciated all the help he got during his illness, especially when and before church services were held in this household. What would we do without a family? I reckon there'd always be a way. Maybe not the best way. We have much to be thankful for in this world, although it seems dreary at times.

Well, I must get breakfast as my husband is in from the barn and the morning hours fly by, especially when I have to leave for the quilting bee soon. You all take care out there and thanks for your encouraging letters, even if not all can be answered.

Fried eggs and potatoes are on the breakfast menu this morning. I usually peel the potatoes (jackets), shred them and fry in a skillet, or I peel raw potatoes, slice, and fry in lard. Season with salt. That is our way of fried potatoes for breakfast.

For the Covington, Kentucky reader about a carrot recipe. Here is a good one:

CARROT BAKE

1 pound carrots, cut into 1/2" slices

3/4 C. mayonnaise
1 T. prepared horseradish
1/2 C. dry bread crumbs
1/2 C. shredded sharp Cheddar cheese
2 T. minced onions
1/3 C. water
1/4 t. pepper
2 T. margarine or butter, melted

Cook carrots until tender. Place in one-quart baking dish. Set aside. In small bowl, combine next 3 ingredients. Mix well. Pour over carrots. Combine crumbs and butter and sprinkle on top. Bake uncovered at 350 for 25-30 minutes. Sprinkle with cheese. Return to oven for a few minutes until cheese is melted.

To the reader in Dodge City, Kansas who requested a chili recipe:

HOMEMADE CHILI

1 1/2 lb. of fresh ground beef
3 C. tomato juice
1 can of kidney beans
2 medium onions
1 T. of chili powder
1/4 - 1/2 C. of brown sugar
salt to taste

Brown hamburger and onion in a deep pot. Add remaining ingredients and bring to a boil. Spaghetti can also be cooked and added to the soup. Cook until spaghetti is done, about 5 - 10 minutes on medium high.

APRIL 1999

This is Sunday morning and the temperature is at a chilly 25 degrees as we head to our church services. They are being held at my nephew's residence. Chores were done and the horse was hitched up to the buggy. Breakfast was prepared and we all were seated at the table to eat. A usual thing, I guess. Beds were made and floors swept. Whatever the morning tasks have to be done. Plenty to do it seems in these early morning hours. My husband, Ben, will finally attend church services after being struck with pneumonia for awhile now.

9 a.m. Church services start off. My brother-in-law is minister but couldn't attend as of sickness. He has two kinds of cancer and wasn't feeling his best lately. The singing takes off in the German song book called the "Ausbund." Our sermons are in German. A treat is passed around during the services for the younger children which usually consists of saltine crackers and a variety of home-baked cookies.

11:30 a.m. Church services let out and a lunch is served to all. Had a good lunch. A big, long table was put up for the menfolks and a table for the women. The children eat at a table as cafeteria-style. A soup is also prepared besides the lunch meal for the children. It was a plentiful meal as I like to see. My Grandpa always said "serve plenty" especially when it comes to church services. After everyone ate, there was plenty of help to gather those dishes and begin the task of washing them. Everyone was invited to come back in the evening for a meal, but I told them my husband won't be able to as of the night in an open buggy would not help his pneumonia. Just good he could come during church services.

1 p.m. We left for home from church services but made a visit with our daughter Leah and family, as Paul Jr. was under doctor's care. But we found him to be in good spirits and feeling a lot better. Some of you readers may have read this column two years ago when he was undergoing open-heart surgery at Riley's Children's Hospital in Indianapolis. He is 3 now. So we headed for home. Was a cold wind sweeping across the fields and into the open buggy. Just hoping it wouldn't make my husband a backset of pneumonia.

2:30 p.m. Arrived back home where three of our family members and their families had come to visit. Verena and Susan had come home with some others from church services.

3:30 p.m. The girls had left to have supper with some friends and then spent the evening there, also daughter and family were with them. The other two families stayed here for supper. It's always good to have our family here for meals.

7:30 p.m. Everyone has left for their homes and the evening was well-spent. Son Albert's and Jacob's (daughter Emma) were here for supper. The girls came home later in the evening which I guess had an enjoyable evening with friends singing and yodeling.

Now here is a good quick, coffeecake recipe that can be prepared the night efore you eat it. Try it!

QUICK COFFEECAKE

1 1/4 C. flour
1/2 teaspoon cinnamon
3/4 C. brown sugar
1/3 C. butter
1/2 C. sour milk
1/2 t. soda

Cream butter with the dry ingredients (except soda). Add sour milk with baking soda. Stir well and pour into a buttered and floured pan. Bake at 350 for 25 minutes until done. Sprinkle top with brown sugar, cinnamon, and butter.

APRIL 1999

It is a cool Tuesday morning and there is lots to do around here: chores, preparing breakfast, and sweeping and mopping the floors. Always good to see everything all clean again. We were out in the garden to clean up and get those flower beds ready for the gardening season. The laundry was also done today and hung out on the clothesline which has really dried nicely. Daughter Leah and her son Paul Jr. stopped in this morning on their way to visit her mother-in-law who lives in northern Indiana. She is not too well at present. Leah had to get her husband at the factory where he works so he could go along.

I am back, a salesman stopped by. Verena left with our horse and buggy to run some errands. Our horse is getting up in years. But still does his duty. Hopefully we can find another horse to drive was safe as he has but with a faster speed. I know we haven't ran the speed limit of more than 55 with this horse. Ha!

1:30 p.m. Dinner is over, dishes are washed and laundry taken from washline.

3:30 p.m. Paul and Leah's other children: Elizabeth and Levi come here after school while their parents are in northern Indiana. Their other son, Ben, was to come here with the horse and buggy after he came home from work. Then they will all go back home and do the chores. He seemed a tired boy. Ben is our oldest grandson who will be 16 on April 15. Life goes on. So he was supper guests were grandchildren Ben, Elizabeth, and Levi, my daughter Lovina and her family, and daughter Emma and hers. So what is the on the menu for this supper?

Well, I made a one-kettle soup of beef chunks, noodles, diced-up potatoes,, one onion, and salt and pepper to taste. Plus rare beef was on the menu. Younce all know what rare beef is? Beef is sliced thin. Then lard is put into a skillet until good and hot. Then slice by slice put well-seasoned of salt and pepper beef slices into the hot lard. Just stir a couple of rounds on both sides and take out. My dad would really have it peppered down which I can recall. They all always liked rare beef, but for me it is like they are eating while I put it through the lard. Ha!

I always like to prepare what the family enjoys to eat. Also on the menu tonight is potatoes (jackets), it always goes good with the hot pork and beans being served. We also are having carrots, pepper strips, celery, onions, chunk beef, cinnamon pudding, fruit, popcorn, and spreads. I reckon the rare beef takes the lead with the adults as they are very fond of it. An easy meal for the evening. I like to cook what they all prefer. They all know they are welcome, whatever hour of the day.

8:30 p.m. Everyone left for their homes and I'm ready to hit the sack. It seems a long, but enjoyable, day. It is always good to have the children home. What would we do without a family?

Here is a recipe for the homemade cinnamon pudding that we had with our dinner tonight.

CINNAMON PUDDING

Step One:

2 C. brown sugar
2 T. margarine
1 1/2 C. of cold water

Mix above in saucepan and let come to a boil over low heat.

Step Two

1 C. of white sugar
2 T. of margarine
1 C. of milk
2 t. of sugar
2 t. of baking powder
enough flour to make a batter

Mix step two ingredients thoroughly in a bowl. Pour step two into the bottom of a greased pan. Pour step one over it and sprinkle with nuts if you wish. Bake at 350 for 45 minutes. Serve with whipped cream.

MAY 1999

𝕿his is a nice Thursday. The laundry has dried on the clothesline. I should get dinner for my husband and I but I need to get this column-writing task done before the mailman comes. My daughters, Susan and Verena, are at work today.

Seems there are no dull moments around this place. Church services are being held among our children so we try to pitch in and help everyone get ready. Daughter Leah had it, and then it goes to Joe and Lovina and then Emma and Jacob., and then to son Albert's. There's always plenty to do at such a time. Daughter Leah had served as their church meal: spaghetti and meatballs, green beans, peaches, cheese, red beets, pickles, margarine, jam, coffee, bread, peanut butter mixture, and hot peppers.

So many spring tasks to be done. I haven't started on the garden yet. I'm never in a hurry as long as the cool weather hangs in. Although I do want to get onion sets into the ground as soon as it dries up outside.

Hello to all! Let me start out this column by going into the mailbag.

To the South Bend, Indiana reader: I would think 2 cups of flour for the cinnamon pudding recipe I had in this column a couple of weeks ago would be plenty. Put it in a loaf pan. Cut in squares and put in a bowl, putting whipped cream in between.

To the Somerset, Pennsylvania reader: I will plant your large cantaloupe seeds you sent me and see what big ones I get. Was greatly appreciated.

Thanks to the Goshen, Indiana reader for sending the recipe for kuchen and to all the rest who took time to send the recipes for our reader from Battle Creek. The reader had inquired about "kooken", which the verdict seems to be that he was inquiring about "kuchen", a German-style coffeecake. Thanks, also, readers for so many encouraging letters. Words can't express my appreciation.

To the Meyersdale, PA reader: I have never heard of what you called "blood sausage." You said it was made with tongue, heart, and perhaps other things and blood). Sorry!

To the 90-year-old woman from Atchison, Kansas and the 97-year-old woman from Columbus, Nebraska, it was nice to reader your letters. Both your writings were good for both your ages, enjoyable reading!

MAY 1999

5 a.m. This is a nice, sunshine-filled Sunday morning. Nature has come back to life here in May. God created it. The leaves on the trees have come back and the grass is a beautiful green. The flowers are in bloom. We have a trampoline out in our yard and that is in use again by the grandchildren who enjoy it much. My daughter Verena bought it some years back. The picnic table has been set outside again for summer use. This is such a lovely time of year! Will any of our family drop by today for dinner? I guess we'll see later.

10 a.m. I made a big loaf pan of meat loaf and then put it in the oven. That way if any of the married children should show up for dinner, we'll have plenty. It is always so nice when the family comes home!

NOON We're eating dinner. Daughter Lovina and husband Joe and daughter Emma and husband Jacob are here to help eat our meat loaf, mashed potatoes, gravy, buttered corn, pork and beans, cheese, and all the rest of the goodies. Emma and Lovina also brought some goodies along!

1 p.m. Everyone decided to go back into the woods which are on the far, far back edge of our farm, which is 1/2 mile back. I said I'm too tired to walk back so a horse and buggy was to haul us or some of us, especially me. Ha! It was such a wonderful beauty to see in God's created woods: there were chirping birds, big trees, wild flowers, which the grandchildren were picking and handing them over to me for Mother's Day. It really felt relaxing back there away from everything. There is wildlife, though, like wildcats, in the woods.

5:30 p.m. Son Albert and his family stopped by for supper to get in on the leftovers from dinner. Joe and Lovina stayed also. The leftovers make it handy to prepare the evening meal.

8 p.m. Daughter Susan's birthday is tomorrow. It looks like another great day ahead of us. It will also be our first day of putting seeds out for the garden. This is a good sign of the moon to plant by. Susan has brought vegetables for a taco supper if any of the family happens to come for her birthday tomorrow night. Good night.

I hope you readers stay healthy, and most of all, happy.

Here is the recipe for meatloaf that we had for dinner.

HOMEMADE MEATLOAF

1 1/2 pounds ground beef
3/4 cups of rolled, uncooked oats
1/4 cup of chopped onion
3/4 cup of milk
1 1/2 teaspoons of salt

1/4 teaspoons of butter
1 egg, beaten

Combine all ingredients and mix thoroughly. Pack into a loaf pan.

Sauce:

1/3 cup of catsup
2 tablespoons of brown sugar
1 tablespoon of prepared mustard

Combine the sauce ingredients and pour over meat loaf. Bake in preheated 350 degree oven for one hour. Let stand five minutes before slicing.

JUNE 1999

With my daughter Susan laid up because of the tri-break in her leg, I've been without her good help around the homestead. The garden just couldn't get its thorough weeding and care without Susan these past few weeks. Susan, age 23, was usually out there other years as she likes working outdoors, caring for our garden. Hopefully, one of these days she'll be on the mend.

While I was away at the wedding in Ohio, of all things our married daughters came over to surprise me by completely tending to our garden. It looks so nice! It was quite a surprise. Then one evening, our son-in-law came over and mowed most of the yard. The help of family is so appreciated!

This morning, I am doing laundry. What a good feeling to be doing the laundry out there. Just got done doing a laundry, which we do using a hand-cranked washer. Then it hangs out on the clothesline on this beautiful sunny day. Daughter Verena is completing our weekly cleaning now and I should be getting dinner ready, but I want to hurry and get this in the mail today. It just really has to be done or I'll be late for this task of writing. But what would we do in life without a family to help us? We just got behind with our work, but there is so much to be thankful for. Good health means so much.

My husband, Ben, went back to work Tuesday on the dairy farm several miles away. He was out of work for most of the winter with pneumonia. But his journey back to work didn't last long, as the dust, he just couldn't handle it, so it's good he's back home to help with repairs. There's always so much to be done when you live on a farm.

This week has been nice, but chilly, out there. But I like it this way for a change after our hot weather. Nicer to work outside.

The garden gives us easier meal planning with all those vegetables out there to prepare. Soups, salads, and cooking of fresh vegetables are just some of the things we can make when the garden is going good. We put out 10 pounds of onions this week. Also, green onions, radishes, lettuce

are so good on the menu right now. Later, we planted another couple pounds of onions. So they coming along nice. This year we're fastening our tomato plants to bamboo sticks to keep them from
leaning towards the ground. It seems to be working, this is the first time we have tried this.

How about some reader mail answered?

To the Logansport, Indiana reader in request of the sandwich spread I mentioned in a recent column. Here is the recipe: 12 green tomatoes, 12 green mangoes, 12 red mangoes, 2 large onions, 1 cup of prepared mustard, 1/2 cup sugar, 1/4 cup salt, 1 tablespoon of celery seed. Stir all of this together and boil for 15 minutes. Take off stove and add 1 quart of your favorite salad dressing. Mix and put back on real low heat so it wont boil. Can and seal while hot.

To the Hays, Kansas reader, and others who have asked. On a rhubarb skillet cake recipe that ran several weeks ago about when to add the egg. I reckon, you mix it how it best suits with the wet and dry ingredients. Add the egg when you add the flour.

HAMBURGER CASSEROLE

2 pounds ground beef
6 medium potatoes, sliced thin
2 large onions, sliced
2 10 ounce cans cream of mushroom soup
1 cup water

Put a layer of each in baking dish, in order given. Pour cup of water over mixture.
 Cover and bake at 350 until potatoes are tender, about 1 1/2 hours.

JUNE 1999

𝕴t's been busy around here lately, especially without Susan's help. She can do hand-sewing work while she is laid up, still recovering from the triple-break in her ankle.

Susan has two screws on one side and five screws on the other side. She is enjoying the cards and gifts that so many wonderful readers have sent to her. So, she's glad to see the mailman arrive each day. Her break happened May 16. On June 9, a boot was put on her. Since then, she has been told to exercise 10 minutes twice a day and keep it washed off. So far, so good, when it comes to not putting weight on the leg. She gets around with crutches.

Well, I have laundry to do and must get with it. Glad my daughter Verena is here to
help this ol' lady. Ha! I will now take some time to answer reader mail.

To the Coshocton, Ohio, reader who requested how I make tomato gravy: Take 1 quart of tomato juice (I use my homemade, home-canned kind) and bring to a boil and add a milk thickening. The milk thickening consists of 2 tablespoons of flour and a cup of milk combined. Bring to a boil and remove from heat. Season with salt and pepper. This is delicious!

To the Michigan and Ohio readers about the Amish friendship bread starter 3 1/2 cups of bread flour, 1 tablespoon of sugar, 1 package of dry yeast, 2 cups warm water. Combine flour, sugar and undissolved yeast into a large bowl. Gradually add warm water to dry ingredients. Beat until smooth. Cover with transparent wrap and let stand in a warm place for 2 days.

Important: Do not use a metal spoon or mixing bowl when making starter or bread, as this can interfere with the fermentation process. Use a wooden or plastic spoon, and preferably, a glass bowl. Do not stir. It is natural for the starter to bubble and rise. Proceed to Part II.

Note: Bread flour may be easily obtained from your local grocer. It is different from all-purpose flour because it contains a gluten-forming protein that is essential to the structure in yeast breads. Also use bread flour in Part II.

Part II
Amish Friendship Bread

Directions for the prepared starter:

Day 1: Do nothing.
Days 2, 3, 4: Stir starter (with a wooden or plastic spoon).
Day 5: To starter add 1 cup each, flour, sugar and milk. Stir, re-cover loosely with plastic wrap and set in a warm place.
Days 6, 7, 8, 9: Stir each day and re-cover.
Day 10: To starter, add 1 cup each flour, sugar and milk. Stir well. Put 1 cup quantities into three separate containers and give to three friends with these instructions. Use remaining starter to make your own bread.

Ingredients for bread:

2/3 cup oil
2 cups flour
1/2 cup flour
1 1/2 teaspoons baking powder
3 eggs
2 teaspoons cinnamon
1 teaspoon vanilla
1/2 teaspoon salt
1/2 teaspoon baking soda
Large box (5.1 ounces) instant vanilla pudding
1 cup chopped nuts, pecans or walnuts

Preheat oven to 350 degrees. Grease and flour 2 (9- by 5-inch) loaf pans, metal or glass, or a bundt pan.

To remaining starter, add ingredients in order listed, beginning with oil and ending with nuts. By hand, mix well.

Divide batter between loaf pans, or pour all into bundt pan, if using. Bake 40 to 50 minutes in preheated oven. (If using bundt pan, the entire 50 minutes will be needed). Toward end of baking time, watch bread carefully and cover with foil, if necessary, to prevent burning. Test center for doneness with a toothpick. Cool in loaf pans for 10 minutes, then invert onto cooling racks, placing bread right-side up to finish cooling. If using bundt pan, cool for 1 hour before inverting onto serving plate.

To the Gas City, Ind., reader who requested a recipe for Mississippi Mud: 1 1/2 cups of brown sugar, 2 1/2 cups milk, 1/2 cup water, 1 teaspoon vanilla, 3 eggs, separated, 4 tablespoons flour, 12 graham crackers, 1 tablespoon butter (heaping). Heat milk, egg yolks and butter in pan until butter is melted. Add sugar and water and boil until thick. Add vanilla and put into a baking dish. Roll graham crackers to crush and spread on top.

Spread with beaten egg whites and a few graham cracker crumbs. Brown slightly in a 350-degree oven.

To the Indianapolis reader who requested the recipe of glazed strawberry pie: 1 quart fresh strawberries, 1/2 cup powdered sugar, 1/2 cup water, 3/4 cup sugar, 1 tablespoon cornstarch, 1 baked pie shell and whipped cream. Wash and stem berries. Mix 3 cups of them with powdered sugar and let stand 1 hour. Crush remaining cup of berries until mushy, add 1/2 cup water and stew for a minute. Then stir in sugar and cornstarch until clear. If not as red as desired, add a little red food coloring. Spread berries over bottom of baked pie shell and pour hot glaze over them. Top with whipped cream.

A Danville, Ky., reader asked how I make apple dumplings. This is one of these recipes I just go by feel so it is hard to write out a recipe, but I make a pie dough and roll out, cut up in 6-inch squares and put half of a peeled apple in it and roll it up. Put into a greased pan and bake at 325 degrees until golden brown.

To the Muncie, Ind., reader about "taco salad." This is a favorite around here. I use 1 head of lettuce (chopped up), 1 onion (chopped up), 2 tomatoes (cut up), 1 1/2 pounds of hamburger, 1 16-ounce bottle of Western French dressing, 1 package of taco seasoning, 1 8-ounce package of shredded cheese, 14 1/2-ounce bag Doritos and a 15-ounce can of kidney beans, drained. Brown hamburger and drain. Then add taco seasoning to hamburger. Simmer a couple of minutes. Cool. Add tomatoes, onions, beans, cooled hamburger and cheese to lettuce. When ready to serve, add dressing and crushed Doritos to lettuce mixture. Toss well.

To the Cincinnati reader, is this the recipe you were wanting for bread?

WHITE BREAD

1 package dry yeast

2 1/2 cups lukewarm water
1 tablespoon salt
2 tablespoons sugar
2 tablespoons lard
Enough flour for a soft dough

Mix ingredients and let rise until double. Punch down. Let rise again. Work down and form loaves. Put in greased loaf pans and let rise.Bake in a 300- to 325-degree oven for 30 to 35 minutes.

JUNE 1999

𝕴t is Thursday morning at 3:30 a.m. as I write this. The calendar shows June 1999. Time has a way of slipping by.

June is the month for weddings around here. We are planning to attend one today. It will be an all-day occasion. Daughter Verena is one of the table-waiters and is to wear a teal blue dress and a white cape and apron. Next Tuesday we plan to attend a wedding which is around a four hour drive by a van. Daughter Susan was to be a tablewaiter and Verena a coffee-server. Their dresses are to be a dark blue in color. Some prefer a royal blue, light blue, etc. as table waiters. The ones who are to cook the meals today are to wear a royal blue dress and a white cape and apron. Table-waiters and coffee-servers wait on the many people who attend the wedding meal.

Wedding services will start off at 9 a.m. today and will be held at the home of the bride. A good noon meal will be served right after the wedding. Also the evening meal is still plentiful for those who stay.

Too bad daughter Susan will not be able to attend both weddings because of her broken ankle She's afraid of making a misstep on the stairs or of someone bumping her ankle. So she plans to spend the day at daughter Lovina's. She has been doing a lot of our hand-sewing since her break of the ankle. I miss her work in he garden. She was always one to hoe and weed all my flowers. What would we've done without the help of our daughter Verena?

We've been having frequent rains this week which is good for the garden, pastures, crops and hay. It is good for filling our cisterns also. So refreshing! Spring is always the best of the four seasons, or so it seems to me. So much to be thankful for.

Will share a recipe as what's usually to be seen on the wedding tables. Yes, the cost now-a-days are high enough to prepare those big wedding meals, but they are enjoyable.

WEDDING NOTHINGS

1 egg
3 cookspoons of cream or Milnot (cookspoons are large kitchen-spoons)
pinch of salt
all purpose flour

Beat egg, cream, and salt. Add flour to make a stiff-like dough. Divide into 6 or 7 balls. Roll out very thin. Cut 3 slits after rolled out. Have a kettle of hard lard or Crisco ready to deep fry them in. Put one by one into the kettle. Turn over with two forks when you see a slight golden in color. Take out and put on a plate covered with paper towels to drain. Stack them on one another and sprinkle each one with sugar. Some call these "knee patches" also.

Our first wedding (for daughter Leah) we served chicken and noodles, 100 quarts mashed potatoes, over 250 pounds of fried chicken, 150 pounds boneless ham, corn (our home-canned), dressing, carrot salad (used 42 boxes of orange jello), 5 gallons of pork & beans, 22 quarts of potato salad, 24 heads of lettuce, 33 cakes, 15 batches of nothings, our own canned fruit salad, over 900 cookies and 16 stalks of celery. We also had coffee, jam, and apple butter. It takes lots of food for two wedding meals.

In the evening, candy bars are passed around. It took over 700 candy bars for Leah's wedding. We served around 1000 people that day. It was an enjoyable day when you think back then. Our first wedding experience.

Well, sounds like the rest of the family is still asleep at this early morning hour. So I will close for now. Have a happy day.

JUNE 1999

We had a long, but enjoyable journey yesterday.

Tuesday morning, 1:30 a.m.: A group from our area left for a wedding, which was a 4 1/2 hour drive by van. It took awhile till everyone from various places were loaded to go. We headed for Fredricksburg, Ohio. Daughter Verena and husband Ben were also along.

7 a.m. We all stopped to eat breakfast at the Dutch Heart restaurant in Apple Creek, Ohio. It was a good restaurant to eat at.

8:30 a.m. Wedding services were to start. It would've been 7:30 a.m. on Indiana time where we live. In the evening to start home it made it good to gain an hour. It was such a beautiful day, but hot.

11:30 a.m. After a three-hour service, held outdoors in a large, well-cleaned out shed, with lots of people, the couple were united in marriage.

Noon - A good dinner was served to all in attendance at the wedding. Lots of good food and desserts The main meat was fried chicken. This area, unlike back home, has only girls for waiting on tables and for coffee-servers. Our daughter Verena was one of the coffee-servers and daughter Susan was to be a table-waiter but didn't attend the wedding because of her tri-break in her ankle. She regretted not being able to attend. Weddings are different in Ohio Amish communities than ours. I guess weddings in each area are somewhat different, but it is interesting to see how others have theirs. They had seven long tables in their shed to serve plus several long tables in the basement. I never asked how many they could seat at one time, but the table I ate at, there were 28. In our area we have a table for the children outside, and the children eat cafeteria-style. At this wedding, tables and benches were set up and men and women took their children along to the wedding tables. So it was interesting to see how this area did their weddings.

In the afternoon, the bride and groom and their attendants opened the many wedding gifts they received. As the wedding gifts were being opened singing and yodeling took place. And then a good evening meal was served to all in attendance. The tables were all filled again. Afterwards singing and yodeling took place before we headed home. We arrived back home at 12:33 a.m. Wednesday morning. It was such an enjoyable day!.

This is now Wednesday and daughter Susan had to be to the Dr. in Ft. Wayne. The Dr. took her coast off and put one of those boots on her foot. She has to wear it for four weeks and use crutches. Hopefully it will all be healed by July. She looks forward to the many cards and letters. Thanks to the many readers who have cheered her days with cards.

A reader wrote asking about blackberries and any good ways to prepare them. Try this good recipe for "blackberry cake."

BLACKBERRY CAKE

3 eggs
1 1/2 cups shortening
1 teaspoon cloves
3 cups flour
1 teaspoon baking soda

1 1/2 cups sugar
2 teaspoons cinnamon
2 cups blackberries, crushed
2 teaspoons baking powder

Combine eggs, shortening, cinnamon, and cloves in a large mixing bowl. Beat until well blended. Add blackberries and remaining ingredients. Pour into a greased 13X9X2" pan. Bake at 350 for 35 minutes or until done.

JULY 1999

This is Thursday morning before 4 a.m., and I want to get this task of writing completed. Guess it shouldn't get neglected. It feels nice and cool this morning after our hot weather.

The gardens and crops are looking so great with our frequent rains lately. We never know with the crops until they're harvested. I am sure you farmers out there understand. Hay seems to be plentiful this year. We have nicer and bigger apples from our yellow transparent trees this year. The apples are bigger than in years past.

I was canning applesauce yesterday afternoon from our fallen apples. I really didn't have that on the list of tasks to be done, but I hate to see those apples go to waste. I will probably process some more applesauce today.

We have plastic two-liter 7-Up bottles hanging from our three apple trees. They really do the job for getting rid of unwanted insects, especially flies. Once the flies enter that bottle, they are done for. It's remarkable how much of those insects are in a bottle. Take one cup of vinegar, one cup of sugar and a couple of banana peelings and put them into the bottle.

Then fill the two-liter bottle three-fourths full of water. Seal and shake well. Then take the cap off and tie the bottle onto a tree branch. It sure does the trick. Makes for fewer flies if you want to eat a meal outside.

We have entered the month of July. This is my birthday month. How this time slips by. Life goes on.

I will answer some reader mail which is more than plentiful.

To the Decatur, Ind., reader: I have never heard of a pie called "Tears on My Pillow." The reader says it is made with brown sugar and canned condensed milk.

To the Danville, Ind., reader: You asked about darning for cotton socks. Try Hilty's Dry Goods Store, Berne, Indiana, 46711.

To all the readers who wrote asking when to add the egg to the rhubarb skillet cake recipe that ran several weeks ago: All you do is, after you cream together the butter and sugar, add the beaten egg, and follow the instructions as given.

To the Logootee, Ind., reader who requested ice box oatmeal cookies.

These are a favorite around here. You'll need: 1 cup of lard, 1 cup of brown sugar, 1 cup of white sugar, 2 beaten eggs, 1 teaspoon vanilla, 1 1/2 cups of flour, 1 teaspoon baking soda, 1 teaspoon salt and 3 cups of oatmeal. Cream together the lard and sugars, add beaten eggs and vanilla. Sift together flour, baking, soda and salt, and add to sugar mixture. Then add oatmeal. Mix well. Shape the dough into 2 or 3 rolls. Chill overnight. Slice vertically into 1/2-inch thick slices and bake at 350 degrees until done (10 minutes) the next morning.

Well, I must get this task to a halt. Daughter Susan is awaiting her doctor appointment this week. Hopefully, she'll get good news about her broken ankle. She's been a patient since May 16. While she has been laid up, she's done a lot of hand-sewing, which sometimes gets neglected around here.

She's been enjoying her many cards sent by readers. God has a purpose for it all, although we shouldn't question why. Without Verena's help, it would be more of a struggle around here. Also, the married daughters have been coming home to help. There's always a way, it seems. Busy time of year, especially busy, it seems. Some of the girls are planning to be here today, so sewing will be on the list.

A reader in Holmes Beach, Fla., requested a good breakfast recipe that uses sausage. Here is one that goes good around here:

SUNRISE BREAKFAST

4 slices bread
1 10-ounce package of smoky links, sliced very thin (or
you can use your own butchered meat like we do)
1 cup shredded Cheddar cheese or 1 10 3/4-ounce can
cheese soup
6 eggs
2 cups milk
1 teaspoon salt

Break bread into pieces and put into a greased 9- by 9-inch baking pan. Lay sausage over the bread and cover with cheese. Beat the eggs, milk and salt together until smooth. Pour over bread and ingredients in the pan. Bake at 350 degrees for 1 hour or until done. It will look crusty brown on the sides and top.

JULY 1999

𝕵t is hot and dry out there. Rain would be welcome and greatly appreciated.

We are happy this morning that Susan got a good report from the doctor about the tri-break in her ankle. He said she can slowly begin putting weight on it over the next weeks. I've missed her good help around here. It is about time to prepare breakfast, a meal that some readers have inquired about.

Breakfast, of course, is the first meal of the day. Shouldn't it be a hearty meal to start the day off? It seems the kitchen is often the warmest room in the house where the food is usually prepared, so during winter we all head in there. The kitchen is always the room where the whole family meets for the morning meal hour and the conversation that goes with it to start the day off.

Mealtime has an interesting part to it. When I was younger, in the home of my parents, the breakfast meal consisted of fried potatoes, coffee soup, cheese and liver pudding. But now we hardly ever have coffee soup (a cup of coffee with bread mixed in). Today, we have bacon, fried eggs, potatoes, biscuits and gravy, cheese, toast and whatever we've got.

Our Christmas family gathering is probably the most special breakfast of the year with fried eggs, potatoes, omelets, cottage cheese, ham, cheese and home -- baked bread, along with biscuits and gravy on the menu. Plus all those other Christmas goodies, which have no calories. Ha!

The family always enjoys those home-baked slices of bread on the table, with butter or jam to go with it. Cinnamon rolls are favored by our family. Coffee and rolls go together great. Coffee, tea and assorted juices are the traditional beverages at breakfast. Hot or cold creamy chocolate also goes good amongst the children.

During the summer, such as now, we have fresh fruits on the table. But in the wintertime, canned fruits are on the table. Also, bananas serve a good purpose anytime. So you all out there keep eating a good, hearty breakfast. Here is a good one to try:

BACON AND EGG BAKE

6 slices bacon   1/2 medium onion, chopped
1/2 teaspoon salt   1/4 teaspoon pepper
1 (10 3/4-ounce) can cream of mushroom soup
5 hard boiled eggs, diced
2 cups shredded cheddar cheese
1/4 cup milk

Heat oven to 350 degrees. Fry bacon until crisp. Remove from skillet; drain fat. Reserve 2 tablespoons of fat from bacon. Fry onions in the tablespoons of fat. Stir in soup, milk, cheese, eggs and seasonings until well blended with onions. Pour into 9- by 9-inch baking dish, and top with crumbled bacon. Bake 20 minutes. Serve over biscuits.
Feeds 5.

JULY 1999

It is early morning as I write this on a hot July morning. The girls are out doing the barn chores right now.

Morning chores have changed a lot from years ago. We still have a cow to milk for our own use of milk. The grandchildren enjoy drinking the milk, and we also use it for cooking. We used to have 12 cows to milk by hand in the morning - no modern milkers involved. It was a real family life at the time for my daughters and I to do the milking. My husband and sons were working on a carpenter crew. Kerosene lamps are used for the light in the barn in the mornings or during evening chores. Some have goats to milk and cattle to feed and provide bedding to. Stainless steel milk cans are in use today as years ago it wasn't. Rules are to keep those milk cans clean just as you would a container for kitchen use. Then there's morning house chores as getting breakfast for all of the family. Wash those dishes then. Make beds, sweep and mop floors. The list can go on and on.

The winter brings more morning chores when the ash pans from our heat-providing, wood-burning stoves, needs to be emptied. Woodboxes need to be filled with wood and coal buckets kept full and the chimneys in good working order. Believe me, there are lots of chores around to be done when you live on a farm.

In the summer-time, the garden needs its care in the morning while it is cool. Year-round, the barn and milk-house have to be kept clean when you milk cows. There's lot of rules when you're milking cows, you farmers know what I mean.

A reader in Mishawaka, Indiana wrote asking about how to store "extra eggs." She said she had heard of packing eggs in salt to preserve them. I had not heard of that before.

In the winter-time we save eggs longer. In the summer we try to use the eggs up within two weeks. If the eggs start to get old, I use them for hard-boiled eggs or in baking. I also make lots of extra noodles. We purchase our eggs from a nearby farmer.

Speaking of morning chores, homemade doughnuts go good in the morning. Here is my recipe:

YEAST DOUGHNUTS

2 packages yeast
4 Tablespoons sugar
1 cup lukewarm water
1 cup scalded milk
2 teaspoons salt
1/2 cup shortening
3 eggs, beaten
6 cups flour

Sift 6 cups of flour in a bowl and set aside. In a small dish, pour water over yeast and 1 tablespoon sugar. Stir and let stand. Meanwhile, pour scalded milk in a bowl and add salt, 3 tablespoons sugar, and then shortening; stir until shortening is melted. When milk mixture is lukewarm, add water and yeast mixture, and 3 cups flour. Beat till smooth and add beaten eggs and rest of flour. Let rise in a warm place until double. Punch down and roll out on floured board until about 1/2 inch thick. Cut out doughnuts with a doughnut shaped cutter and let rise. Then, in deep skillet, fry in about two inches hot hard lard or shortening, turning once after rising and becoming light brown. Remove when doughnut has risen and is slightly brown on both sides and
drain on paper towels. Makes about 75 doughnuts.

AUGUST 1999

𝕿omatoes are still on the menu for every meal. Our garden is going well, especially considering how dry it has been lately. But we had some rain during the night, so it's a dreary day.

However, the flowers are still beautiful and with our rhubarb, I've made five batches of jam. That takes five cups of diced rhubarb and 4 cups of sugar to a batch. You have to let it stand overnight. In the morning, it has to be cooked for 5 minutes and a 6-ounce package of strawberry-flavored gelatin added. I put the mixture in the jars and seal (Refrigerator storage is best if the jam jars are not processed in a water-bath canner).

We've also canned some hot peppers -- long banana ones and jalapeno peppers. We have them on the menu for every meal. They go so well diced into fried eggs and potatoes for breakfast with bacon, cheese, and toast.

Some of our garden peppers are really hot. I wonder if the weather being hot and dry causes them to turn hotter?

Want to try this recipe for hot-pepper butter. It takes 45 hot peppers, which you grind, then add 1 quart of vinegar, 1 pint of yellow mustard, 7 cups of sugar, and 1 tablespoon of salt. Put all in a non-reactive saucepan and bring it to a boil. Then make a paste with 1 cup of flour and 1-1/2 cups of cold water. Add that to the boiling mixture and cook for five minutes. Pour into jars and seal. It makes 7 pints (Process in a water-bath canner for safe on-the-shelf storage. Or refrigerate the jars to share with friends).

We're still enjoying corn on the cob from the garden.

Well, I will share some more recipes with you great readers out there.

EASY-BAKED FRENCH FRIES

Potatoes (as needed)
Cornflake crumbs
Salt
Melted butter
BAKING TIME: At least five minutes

Peel as many potatoes as you need. Cut lengthwise into 3/8-inch strips or 3/8-inch slices. Dip into melted butter, sprinkle with salt and roll in cornflake crumbs. Place potatoes in a shallow baking dish or on a cookie sheet in a single layer. Bake at 375 degrees at least 5 minutes or until golden brown.

MOTHER'S RHUBARB CAKE

5 cups of freshly chopped rhubarb (I use fresh from garden, but frozen is okay)
1 (3-ounce) package of dry strawberry-flavored gelatin
1 tablespoon of cornstarch
2 cups of miniature marshmallows
1 box (2 layer-size) of yellow or white cake mix

YIELD: 9 servings
PREP TIME: 30 minutes
BAKING TIME: 1 hour

Thaw and drain rhubarb, if using frozen. Toss rhubarb with the dry gelatin and cornstarch. Spread evenly in a 13X9 inch baking pan. Top with marshmallows. Then prepare the cake mix to the batter stage following directions on the box. Pour batter evenly over marshmallows. Bake at 350 degrees for 1 hour or until done. Serve with whipped cream.

AUGUST 1999

We had a welcome rain this week. It's been so hot and muggy. I reckon that's why those unwanted tomato worms are so plentiful on our tomato plants.

My son-in-law has gotten 47 worms off their plants. The tomatoes are of good taste, though, which are so good with sandwiches, salads, soups and other summer goodies this time of year.

The cucumbers are still plentiful here but lots have lost their plants from the hot and dry weather. So good to make salads with them too. Sweet corn on cob is going good now. We helped our daughter Liz on Monday with canning all their sweet corn, which was a relief on her to have help.

To the Indianapolis reader, and others, who wrote asking about the "fly traps" I wrote about these several weeks ago. Let me provide a bit more detail. Some people wrote saying that no flies were caught.

We have plastic two-liter 7-Up bottles hanging from our three apple trees. Once the flies enter that bottle, they are trapped. It's remarkable how many of those insects become trapped in the bottle. The instructions are: Take one cup of vinegar, one cup of sugar and a couple of banana peelings and put them into the bottle. Then fill the 2-liter bottle three-fourths full of water. Seal and shake well. Then take the cap off and tie the bottle onto a tree branch. It sure does the trick. Makes for fewer flies if you want to eat a meal outside.

We always use the green two-liter 7-Up bottles and use the apple cider vinegar and plenty of banana peelings. Some wrote saying they used white vinegar. I don't know if the type of vinegar makes a difference, but we use apple cider vinegar. Also, it takes a couple of days until you see a fly in those bottles hung under the trees. But once they start going in, you see all kinds of insects in those bottles. Remember, the bottles are only to be filled three-fourths of the way. I hope this helps. Give it a try to get rid of bugs!

Daughter Susan is still going around with the aid of crutches. Hopefully, soon She'll be putting them away.

To the Highland Heights, Ky., reader who asked where you can get alum. I'd think you can buy alum in drug stores.

Daughter Verena is doing our huge stack of ironing this morning. She assisted daughter Lovina on Monday with her household duties, as Lovina and her family continue to enjoy their newborn bundle. Lovina and Joe's baby seems to be gaining weight now. It is good to have Verena's help here at home again.

Daughters Liz, Lovina and Emma spent the day here yesterday helping clean the house. I was glad for their help. There's always plenty of work around here. The grandchildren are always glad to see grandma's candy dish. Ha!

Well, I had best get this in the mail as I guess I was out in the garden too long before I took up the task of writing.

I will try and answer some more of the reader mail in this column next week, hopefully. Don't let this hot weather get the best of you readers out there.

Here is a good recipe to use those garden green beans:

PICKLED GREEN BEANS

3 to 4 slices bacon
3 to 4 tablespoons chopped onions
2 tablespoons sugar
2 to 3 tablespoons vinegar
2 tablespoons water
1/4 teaspoon salt
1/4 teaspoon pepper
1 quart green beans

Fry bacon and onions. Add sugar, vinegar, water, salt and pepper. Add green beans and simmer 5 to 10 minutes.

This recipe ran in my column earlier this year, but it was mislabeled as "Rhubarb Crunch Cake." It is actually just called "rhubarb crunch." So many have written about this one, so here it is again.

RHUBARB CRUNCH

3 cups rhubarb (cut into small pieces)
1 box strawberry or cherry Jell-O
1 box cake mix (yellow or white)
3/4 cup melted margarine
1 package marshmallows

Put rhubarb cuts in buttered 9- by 13-inch baking dish. Pour dry Jell-O and marshmallows over this. Pour dry cake mix over all of this and drizzle margarine on top. Bake at 375 degrees for 45 minutes.

AUGUST 1999

𝕴t is a nice Thursday morning as we progress through August. We had a much-needed rain of 1 3/10 inch last night, but we need more. My thoughts today go back years ago when my daughters Leah and Verena were born during this month. Leah was born in 1959 and Verena in 1966.

I've got two 20-quart cookers of tomatoes ready to put into juice. The tomatoes from our garden will be turned into homemade V-8 juice, good and hot. To make the juice, I cooked tomatoes, adding celery, green beans, onions, sweet peppers, hot peppers, banana hot peppers and cabbage to it. I would've added carrots if I had some ready from the garden but they are too mall as yet.

The juice will be put into sterilized glass jars and processed. Be a good drink for those cold days when tomatoes won't be available. So good to fill those jars for the winter ahead. It is lots of work but worth it to fill those jars now and prepare those meals ahead of time for the long winter.

It is very important to keep everything clean in the kitchen when processing food. You have to keep the jars clean and sterilized. Mother never even let the children have cracker crumbs around as it could cause the food to spoil later on. I have good memories of how my mother taught her daughters how to clean. She's gone to a better land but not forgotten. Life goes on, right?

It's two years ago our 6-year-old granddaughter Mary Shetler left us for a better home. God makes no mistakes. Her brother Paul Jr. seems to be getting along well.

Thanks to all you readers out there who sent me a birthday card. I have found out I have some "twins" out there also born on July 18, 1936. Good month, good day, good year. Ha!

Daughter Susan had good results yesterday when saw the doctor again about her tri-break in her ankle. She can get around now without the aid of crutches. It's like walking all over again, not fast. She had some long, but patient days. A lot of cards and visits from family and friends kept her spirits up through all this.

Well, I had best get the tomato juice into the jars to be processed. Time goes on and it seems to not wait at such a time. A reader in Decatur, Ind., requested a recipe for this pie, which I'm not sure how it got its name. Does anyone out there know?

TEARS ON YOUR PILLOW PIE

1/3 cup butter, melted
1 1/2 cup brown sugar
2 eggs
1 Tablespoon all-purpose flour
1/2 cup evaporated milk
1-9 inch unbaked pie shell

Preheat oven to 350 degrees. In a large bowl, beat together the butter, brown sugar, eggs, flour, and milk until well-blended. Pour the filling into the pie shell. Bake at 350 for 15 minutes, or until crust is golden brown. Turn off oven and leave the pie for 45 minutes to 1 hour. Serves 6 to 8.

AUGUST 1999

Sunday, Aug. 15, is when our first newborn, Leah, now Mrs. Paul M. Shetler, was born 40 years ago. Then followed two sons and then five girls.

For those who write wondering about their ages it is: Leah, 40; Amos, 38; Albert, 35; Verena, 33; Liz, 30; Lovina, 28; Emma, 26, and Susan, 23. Susan and Verena still live with us at home; the rest have families of their own but all live nearby.

It was hard to see our daughter Leah attend her first year in school and more yet when our youngest daughter had her last day of school. These years flew by. But it was enjoyable to attend parties and programs the children would put on at school. Now the grandchildren and all the other children are gearing up for the start of school around here in the coming days.

This morning I have been out in the garden. A reader in Somerset, Pa., sent me some melon seeds that she said made great big melons. They are doing great so far. The garden has been good, considering the hot, dry weather we have had. We canned some more homemade V-8 juice yesterday. I should can pickles or share them with someone as I really don't need them. We had corn on the cob last night for supper, which I had put out as a second patch.
Was good eating. Yummy!

Friday evening we had a belated July birthday supper for the July birthdays. A total of 100 family members came for a taco supper. Also some other cooked food and desserts were brought. Had such a nice evening.

This morning, daughters Emma, Lovina and Liz, and nine grandchildren dropped in. They were attending a nearby garage sale. So we had breakfast together -- very enjoyable.

Lovina's newborn son, Benjamin, was in the hospital over the weekend from being dehydrated and having gastroenteritis. He seems better now. So while he was in the hospital, we had Lovina and Joe's three little girls with us over the weekend. We took them to church services Sunday and to the hospital in the evening.

A reader in Alexandria, Ky., wrote in asking to share my raisin bread recipe, which makes for a delicious start to the day.

RAISIN BREAD

1 1/2 cups milk
1/4 cup sugar
2 teaspoons salt
1/2 cup butter
1 cup unseasoned mashed potatoes
1/2 cup warm water
2 packages yeast
7 1/2 cups flour
1 1/2 cups raisins

Scald milk, remove from heat, and add sugar, salt, butter and mashed potatoes. Let cool. Dissolve yeast in water, then mix with milk. Add raisins and flour. Stir. Let rise in warm place 1 1/2 hours. Divide dough into 2 loaves. Then mix the following separately:

1/2 cup sugar
2 teaspoons cinnamon
1/2 cup butter or margarine (melted)

Then roll the set aside loaves out on a board and put half of butter, sugar and cinnamon mixture on each roll. Roll up as for a jelly roll and pinch edges together. Bake in loaf pans at 350 degrees to 375 degrees for 45 minutes.

AUGUST 1999

It is a nice Tuesday afternoon as I write this. After I am done writing, I will begin helping my daughters prepare dinner. We're having mashed potatoes, pork chops, gravy, corn and cheese. From the garden, I got tomatoes, hot peppers, cucumbers, muskmelons and lettuce.

This all together will make for a nice meal. The seeds have done so well considering the dry weather. We planted seeds for turnips and radishes last week and they are up already. I also planted some more tomato plants, just hoping to get tomatoes yet this fall. They are a big yellow and pink in color. I saved tomato seeds from last year. I had forgotten I had saved them. So time will tell if I'll get tomatoes from them.

Daughter Leah and her children walked over this morning. They live about one and one-half miles form here, so it was a surprise to see them walk in.

My daughters Verena and Susan went to my daughter Emma's this morning to get Verena's new teal dress and apron, which she will wear to a wedding Thursday. She is a tablewaiter at the wedding. Susan, Verena and I have to go to the wedding location tomorrow (Wednesday) to help with preparations.

The young, unmarried women always serve as tablewaiters for the meal after the wedding. They make sure dishes are cleared and everyone gets enough food.

While I am writing this, Leah is getting our pork chop dinner ready, and Verena is doing our huge stack of weekly ironing. Susan is doing the finishing touches to the new dress.

Ben is at the place where our horses are shod. So our horse had to get new shoes put on. The horse didn't need gas -- he needed shoes. Ha!

After coming home, the horse got well fed to make up for those miles. We feed it hay and grain.

Some of the family went to Paul and Leah's on Sunday for dinner in honor of her 40th birthday. Leah was our first born when we started out to raise a family. So everyone decided to be here for Sunday supper then. Always enjoyable to have family come home.

There will be several birthdays in the family Sunday, Aug. 22, including daughter Verena and grandchildren Elizabeth of son Albert's family and Paul Jr. Also I have a brother-in-law, Joe, and several other friends I know who have birthdays on that date.

My son Amos, his wife, Nancy, and their family, and son Albert, with his wife Sarah Irene and family, Ben, myself, and Susan visited a friend Saturday evening as he has cancer. Was good to see their families again. Had a nice visit.

The smell of dinner is in the air now. Smells yummy. So I must hurry to get this written.

A reader in Hutchinson asked about "wigglers," a popular dinner among some. Here is that recipe. Also, a reader in Danville, Ky., asked to repeat my nacho dip recipe.

NACHO DIP

2 pounds hamburger
1 1.25-ounce package taco seasoning
1 pound Velveeta cheese, cubed
1 15-ounce can Armour chili

Fry hamburger; drain. To cooked hamburger, add taco seasoning, chili and cheese. Mix and heat just until cheese is melted. Pour over chips.

WIGGLERS

2 pounds hamburger
2 onions, diced
5 slices bacon
1 1/2 cups celery
1 16-ounce package spaghetti, broken
2 cups cooked potatoes
2 10 3/4-ounce cans tomato soup, prepared according to instructions
1 15-ounce can peas, drained
1 15-ounce can sliced carrots, drained
1 10 3/4-ounce can mushroom soup

Fry bacon and crumble. Take out of skillet, and fry hamburger and onions in the bacon grease. Put bacon, hamburger and onion in the bottom of a deep 9- by 13-inch roaster. Put the spaghetti, potatoes, carrots, celery and peas on top of hamburger. Pour tomato soup over ingredients. Put mushroom soup on top. Bake for 1 hour at 350 degrees.

AUGUST 1999

I am sitting outside on a beautiful day writing this. I am at my daughter Lovina's and her husband Joe's.

The whole family was at Lovina's this morning for breakfast, which consisted of omelets, bacon, tomatoes, toast, hot peppers, cake, cereal, milk, coffee, tea and cheese.

The women are washing dishes now. The dishes, of course, are all washed and dried by hand. Makes for a big job in the morning. I am taking a break to write this column. While I am sitting outside writing this, the grandchildren are playing out here in the yard. Reminds me of short years ago when our children were at a tender age. The older grandchildren are in school right now as the year has begun for them, but it was delayed almost three hours this morning with a thick fog in the area. It has cleared out quite nicely now.

Another memory, with the cornfields being tall this time of year are corn-husking bees.

Who knows what a corn-husking bee is?

Well, we used to go to these bees years ago. There are still some people around here who have them, but they aren't as common.

Menfolk take the team of horses and wagon to the corn field when the harvest is ready to be husked. They jerk the ears of corn with the husk on and haul it back to the barn or a shed. This makes a long pile of corn ready to be husked. In the evening, the young people are invited to help husk the corn by lantern light. Benches are set up in front of the corn, so the job can be done sitting down. The husk is sorted. The clean white husk goes into a box and is put into a place to be kept clean.

Then the white husk is taken into the house to be put in a big sack (size of a bed) with four openings in it. They stuff the husks inside 'til the sack is full. This is then used as a mattress.

There's lots of singing and yodeling going on all evening. After this is completed, everyone goes in the house for soup, sandwiches or something to drink. There are still corn-husking bees today, but most people use regular store bought mattresses now -- although a few still have the husk-filled ones. Lots easier and less dust with a store-bought one, I'd say.

My children have never been to a corn-husking bee, so all I can do is explain how it was when I used to go to them -- it was lots of fun.

A reader in Battle Creek, Mich., and in Danville, Ky., wrote asking about a good zucchini casserole recipe.

ZUCCHINI CASSEROLE

3 cups shredded zucchini
1/2 cup cooking oil
1/2 cup shredded cheddar cheese
4 beaten eggs

1/4 cup chopped onion
1 cup Bisquick
1 teaspoon salt
1/4 teaspoon pepper
1 tablespoon Parsley (optional)

Beat eggs, add oil, and seasonings. Add rest of ingredients, except parsley. Pour into 9- by 9-inch baking dish. Sprinkle parsley on top. Bake 40 minutes at 350 degrees.

SEPTEMBER 1999

It is Monday morning as I write this. It was a busy weekend that just finished.

On Thursday, our water pump stopped on us. It would no longer throw water up from the well. What is it to be without water? So my husband got our five-gallon jug and went over to the neighbors for water. Some of the family said they would come over Friday evening to repair the pump. But, a nice surprise, son-in-law Paul and his son Ben came Friday morning and my husband, Paul, and grandson Ben got it repaired, without pay. So they had a late dinner.

I wanted them to come back here in the evening for supper, but I reckon they were too tired to come back. So the rest showed up in the evening, as promised, to repair the pump but by then it had been fixed. They did stay for supper, though.

Here for supper were: son Albert's, Joe's and Jacob's families. Joe got the grill in gear for barbecued chicken. Only Johnny salt was added and was so good. Good eating!

Then Albert told us to all come to their place on Sunday morning for homemade biscuits and gravy before church.

Amos and Nancy dropped in for Saturday night supper and stayed here for the night. What a treat to see son Amos and Nancy and seven children here for the night. We then all got up early on Sunday morning, got dressed for church services, and went to Albert's for breakfast. It was relaxing to ride in Amos' two-seated buggy on such a beautiful morning and to go to son Albert's for breakfast, where we met Joe's and Jacob's families. Paul and Leah didn't make it. After the biscuit and gravy breakfast we headed to church, arriving there early. The only bad thing: the weather has been too hot and dry. The gardens could use the rain.

Today, daughter Leah, Lovina, Emma and their children are here. So daughter Verena made pizza for dinner, topped with sliced tomatoes, sweet peppers, and mashed potatoes and gravy on the side. The list will go on, depending on what food we have.

We're canning tomato juice together today. Keep canning these tomatoes as to not leave them go to waste. Go good to fill those jars for the long winter ahead. So glad when the children fill their jars for the winter also. I think my jars are all full enough now but I am sharing with children what is from my garden. It just doesn't take as much for us anymore since we are not that many at the table, although the children and their families still come home for meals, which we so enjoy.

I can't believe as I look out the window how the trees are changing color. The leaves look beautiful already. The soybean fields are really turning colors and some are being combined.

Well, dinner is ready and I must meet the rest as my daughters are here. Always good to have them here.

A reader from Queensbury, N.Y., requested a lasagna recipe. This is a good one to use:

LAZY LASAGNA

2 pounds ground beef
1/2 onion, finely chopped
8 ounces tomato sauce
6 ounces tomato paste
1 teaspoon oregano
2 teaspoons sweet basil
1 tablespoon parsley
2 cloves garlic, minced
3 1/2 cups water
32 ounces cottage cheese
2 eggs, slightly beaten
2 pounds mozzarella cheese
1 16-ounce package lasagna noodles

Brown ground beef and onion in large skillet. Drain. Add tomato paste, sauce, 1/2 cup water, garlic and seasonings to meat mixture. Simmer for 10 minutes. Combine cottage cheese and eggs together. Layer half the meat, noodles, cottage cheese and cheese in 9- by 13-inch deep baking dish. Repeat. Pour remaining water over entire dish. Cover with foil and bake at 350 for 1 1/2 hours.

SEPTEMBER 1999

It is Sunday morning and our son Albert, his wife, Sarah Irene, and their seven children spent the night here. They had put a treatment on their new floors yesterday so it left a smell in the house.

The children were so glad to have spent a night here. It makes life happier to have our children and families spend a night here.

7 a.m. -- Breakfast was on the list for all of us. We had fried eggs, potatoes, bacon, cheese, toast, cereal and you name it. Glad when the grandchildren will eat whatever we prepare for a meal.

Noon -- More family dropped in, which is a wonderful way to spend a Sunday. A dinner was prepared with barbecued pork chops on the menu. Those here for dinner were Albert's family, Paul and Leah's family, Joe and Lovina's family, and Emma and Jacob's family.

Joe and Lovina's little son, Benjamin, seems to be gaining weight now. He was only 4 pounds 13 ounces at birth and later entered the hospital from being dehydrated. They caught it in time. He seems a good baby.

5: 30 p.m. -- It is suppertime and everyone has left, except for Joe's family. We got them to stay for leftovers. So this does it for today, the last Sunday in August. Where did time go? Many happenings have taken place this year: weddings, funerals, birthdays, reunions. Happy and sad events.

The grandchildren are once again back to school. We have 10 grandchildren of school age. I remember when our daughter Leah started her first day of school. It was a sad feeling to see her go. And it was such a sad feeling many years later when our youngest daughter Susan had her last day of school.

But they all liked their teachers at the public schools.

(Editor's note: While some people unfamiliar with Amish ways may be surprised to hear The Amish Cook talk about attending public schools, it is a very common practice among the Amish. Some Amish communities have their own, private "one-room" country schools, but many send their children to public entities through the eighth or ninth grade. Coblentz attended school through the ninth grade.)

When I was at school age, we went to a two-room public school. First to fourth grade were in one room (the little side), and fifth through eighth was called the "big side." A room for lunch buckets and coats divided the two. Then we moved to a different place, which brought us to grade nine and a high school. Was so different from a country school of eight grades. At the high school, they served a noon lunch, but who could almost afford it?

Money just wasn't that plentiful then. I remember this one school, the meal was 15 cents where we attended, but money wasn't there. So we packed lunch buckets back then, and it wasn't anything fancy. But we enjoyed it just the same, and mother made sure we had plenty to eat. I suppose some children today would turn their nose up if they'd have to eat out of lunch buckets what we used to eat.

When our eight children went to public schools where lunch was prepared, I thought it was healthier to leave them eat a warm meal at school. Made less work to pack the lunch and keep those buckets clean.

A couple of readers have written to me asking if I have heard of "watermelon preserves." I have not heard of those before. Maybe someone out there has and can share.

Also, a couple of weeks ago I talked about how we drink coffee or tea around here in the morning. I like to make a tea of fresh peppermint. Some have written in asking about how to make that tea.

Take leaves from peppermint and pour boiling water over it in a kettle. And turn on very low heat for 10 to 15 minutes. Do not boil. The amount of peppermint you use depends on how strong of a peppermint taste you want.

Try this recipe for another good way to start your day.

CREAMED EGGS ON TOAST

4 hard-boiled eggs, sliced
1/4 cup margarine
1/4 cup flour
2 cups milk
1/2 teaspoon salt
6 slices of bacon, fried and crumbled
4 slices of toast

Melt margarine and blend in flour in large sauce pan until smooth and bubbly. Add milk all at once and salt, stirring continuously over high heat. Continue stirring until thick and creamy. Add sliced eggs and crumbled bacon. Stir to blend. Pour over prepared toast and serve.SEPTEMBER 1999

A reader from Catlin, Illinois requested a recipe for "saw-dust pie", I have never heard of that. Does anyone out there know what that is?

A reader from Sherwood, Michigan wrote to me and was surprised that I had never heard of keeping eggs stored in salt. In her letter she writes about how she remembers going into the her dirt-floor basement for eggs that she had helped salt down. She wrote that her mother used a 20 gallon crock and layered the salt, then eggs (small end down) as in a carton, another layer of salt, and so on until the crock was filled. She wrote the eggs were ice cold and her hands felt frozen digging for eggs. She said they did this as the hens didn't lay in the winter due probably to chilly houses and poor feed. Interesting to read that letter.

To the Kewaunee, Wisconsin reader: about the comfrey tea that I make. Yes, we used the fresh leaves. Pour boiling water over it. Do not boil. Use as much comfrey as you prefer for the strength you like. Y ou can also dry the leaves for the winter use. I feel it makes such a healthful tea.

To the Indianapolis reader who asked for my macaroni and cheese recipe: 3 tablespoons butter or margarine, 2 1/2 cups uncooked macaroni, 1 teaspoon salt, 1/4 teaspoon pepper, 1/2 pound Velveeta cheese, 4 cups milk. Melt margarine in 9x13 baking dish, pour in macaroni. Stir until macaroni is all buttered. Slice cheese and cut each slice into 4 pieces. Add salt and pepper, cheese and cold milk to macaroni. Bake uncovered at 350 for 1 1/2 hours. Do not stir when baking.

To the Dansville, NY reader who requested a recipe for caramel icing: Here's one - 1/4 cup margarine or butter, 3/4 cup firmly packed light brown sugar, 1/4 cup evaporated milk, 2 1/2 cups powdered sugar, 1 teaspoon vanilla. In medium saucepan, melt margarine. Add brown sugar and milk. Heat until sugar is dissolved. Cool slightly. Beat in powdered sugar and vanilla.

To the Bettsville, Ohio reader, I have never heard of bumbleberry pie. She said it has many fruits. Has anyone heard of this?

Well, I've got tomato juice canning to get back to. I am canning using tomatoes, celery, onions, hot peppers, and cabbage. Carrots are too small to use to can. But we are thankful for what the garden produced this year. So good to fill those jars for the winter

A reader in Plainville, Kansas requested my apple pie recipe. This is a good one for those still in-season apples.

DUTCH APPLE PIE

1-9 inch unbaked pie shell
4 - 6 apples (enough to fill pie plate)
1/2 cup brown sugar
2 tablespoons milk
1/4 cup margarine
1/2 cup flour
1/2 cup sugar

1 teaspoon cinnamon

Peel apples and slice in pieces; put in unbaked pie shell. Combine brown sugar, cinnamon, and milk. Pour over top of apples. Combine flour and sugar. Cut in margarine until crumbly. Sprinkle crumbs on top of apples in shell. Bake 5 minutes at 425. Then lower heat to 350 and finish baking about 40 - 45 minutes or until apples are tender and bubbly.

SEPTEMBER 1999

It is a nice, sunshiny morning. I should do another load of laundry, although it is not as if I have been doing nothing.

I have been washing curtains this week. I am also in the middle of processing grapes, 104 quarts, which will be good to have this winter to drink. Homemade grape juice always goes good with breakfast. Grapes are usually ripe in early fall and make for excellent juice and jelly.

We are still enjoying our peppers, which are mild and hot. Mild green bell peppers may become mild red bell peppers if they are left on the plant long enough, but I guess early picking of green peppers will encourage further production. In some areas -- like around here -- bell peppers are called mangoes. I have heard peppers are an excellent source of vitamin C. And fresh peppers look so good on a relish plate when they are in season.

Peppers combine well with other vegetables, such as tomatoes, celery, carrots, onions and lettuce. Well, it is a colorful dish on a table to eat with a well-cooked meal. I never froze them, but I heard and read that peppers are one of the few vegetables that require no blanching before freezing.

We have probably had our last meal of fresh from the garden corn on the cob for the season, which was Sept. 14 at daughter Emma and Jacob's home. We were over there for the evening meal. My husband was over there on that day helping them put up a fence at their new place. Our corn crop is done for the season of '99.

I hope all of you out there are healthy and happy, as life goes on. Our daughter Liz and her children are here today. So the windows are getting a good cleaning with their help. Emma and her daughters were here yesterday. They helped out with sewing, cleaning windows and working in the garden.

I will share a good pepper recipe with you. Sometimes we like to cut and hollow out pepper halves and stuff them with a delicious tuna salad, and then bake it. Makes for delicious tuna-stuffed peppers. Here is a yummy stuffed pepper recipe using beef.

STUFFED PEPPERS WITH BEEF & RICE

6 to 8 green peppers
1 cup rice, parboiled
1 pound ground beef
1 medium onion, chopped
1 tablespoon chopped parsley
1/2 teaspoon salt
1/4 teaspoon black pepper
2 cups fresh tomato pulp or 15-ounce can diced tomatoes

Cut off tops of green peppers, remove stems, seeds and membranes. But save the tops. Precook rice and drain. Brown ground beef, add chopped onion, and cook until tender. Mix beef, rice, onions, parsley, salt and pepper, together. Stuff peppers, put on tops, and stand upright in casserole or Dutch oven. Pour tomato pulp over peppers and cook slowly for 30 to 40 minutes.

Serves 6 to 8. One teaspoon chili powder may be added to the stuffing mix.

Editor's note: Parboiling is to cook partially. In this case rice should be about half cooked. Suggested rice cooking time 10 to 15 minutes.)

OCTOBER 1999

It is hard to believe that we are into October. Time sure has a way of slipping by.

This is a time of year when tomatoes are being processed in so many ways. We processed homemade V-8 juice at Joe's (daughter Lovina's husband) last night. We also made a homemade pizza sauce from our tomatoes.

For the sauce, I use one large onion, four bay leaves, 10 cups of tomato juice, one-half cup salad oil, two teaspoons oregano, four teaspoons salt, one and one-half teaspoons garlic powder, four teaspoons sugar, one-fourth teaspoon red pepper, one-half teaspoon pepper and three-fourths cup Clear-Jel. Then I cook the onion and bay leaves in the tomato juice. Strain. Add salad oil, oregano, salt, garlic powder, sugar, red pepper and pepper. Bring to a boil and add a paste of Clear Jel and water. Boil five minutes. Makes five pints.

I helped daughter Emma (Jacob's family) on Saturday with processing homemade thick and chunky salsa.

Can you imagine a summer without fresh sun-drenched tomatoes? Tomatoes lend themselves to serving fresh sliced in salads, and canning in all kinds of ways, such as salsa, tomato juice, V-8, spaghetti sauce, catsup, gazpacho, chili sauce, chili soup, vegetable soup, tomato chunks, barbecue sauce and the list can go on and on.

We are glad to have tomatoes for our meals of tacos, which we eat with chopped onions, peppers and lettuce. Salsa and shredded cheese with it makes a good meal.

Fried green tomatoes are a delicious delicacy for us after a frost. You can wrap the green tomatoes in newspaper and place them in a single layer in a dark place in your cellar. But keep checking frequently and use them before they ripen, while they are still green. You can fry or bake them. When a frost is near, I usually like to pick all my green tomatoes to let them ripen and use to fry and bake. In a skillet of grease, slice and roll in flour and put in skillet. Add salt and pepper and fry until brown. Delicious.

Or try this recipe for baked green tomatoes.

BAKED GREEN TOMATOES

6 medium green tomatoes
2 tablespoons shortening, melted
1/2 cup seasoned bread crumbs
1/2 teaspoon salt
1/4 teaspoon pepper

Wash and remove stems and ends of tomatoes. Place in greased 9- by 9-inch baking dish. Brush with melted shortening, salt and pepper. Add enough hot water to cover the bottom of baking dish. Sprinkle with bread crumbs. Bake in preheated oven at 375 degrees about 20 to 30 minutes, until tender.

HOMEMADE SALSA

14 pounds tomatoes, scalded, peeled and cut up
5 cups onions (chopped)
10 green peppers (chopped)
2 ounces Jalapeno peppers (chopped)
1 cup vinegar
1/2 cup brown sugar
1/4 cup salt
2 teaspoons oregano flakes
3 teaspoons cumin
3 teaspoons chili powder
1 teaspoon garlic powder

10 teaspoons Clear Gel

Mix all of the above together, except Clear Gel. Cook on low heat in large stock pot for 45 minutes, stirring frequently to prevent sticking. Thicken with Clear Jel. Hot pack for 20 minutes. Makes 15 pints.

OCTOBER 1999

It is a crisp 33 degrees this beautiful morning, and I must get this written.

There's always plenty to do, it seems. Maybe it would be best to take a break from some of this work soon to visit our aged or shut-in neighbors. Good health means so much. This year has been stressful with health problems in the family, but there is also so much to be thankful for. God, the "One" who makes no mistakes, has a purpose for it all.

Our crops are all harvested now, crops of corn and soybeans out of our fields. Our neighbor has farmed for us since 1958. The years have a way of slipping by. Wonder what the winter will hold. Will it be cold and snowy? With plenty of snow, our horse-drawn sleighs can be used. Being snowbound too long isn't my favorite thing. I often wonder what 2000 holds? God only knows.

Sewing has been our focus the past couple of weeks. As all our clothing is made by hand, it takes a lot of time. My daughter Lovina, her children, Emma and her daughter spent the day here yesterday. Our sewing machines were in gear. The last two weeks, they've made two dresses and aprons for Susan and one outfit, almost completed, for me.

Also, they have made six children's dresses and aprons, and Emma tried her luck with cutting out and sewing a coat. Emma used to work at a sewing factory, so she knows how to put it all together.

I am so glad this sewing is getting done. Two men's shirts were also made. While Lovina and Emma have been at the sewing machines working, I usually am in the kitchen preparing meals, washing dishes and canning. It has been wonderful to spend all this time together.

Well, I must eat some breakfast. Verena has prepared it, and it smells so good. Susan is doing the sweeping. Susan has been unable to work since the tri-break of her ankle May 16, and then an infection set in. Hopefully it will heal completely soon. We just try to take one day at a time.

I continue to harvest late-season goodies from the garden. Turnips and radishes are continuing to go good. A reader in Jacksonville, N.C.,

sent me some turnip seeds earlier this season. They are coming up nicely. A hearty thank you to people who have sent seeds. There are also a few pumpkins that need to be harvested.

A few weeks ago, a reader wrote asking about "watermelon preserves." I said I had never heard of them, and dozens of people sent in their recipes. Thank you very, very much for your recipes and kind words. I had heard of these. We just always called them "watermelon pickles." Following is a recipe for watermelon pickles.

WATERMELON PRESERVES

3 quarts watermelon rind, peeled
1 Tablespoon salt in one quart of water
4 cups sugar
1 quart water
1 lemon
Allspice nuggets, if desired

Peel watermelon rind, and cut into strips 2 inches long and 3/4 inch wide. Cover with brine made by dissolving 1 tablespoon salt in 1 quart water. Let stand overnight. Drain.

Cover with fresh water, and boil 10 minutes. Drain.

Cover with a heavy syrup made of 1 part water and 1 part sugar. Make enough to cover.

Add 1 thinly sliced lemon to each 3 quarts rind. Cook slowly until rind is tender and clear.

Add whole spices, if desired. Mother always left a bit of the red on the rind. Watermelon rind is difficult to peel. Cut it into strips before attempting to peel. Use a good knife, and try not to cut your hand. The results (preserves) should be well worth the effort. Hot pack in pint jars for 15 minutes.

OCTOBER 1999

We canned some more V-8 tomato juice this week, instead of letting our tomatoes go to waste in the garden. So we used the red and yellow tomatoes; red, yellow, and green sweet peppers;

hot banana peppers and jalapeno peppers, and plenty of onions, celery, carrots, and cabbage. It will go good this winter to have all of those vitamins in one drink homemade V-8 juice drink. It is always good to fill those jars for the coming winter.

Red beets are to be canned yet. They are so good to cook and eat fresh. I boil them until they are soft, then peel them, slice and fry in butter or margarine, and add salt and pepper to them. Good eating. Also, we can them with vinegar, sugar, and salt, and pickling spices. We helped daughter Emma can her red beets and V-8 tomato juice earlier this week. We added plenty of red beet juice to her homemade V-8. It made for a more red-colored V-8 juice than usual, but it tastes better than it might look. Ha! So the garden of 1999 will be history soon. I put more tomato plants and turnip plants out in August. I wonder if I'll get anything from them. Time will tell if the gardening season holds out long enough. The pumpkins are still hanging on the vines. Muskmelons done well this year even as our drought hung in for some time, but we had several frequent rains lately. First time we could eat muskmelons from the garden. I had never had luck with them, until a reader from Somerset, Pennsylvania sent me some of her seeds this year. Thank you!

It is our 42 wedding anniversary for Ben and I on Oct. 17. Anyone having an anniversary on that date? Levi's (daughter Liz) had one on Oct. 4 and son Albert's on Oct. 2 and the birthday of son Amos, on Oct. 30. Their son Ben's birthday is on Oct. 6.

Daughter Emma and her daughters are here today so we done a huge laundry. I should get dinner on the table now.

We attended a funeral yesterday, Wednesday, of a daughter of my cousin. She was 15 years old and dropped over dead Saturday evening while playing with family members. Must've been quite a shock on the family to see she was gone. Death is so final.

Mail-time so I must get this in the mail, hoping to beat the mailman to the box.

To the Catlin, Illinois reader who requested a recipe for "sawdust pie": I had readers from everywhere send me the recipe. I want to thank all the readers who took their time to send it. For the reader who wanted to know, here is that recipe:

SAWDUST PIE

1 1 /2 cup coconut
1 1/2 cup graham cracker crumbs
1 1/2 cup pecans, chopped
1 1/ 2 cup sugar
1 cup egg whites (unbeaten)
1 unbaked pie crust

Combine coconut, graham cracker crumbs, pecans and sugar. Mix with egg whites. Pour mixture into pie shell. Bake at 350 for 35 minutes. Good luck!

Also for the Bettsville, Ohio reader who requested bumbleberry pie:

BUMBLEBERRY PIE

2-9 inch pie crusts

Filling: 2 cups each blueberries, raspberries, and sliced strawberries (any kind of fruit may be used)
2 cups chopped rhubarb
4 cups chopped, peeled baking apples
2 cups sugar
2 /3 cup flour
2 tablespoons lemon juice

Mix and spoon into the pie crusts. Cover with top crust which has been slit. Sprinkle with sugar or egg wash of 1 egg with 1 or 2 tablespoons water.

Thanks again to all the readers out there who took their time to write and send recipes.

NOVEMBER 1999

It has been a busy time around here, but when isn't it?

Daughters Lovina and Emma are here today. My husband Ben, Lovina and daughter Verena are out in our 16-acre cornfield picking up corn that was left from the combine when it came through to harvest. A neighbor farms our fields for us. Emma is inside doing some sewing for me.

Daughter Liz and children were here helping yesterday when 26 students and two teachers from the local Amish school came in the afternoon to sing for daughter Susan. It was a big, pleasant surprise for her. She received two scrapbooks from the school. It's interesting to see all of the activity ideas one has on each sheet.

Susan hasn't been working since May when she broke her ankle in three places and since then infection has set in. But it is looking lots better. I keep telling her to keep looking ahead. Hopefully, she can get back to work soon. The visit from the schoolchildren cheered her up.

In the evening, we went to Lovina and Joe's house. Joe, Jacob (Emma's husband) and Levi (Liz's husband) put up a ceiling at Joe's. It will make it warmer for the winter.

We've had several light frosts recently, so the garden will soon be history for

1999. I dug some of the carrots and was surprised that in the dry and hot weather they did so good. Celery is still out there and some red beets, cabbage, tomatoes, radishes, turnips and Chinese cabbage. So I must go get these in before our killing frost.

Some readers have asked what Clear-Jel is, which I have mentioned in this column. Clear-Jel is used around this household as a thickening in salsas, pie fillings, etc. Clear-Jel is used in much the same way as cornstarch is, as a thickener. Clear-Jel is available at grocery stores.

Being in the Halloween and autumn season still and the pumpkins are now out of the garden, how about this recipe?

HOMEMADE PUMPKIN BARS

> 2 cups of flour
> 2 teaspoons baking powder
> 1/2 teaspoon salt
> 1 teaspoon baking soda
> 2 teaspoons of cinnamon
> 2 cups of sugar
> 4 eggs
> 2 cups pumpkin
> 1 cup oil
> 1 cup walnut pieces (optional)

Mix dry ingredients together and set aside. Combine eggs, pumpkin and oil, and mix well. Add dry ingredients, and blend until smooth. Add walnut pieces, if desired. Pour onto a 10- by 15- inch cookie sheet that has been greased and floured. Bake at 350 degrees for 25 to 30 minutes. Ice with cream cheese icing.

CREAM CHEESE ICING

> 1/2 stick margarine or butter, softened
> 8 ounces cream cheese, softened
> 1 teaspoon vanilla
> 2 cups of powdered sugar
> 2 to 4 teaspoons milk, if necessary

Beat together margarine, cream cheese and vanilla. Mix in sugar until smooth. Add milk until icing consistency. Ice pumpkin bars after cooling.

NOVEMBER 1999

$\mathfrak{N}$ovember is now on the calendar and we are still having beautiful days in the 70s.

The laundry is drying well out there on the clothesline, and work is able to continue in our garden. I have been taking the celery, carrots, red beets, cabbage and pumpkins out from the garden today. Hopefully, the weather will stay nice and some vegetables will grow even larger. To the reader who sent me radish and turnip seeds to plant: I did plant them in August, and we are now feasting on them. Very good and tender, which was surprising considering our hot, dry summer. I put some leftover small potatoes in the ground, and the yield was good. I should have put more sweet potato plants in the ground, but at least we have enough for a good taste this winter. We'll be glad for all this hard work in the garden during the long, cold, dark days of January when we can open those canning jars and taste the bounty of summer.

On Oct. 31, we went to church services nearby. The services were in a large, cleaned-out shed. It is unusual the weather is warm enough Oct. 31 to have services outside. But conducting services in an outdoor shed is a lot easier, because furniture indoors does not have to be rearranged to make room for the church benches. Afterwards, Ben and I stopped at Emma and Jacob's since they were unable to attend.

On Sunday evening, we planned a favorite around here for supper: tacos. We had my daughter Leah and family, son Amos and family, daughter Lovina and family, and Emma's family over for supper. So we had a large gathering, but having family over is the best of times. Those sweet, precious grandchildren are always welcome here, so the house was full of children.

We all enjoy a taco supper. The tomatoes, mangoes (peppers) and onions used on the tacos were all from our garden. Canned hamburger was browned for the tacos, and there was lots more to feast on because everyone else brought a covered dish.

As the family gets bigger and older, we have to use larger containers now.

It's always good to see the family come home. Our son Albert and his wife, Sarah Irene, stopped in during the afternoon on their way to her sister and family for supper. So we saw all the family yesterday (Sunday) except for my daughter Liz and family who were at her husband's folks.

Today (Nov. 1) is son-in-law Jacob's birthday, and Oct. 30 was Amos' birthday. Also Liz's daughter, Rosa, turned 2 Oct. 30.

This is the time of year when mother was still living that we would have her family reunion. One of the last reunions before she passed away was on Oct. 31, 1993. That morning was our first snow of the season. But the day was enjoyable in spite of the weather, with 279 family members present.

Now, here is a good dessert to use those beets from the garden.

RED BEET CHOCOLATE CAKE

1 1/2 cups sugar
3 eggs
1 cup oil
1 1/2 cups cooked, pureed, fresh beets
2 (1-ounce) squares unsweetened chocolate, melted
and cooled
1 teaspoon vanilla
1 3/4 cups flour
1/2 teaspoon salt
1/2 teaspoon baking soda
Sifted confectioner's sugar

Mix flour, soda and salt. Set aside. Combine sugar, eggs and oil in mixing bowl. Stir vigorously (those who use electric mixers can use them here at medium speed for 2 minutes). Beat in beets, chocolate and vanilla.

Gradually add dry ingredients, beating well after each addition. Pour into buttered 9- by 13-inch cake pan. Bake at 350 degrees for 25 minutes or until cake tests done. (For testing, a toothpick, when inserted into center of cake, comes out clean.) Cool in pan. Cover and let stand overnight to improve flavor. Sprinkle with powdered sugar.

P.S. You can put cream cheese icing on instead of powdered sugar.

NOVEMBER 1999

The highlight of Wednesday, Nov. 17, was when a baby boy was born to daughter Emma and her husband Jacob.

He weighed 6 pounds, 10 ounces and arrived at 10:08 p.m. They named the newborn Jacob. He's greeted by two sisters, Elizabeth and Emma. My daughters Verena and Susan are assisting her with household duties, and sometimes so is Grandma. Ha!

For us, this makes 12 grandsons, but the girls are still ahead with 18. That makes 30 grandchildren, 29 living. Granddaughter Mary is at peace.

What's the next holiday on the calendar? Thanksgiving Day!

When I was younger we always used to recite the poem: "Over the river and through the woods to grandfather's house we go, the horse knows the way to carry the sleigh over the white and drifted snow."

Doesn't this poem sound as if those were the good old days? They were good, although times could have been easier back then. We have lots to be thankful for when Thanksgiving Day arrives each year.

Especially when we think about the struggles those early Pilgrims endured long, long ago. We'll never know the terrors that they braved years and years ago. Shouldn't we be so thankful to our Heavenly Father for our bounteous harvest of 1999? And yet, too often, we forget to be thankful for our plentiful harvest.

On Thanksgiving day, we will have turkey on the menu. Also on the list, chicken and ham, along with sweet potatoes, pumpkin pie and pumpkin bread. Pumpkins are taken from the garden, and they can be cooked and processed. Cookies and bread also can be baked using pumpkin. Sweet potatoes with butter, salt, pepper and brown sugar are another favorite around here on Thanksgiving day.

Family gatherings or weddings are usually on Thanksgiving day. A 20-pound stuffed turkey is usually put in the oven for whenever some of the family members come. Often we have our garden plowed on Thanksgiving day, so we'll see what the weather holds. Last year, we attended a wedding at La Grange, Ind., of the daughter of my niece. It was an enjoyable day, although the garden did not get plowed. It was so good to be with family members that we don't get to see too often.

This Thanksgiving Day will be spent with family coming and going from our home. Lots to be thankful for.

Lately, I think of what or how one would feel being alone in a house when a partner has gone to that Great Beyond. So we take one day at a time. God makes no mistakes and who will do the judging someday. Right?

I'm wishing all you readers out there a happy Thanksgiving day in 1999 and many more to come. What will 2000 hold? Only God knows. Let's keep "Him" in our thoughts and prayers.

With the holidays here, I've had many readers asking about a bread pudding recipe.

Here is a delicious bread pudding:

HOLIDAY BREAD PUDDING

4 cups bread cubes
1 quart hot milk
3 tablespoons butter
4 eggs
Dash salt
1 cup sugar
1/2 teaspoon vanilla
1 teaspoon cinnamon

After the milk has been boiled, combine it with bread cubes and butter. Then allow it to stand for 10 minutes. Beat eggs with salt until light. Add sugar, cinnamon and vanilla; beat until lemon-colored. Add bread mixture. Pour into greased 2-quart baking dish and bake at 350 degrees for 50 minutes.

Serves 6 to 8 people.

NOVEMBER 1999

It is 5:30 a.m., and I had best get some breakfast ready as it looks like a full day ahead. I do want to take some time to get caught up on some reader mail this week.

To the Indianapolis reader who requested a recipe for homemade mayonnaise: 2 cups sugar, 1/2 cup flour, 1 teaspoon salt and 1/2 teaspoon ground mustard. Add 1 cup water, 4 beaten eggs. Blend. Then add 1 cup vinegar and stir. Add 1 tablespoon butter. Boil until mixture thickens. Will keep for many weeks in a covered jar in the ice-house or, for those who have them, the refrigerator.

To the Ashland, Ohio, reader who wants pickled yellow egg recipe (most people call them simply deviled eggs) to which mustard is added: I can tell you how I make them. Boil eggs until done. Naturally, remove the shells and cut in half, length-ways. Take the yolk part and mash it up with mustard and salad dressing and also salt and pepper to your taste. Put back in the white of the egg.

To the reader in Forest, Ohio, who wants a recipe for pickled red beets and old-fashioned apple pie:

Is this the apple pie you are wanting? Apple pie: 3/4 cup sugar, 1 teaspoon cinnamon, 6 to 7 cups sliced apples, 1/2 cup margarine, 1/2 cup brown sugar and 1 cup flour. Mix sugar and cinnamon with sliced apples and put into an unbaked nine-inch pie shell. Mix margarine, brown sugar and flour for topping. Sprinkle over pie. Bake 15 minutes at 425 degrees. Then lower oven temperature to 350 degrees and bake for 30 minutes or until apples are tender.

Apples can be used in so many ways, especially at this time of year. Some process them with a thickening, so they can open a jar of fresh apples later for baking a pie. But I usually like to just peel and slice them when baking pies.

Pickled red beets: After beets are cooked and skins removed, put beets in a kettle or dishpan and add vinegar, sugar, salt and pickling spice to your taste. The amounts depend on how many red beets you've cooked. When heated, put in jars and seal.

To the reader who wanted watermelon preserves: 4 cups diced watermelon rind, 3 cups sugar, 1/2 lemon and 1/2 cup crushed pineapple (optional). Use the white part of the rind and add thin strip of the pink melon for color. Cut into 3/4-inch cubes. Add sugar to the melon, and slowly bring to a boil. Slice the lemon into thin strips, and add along with crushed pineapples. Cook faster after the sugar is dissolved. Cook until the fruit is clear and the syrup is thickened. Pour into jars and seal. Hot pack pint jars for 10 minutes.

Lots planned for this Saturday. Emma and Jacob's new baby boy seems so happy and healthy. It made for a joyous Thanksgiving to have all the family come home during the day and to see the grandchildren. We are entering the holiday season, which means family and special holiday goodies, which I'll share more of in upcoming columns.

To the reader in Jetmore, Kan.: I have never heard of a pronghorn deer. I reckon some readers out there have?

To the Indianapolis and the Columbus, Neb., reader, and all the others who have asked: Yes, a cookbook will be out in the future. More about that in this column later.

NOVEMBER 1999

It looks like my tomatoes are now history for 1999 from our garden.

I'll miss them as they were used fresh in so many ways: in salads, vegetable chili and tomato soup. They are sliced to use with meals three times a day and good for sandwiches. We processed many jars of tomato juice and chunks. Didn't process any homemade catsup this year and still had plenty of jars of hot pepper butter and salsa from last year.

Root vegetables, such as red beets, carrots, radishes and turnips, are all still in the ground. Some I pulled to let the others grow more. We like the buttered red beets. That is what was on the menu for dinner and supper today, plus onions, radishes and carrots.

This was a busy day cleaning out the tool shed and wash-house while the weather is so nice and warm. I washed the buggy blankets and the buggy robes. The buggy covers make for a more comforatable ride.

The ironing was also completed, and a lot of canning jars were washed, probably around 18 dozen, which were bought recently at a public auction.

Those were for daughters Lovina, Emma and us. Always like to store away those jars when washed. It's easier when canning jars are clean when you want to process in them.

A 1,000-piece jigsaw puzzle was completed by daughter Verena. It was a gift from Joe and Lovina some time ago. The family gathered here to put this puzzle together on our card table. It's Amish country; the photo was taken near Becks Mills, Ohio, of an Amish farm with a main house, dawdy haus, and large barn and fields full of livestock and crops. The puzzle's size is 20 by 27 inches.

Some may wonder what a "dawdy haus" is. Right? Well, when parents get older, one of the children will take over the main house and a smaller house is built for the older parents to live in. But some don't look that small compared to the main house.

So our puzzle is now done. No wonder there are some pieces still missing with so many children around here at times. Now it is complete and looks like beautiful scenery. I didn't put a single piece together in that puzzle, but the family enjoyed putting it together when they were here.

Speaking of family, Thanksgiving is coming soon. More on that next week. Here is a good, simple stuffing recipe!

STUFFING FOR THANKSGIVING

1 whole loaf bread
3 eggs, well-beaten
2 tablespoons butter
3 cups chicken broth or chicken bouillon
4 tablespoons chopped celery
1 medium onion, chopped
1/2 teaspoon poultry seasoning
1 teaspoon salt
1/2 teaspoon pepper

Toast bread, and cut in cubes. Combine celery, onion and seasonings, and add to bread cubes. Bring broth to boil, add butter and stir until melted. Add broth to bread and celery mixture. Add eggs last and stir until mixed well.

Pour into greased large casserole dish. Bake 1 hour at 350 degrees. Serves about 8 to 10 people.

DECEMBER 1999

𝕴t is 4 a.m. as I write this, and the thermometer reads 22 degrees outside. Cold, but we expect all kinds of weather in December. We had snow flurries yesterday.

Thanksgiving day was a workday for us, preparing for having church services here in our home in December. The manure was hauled from the barn to our garden. Trim was put around our new windows. Six old windows were replaced. Still a few windows to have the trim yet, and our garden was plowed for spring of 2000.

Toward evening, our son Albert took our team of horses and manure-spreader to plow their own garden and some of their yard with the assistance of son Amos. We had fried chicken and also chicken and dressing in the oven for both meals on Thanksgiving day. A change from turkey.

Those assisting us on Thanksgiving Day were son Albert's, Joe's and Jacob's families. Son Amos' family also came for supper and got in on helping Albert with his plowing. Daughter Leah and her husband Paul were busy as they were having church services in their home the Sunday after Thanksgiving. He also was occupied with making a new buggy box to be put on our new running gears.

On Sunday, we were able to drive to Paul's for church services in our brand new buggy. Paul put a lot of labor into it. We are so pleased with it. Daughter Liz and husband Levi also were preparing for church services to be at their place the first Sunday in December. So it was a busy Thanksgiving Day!

Levi will be another year older Sunday. Some of the family plans to help with their cleaning today in preparing for church services. So many of the family are having church services in December. Makes for a busy month, so everyone is helping each other clean their houses and prepare food.

(Editor's note: For those new to the column, Amish families have church services in the homes of church-members on a rotating basis, there is no formal church building.)

Our family Christmas gathering will be held this year on New Year's Day of
2000. That is when the family is together here for breakfast, dinner and supper
-- all day. One day of the year we do this and everyone looks forward to it.
Tables are set up for the 45 of us as to eat all at one time for both meals. Yes, we can say 45 as of
now, but lots can take place by then. We've learned to
take one day at a time.

To the reader who asked about "schnitz pie." I thought you might be referring
to dried apples, sliced thin. Grandpa did this. Out in the orchard, a small tin
shanty-like structure with lots of trays in it is where they dried their apples. This was used before
any processing in jars was done. I guess back then they dried most of what is processed now.

Several have written asking about homemade V-8 juice. We add anything to
ours: such as tomatoes, onions, carrots, hot banana peppers and jalapeno
peppers, sweet peppers, celery and cabbage. At times, we added green
beans. Season with salt after it is in the jars. I make my own recipe when it
comes to V-8. Sometimes it is really hot to drink, but good in winter-time
when some have colds. If they can drink that hot it makes them feel better.
Some process it very hot, others not so hot.

A reader in Kansas City, Kan., wrote a while back asking about whoopie pies,
a favorite in some communities. Others also have written asking about this
recipe. The pies are actually two cookies with filling in between.

WHOOPIE PIES

Cookies:

2 cups white sugar
4 cups flour
1/8 teaspoon of salt
1 cup sour milk
1 cup shortening
2 eggs
1 cup hot water
2 teaspoons vanilla
2 teaspoons soda
1 cup cocoa

Sift dry ingredients together; cream eggs, sugar and shortening
together. Add sour milk (combine 1 tablespoon vinegar with
enough milk to make 1 cup to sour it). Mix dry ingredients, egg
mixture and milk alternately until blended. Then add hot water
last. Drop onto cookie sheet and bake about 8 minutes at 350 or until done.

Filling:

3 tablespoons all-purpose flour
1 cup milk
3/4 cup shortening
1 1/2 cups confectioner's sugar
2 teaspoons vanilla extract

On a stovetop, add flour to a saucepan. With a whisk, gradually add milk until smooth; cook and stir over a medium-high heat until thick, about 5 to 7 minutes. Remove from heat. Cover and cool refrigerate) until completely cool. In a mixing bowl, cream shortening, sugar and vanilla. Add chilled milk mixture; beat for 7 minutes (electric mixers can be used here) or until fluffy. Spread filling on half of the cookies; top with the other half. Store in a cool, dry place.
Yield: 2 dozen.

DECEMBER 1999

It's 4 a.m., and I am ready to write, as this column needs to go into the mail today.

We have church services in our home this Sunday, so there is still plenty of cleaning to do. It looks like a busy day ahead. Chores include washing off walls and windows. Most of the cleaning has already been completed, but there are always plenty of odds and end jobs on the last days before church that need to be completed.

We also have preparations to make for Christmas. Christmas has to be, without a doubt, the most widely observed holiday in the world today. Around here, there are lots of family gatherings. Some do a lot of baking and candy making.

I just don't do too much candy making anymore. Eating too many sweets doesn't go with this family anymore. We enjoy the fresh fruits and vegetables, which are probably healthier anyway.

Lots of "secret pals" reveal their roles at this time of year. My daughter Leah and her husband, Paul, divulged themselves Tuesday as the "99" secret pal for my sister Lovina. (I also have a daughter named Lovina.) Her husband died from cancer in April, so the secret pal was cheer to her. Paul and Leah hosted a very delicious meal for her, her daughter and family, who reside with my sister.

And, to my surprise, they also had invited my family. We are six living sisters and one brother. So it was good to all be together. Singing and yodeling took place after supper. The New Year's Song was sung before everyone left for their homes. The New Year's Song is a traditional song for New Year's Day sung in German.

Our family used to all gather at Grandpa's for New Year's. Lots of memories of our gatherings at Grandpa's. They had 14 children and more than 100 grandchildren when Grandma died. We looked forward to attending the annual gathering. There's only four of that family living now.

Some may wonder: "What is a secret pal?" Right?

To cheer up older people, widows, etc., someone chooses a friend or relative and they -- anonymously -- keep sending them gifts, money and groceries all year, especially during holidays. The person receiving them has fun all year trying to guess who their "secret pal" is. At Christmas-time, the "secret pal" reveals themselves. They always pass gifts through other families to deliver from their "secret pal." So it's usually guess, guess, guess as to who could it be.

Daughter Susan has a secret pal also this year. So she's guessing who it could be. She'll have to wait until her secret pal steps forward.

Daughter Susan also received a scrapbook Tuesday evening at Paul's from her cousins, Adeline and Miriam Schwartz, to cheer her after having a rough year with her tri-break ankle. It's a very nice scrapbook. Friends and relatives had good ideas on each sheet.

We have our kitchen cook-stove in gear now. Temperatures are at 35 degrees this morning. We had some cold, windy days, but you can expect this at this time of year. We have not received much snow as yet. Dread to have our stove going again. That means fuel to carry, ash pans to be emptied, but it is good we have fuel to carry in to keep the house warm. I will close this letter now, but enjoy these good Christmas cookie recipes:

AMISH CHRISTMAS COOKIES

2 cups flour
1 cup sugar
1 teaspoon soda
1/2 teaspoon salt
1 teaspoon cream tartar
1 1/4 cup margarine, softened
3 tablespoons milk
2 eggs, slightly beaten
1 teaspoon vanilla

Mix dry ingredients. Add remaining ingredients and stir until blended. Roll out thin (about 1/8 inch thick). Cut in any shape desired. Bake at 375 degrees on ungreased cookie sheet for 8 to

10 minutes or until slightly brown around the edges. Let cool and decorate as you wish.

SOFT CHRISTMAS CUT-OUTS

3 cups flour
1/2 teaspoon baking powder
1/2 teaspoon baking soda
1 cup margarine
2 eggs, beaten
1 1/2 cups sugar

Mix all ingredients together until soft dough forms. Chill dough overnight in a refrigerator or cool cellar. The next morning, roll out to about 1/8 inch thick and cut into shapes you wish. Bake at 375 degrees. When cool, spread with icing.

DECEMBER 1999

It is Wednesday, Dec. 15, as I write this. It has been a rainy week so far. Rain, rain, rain. I did a huge laundry on Monday. It is always an extra large amount the day after having church services here.

I hung the laundry out in the morning, but then it began raining in the afternoon. Some clothing had dried before the rains came, and we were able to get those in.

Other clothing remained on the clothesline all night. There was a powerful wind and plenty of rain during the night, but by morning the clothes were dry. Without an electric dryer, it takes longer for us to dry clothes, but I guess we are used to doing it the hard way. Ha! But to think that it is December and we are still able to do our laundry in our wash-house. When it gets wintery cold, we take our clothes-washing equipment inside the enclosed porch of our house where it is warmer. Well, enough of this for now.

Through this rainy week, my daughter Susan has completed a 1,000- piece jigsaw puzzle. The jigsaw puzzle was of an Amish barn-raising near Farmerstown, Ohio. Two weeks earlier, a barn burned down from a lightning strike. To help the owners, neighbors gathered by the thousands to rebuild that barn in half a day. So they must've done quicker work at the real barn than it took us to put this 1,000-piece puzzle together.

It was hard to put together, but I never put a piece in it. Others in the family helped with that. This puzzle was a gift to daughter Susan some time ago from our daughter Lovina and husband Joe. I guess I am just not a puzzler when it comes to such small pieces.

Our turn to have church services is over with for a while, but we'll have services here again next week, though. That turn is for daughter Jacob and Emma. We took it for them as to not lose out on a turn, otherwise they have to take it twice when their turn comes around again. Church rules. Everyone gets their turn. So it has been a busy time around here cleaning and getting our house in order. Next, Lovina and Joe will have services at their house and after, that son Albert and his wife, Sarah Irene.

We had a nice attendance at church on Sunday. Lunch is served at noon after church. Some of you may wonder what is served? It varies from place to place, but we served ham, two kinds of cheese, bread, coffee, milk, red beets, dill pickles, lettuce, cottage cheese that I had made and hot peppers.

For the small children, a cafeteria-style meal was prepared and served with crackers. The small children eat cafeteria-style, while the older ones and adults are seated at several tables and the single girls help serve everyone. Dinner dishes are washed afterward, and visiting takes place until the evening meal gets prepared, which is a hot meal. We had everyone invited back for a hot evening supper who attended church. Quite a few came back to enjoy the meal.

Daughter Liz and husband Levi live in another church district, where they serve a chili soup, potato salad, cottage cheese with the rest of the after-church noon lunch being ham, cheese and other items. Levi turned another year older this past week. They also had services at their home this week.

Their church district is larger than ours, so it just takes more food. Levi's family had quite a few families there for supper.

The bench wagon is still sitting outside our home in preparation for our upcoming church services for Emma and Jacob's turn. The church benches and songbooks are stored in the wagon, which goes from place to place, according to which home is holding the services.

Son Amos and wife Nancy Jean also live in another church district, but our and Paul's (Leah), Albert's, Joe's and Jacob's families belong to say church district.

I hope you readers have a wonderful Christmas. Enjoy this recipe!

NUT PIE FOR CHRISTMAS

1 cup white sugar
1/2 cup of raisins
1 tablespoon of flour
1 tablespoon of vinegar
1/2 cup of walnuts or pecans
2 eggs, beaten
1/2 cup of butter, melted

Mix all ingredients together and pour into 8 or 9 inch, unbaked
pie shell. Bake at 350 degrees until golden, about 45 minutes.

DECEMBER 1999

This is a cold Wednesday morning, Dec. 23, at 4 a.m. The temperature is at 8 above right now.
I hope it warms up as we plan to go help at Joe's (daughter Lovina) today.

We will wash off walls and floors, and help them get their house ready for church. Church
services are to be in their home in January of 2000.
Meanwhile, my daughters Liz, Lovina and Emma were to our house yesterday
to help get ready for church services, which will be here on Sunday, Dec. 26.
As I mentioned in last week's column, we are having services here for Emma and Jacob. My
daughter Emma and husband Jacob were going to have them in their house this Sunday, but with
their new baby, we offered to have it here for them.

By the time you readers read this, Christmas will be over. What will Christmas
hold? God only knows. It would be nice to see those snow flakes fall and
cover the ground at Christmastime.

On Sunday, we tried our new hand-crank ice cream freezer, which was a
birthday gift to Ben and I. So homemade ice cream was on the menu for
supper. The hand-crank ice-cream maker was a gift from Joe's (Lovina) and
Jacob's (Emma) families.

Speaking of Joe, he turned another year older today. So, on Sunday, we were
making ice cream in celebration of his birthday. In addition to homemade ice
cream, chicken was grilled and barbecued for a special birthday dinner.

Also on Sunday, son Albert and his family came here to join us for the
occasion. You never know who from the family will arrive. So we had mashed
potatoes, gravy, chicken and the homemade ice cream for dessert.

We had not made homemade ice cream in quite some time. It was delicious, and we plan to make some at our family Christmas gathering. Albert's family and daughter Leah also will bring some homemade ice cream. Everyone thought the ice cream was very yummy, using cream, milk, salt, sugar and vanilla. It's my own recipe. Our family Christmas gathering is Jan. 1.

The two stoves are in full gear this morning. Several stoves help keep our home warm in the winter. The cook-stove takes only wood fuel and is located in our kitchen, and the much larger Hitzer (living room stove) takes wood and coal. So there's extra work with those stoves. You have to keep fuel in them and empty those ash pans. You also have to see that the chimneys are in good working order as to not have a chimney fire. Those scare me.

Our cook-stove ash-pans only have to be emptied about once every five to six weeks when in use. The cook-stove does a lot of help in wintertime. You can prepare a meal, you can bake with it, and there is always warm or hot water in its attached tank. The tank needs to be kept filled with water. Our kerosene heater hasn't been in use thus far. We only use it when extra heat is needed.

We had a nice fall and only took a turn for colder weather this week. Last week, it was warm and rainy. The stoves do a good job of keeping the place warm during winter.

Well, I must get some breakfast, as the girls are not home. So it's just for hubby and me, which a cup of coffee would do. Ha!

Yesterday, daughters Lovina, Emma and children were here for breakfast and here to help for the day. So the girls made a breakfast casserole and had fried potatoes, oatmeal, toast, bacon, cheese, bananas and coffee.

Here is a delicious, simple recipe for homemade banana bread. Thank you readers for all your Christmas cards.

BANANA NUT BREAD

1 cup sugar	2 tablespoons margarine
1 egg	3 teaspoons thick, sour milk
1 teaspoon baking soda	2 cups flour
1/2 cup nut meats	1 cup mashed bananas

Mix sugar, margarine, egg, milk and soda very well in a large bowl. Then sift in the flour, nut meats and bananas. Mix very well. Pour into lightly greased loaf pan and bake at 350 degrees for one hour.

2000-2001

The world made it into the new millennium without the meltdown and chaos many had feared. The power grid blinked in Seattle, gaming machines shut down in Delaware, and an apartment complex in Seoul, South Korea lost power. But most people felt the new millennium enter with little more than a whimper and ripple.

The United States made its mark in sports, with cancer-survivor Lance Armstrong capturing the Tour De France, and the USA Women's soccer team captivated the country with their world champion win.

While the United States scored decisive victories in sports, neither Al Gore or George W. Bush could muster enough votes in the Presidential election to claim a clear win. After numerous recounts in Florida, and the term "hanging chad" entering into the national dialogue (referring to tiny paper particles on an old-fashioned voter punch card), the outcome of the election remained in doubt for weeks before finally being settled by the Supreme Court. George W. Bush was declared the victory.

Meanwhile, the United States economy began to grind to a halt in early 2001, as dot.coms went bust and the stock market began a slide.

On the Coblentz farm, Elizabeth dealt with the biggest heartbreak of her life when her husband, Ben, passed away suddenly in the spring after suffering a stroke. He was 69. Thousands of letters, cards, and emails poured in from readers of The Amish Cook column. The rest of the year and the early part of 2001 were spent grieving and, slowly, recovering. Elizabeth continued to pen her weekly column, and the arrival of new grandchildren added a renewed sense of life.

JANUARY 2000

𝔍 am writing this two days after Christmas. Snow flurries are in the air, so it seems like the season.

We spent Christmas Day at son Albert's home. Paul and Leah's families were there also. Joe and Lovina came later. A stuffed turkey was on the menu and home-made ice cream. Yummy!

Yesterday, Sunday, we had church services in our home. Daughter Liz and her husband, Levi, daughter Emma and husband Jacob spent the night here Sunday night. They helped clean up the house after church services.

Verena and Susan went to work this morning. Both of them clean rooms at a motel in town as a part-time job. This will be the first time Susan has been into work since the tri-break of her ankle last May. I wonder how she will do. She has had a hard year, health-wise. We've learned to take one day at a time.

Some of the family could not attend church services here yesterday because of family Christmas gatherings. So many family functions are conducted in this area at this time of year. Because of all the obligations, our family Christmas gathering is on New Year's Day. So today is just a clean-up day. It feels so good to have the place clean again after church.

Verena and Susan made pizza last night with plenty of other foods on the menu as well. Then the family started to put together another 1,000-piece puzzle. This was a picture of children walking to church. This photo was taken near Fredricksburg, Ohio. Sometimes when church services are in a home nearby, people will just walk to services instead of taking the buggy.

The puzzle was a gift from Joe and Lovina to Susan some time ago. Wintertime brings this on, I guess. I am not much of a puzzler. Daughters Liz and Emma were doing a good job on it. At 1 a.m., they finally went to bed. Quite a lot of pieces were put together on that puzzle. It seems amazing how many of the family takes an interest in it.

Well, I should help daughter Emma with dinner as I sit here writing this. You readers have a happy year as we enter 2000.

Try this yummy recipe:

CREAM STICKS

2 packages yeast (1/4 ounce), dissolved in 1 cup warm water
2/3 cup sugar
1/2 teaspoon salt
6 cups flour
1 cup milk, scalded
1/2 cup margarine, softened

139

2 eggs
1 teaspoon vanilla

Mix all ingredients together until smooth. Let dough rise until double in size in warm place. Knead and then form dough into sticks 3 1/2- by 1 1/2 inches. Let rise again, in a warm place, until doubled in size. Deep fry in fat or oil. Remove when golden.

Frosting: 1/2 cup of brown sugar, 2 tablespoons of milk, 4 tablespoons of butter, softened. Mix until sugar is dissolved, and spread over cooled sticks.

JANUARY 2000

January of 2000 has appeared on the calendar. It was somewhat scary to see the New Year come in with all the talk of calamity. But it was calm. We had our Christmas family gathering on New Year's Day. We were glad to have everyone present, which we total to 45 now. We had four folding tables and benches so everyone could be seated for the meals, which were served in our living room this year. We had a nice breakfast, our usual larger noon meal and a dinner. I think the children all enjoyed eating together at one time.

The New Year's Song was sung at different times through the day. The song is in German. It was a different dinner this year, as the family had plans to go with a haystack (a simple, taco-style casserole piled in layers).

The girls thought I probably would not expect this kind of dinner on New Year's Day. We usually have something fancier. But this was an easier dinner for us women and girls to prepare.

There were plenty of other goodies also. It was decided to make homemade ice cream, which tasted good after the haystack. So I stirred three six-quart helpings of ice cream together, and that was the job for the men and boys to see that it got frozen. Ha! So there was more than plenty to feast on for supper and the rest of the day.

In the evening, everything was put back in order. Then daughter Verena did the job of mopping the floors. By then, we were ready to relax for New Year's night.

Paul's family then had us all invited for whoever had no plans for the next day, Sunday, as Leah said she is going to put a turkey in the oven.

Son Albert's family, Joe's family, Jacob's family, Ben, daughters Verena and Susan, and I were present for their delicious dinner. There was turkey and plenty of food on the menu. We were glad to see our two nephews and families when we arrived at Paul's. They had moved to Hudson, Ky., some time ago and had come to this area for their family gathering, which was also on New Year's Day.

New Year's Day always brings back memories of when my Grandpa had their gatherings. They had 14 children and families. It used to really be a big group together. Then us eight children and families gathered at my folks' place after Grandpa died.

Now my parents are gone and we're in line with our children and families. Life goes on!

Well, enough about New Year's. Wishing all you readers a Happy New Year as we've entered 2000. What will this year hold? God only knows.

Try this recipe, popular around here on New Year's.

CABBAGE ROLLS FOR NEW YEAR'S

2 pounds cabbage (24 cabbage leaves)
2 pounds pork sausage, ground
1 large onion, chopped
1 teaspoon garlic salt
1 cup raw rice
2 slices milk-soaked bread
4 pounds sauerkraut
3 cans tomato soup

Separate and dip enough cabbage leaves in scalding water for a few minutes to soften. Mix sausage, onion, garlic salt, rice and bread, and wrap in softened cabbage leaves. Blanch remaining heads of cabbage in

hot water for about 10 minutes. Put a layer of cabbage leaves in bottom of large baking dish. Alternate cabbage rolls and layers of sauerkraut. Add about 3 10 1/4-ounce cans of tomato soup over top. Bake covered in 300-degree oven for 4 hours.

Serves 8 to 10.

JANUARY 2000

It is a cold, windy day in the low 30s. Wind is what makes it feel so cold. But I must say we've had a mild winter thus far with hardly any snow. No sleigh-riding this season.

But I guess there's no reason to complain if there's plenty of fuel for the stoves. Wood that has been cut and mixing it with coal makes a good heat. Also, it feels comforting to face the winter with plenty of food to eat. It is good to open those jars, which were filled and processed last summer and autumn. We have to do our part. Just like the birds, they can't just sit on their nests all the time. They scratch for food too. The Good Lord supplies all their needs and also gladly our needs too. Those birds have a great feast on those bird feeders or seeds, which are thrown on the ground. Those busy birds live from day to day to be fed. Wouldn't it be hard for us to find our food from day to day? How blessed we are to have a bountiful harvest.

It seems in the wintertime, many around here have their ice-cream freezers in gear when there is plenty of ice around. Ice cream makes for a refreshing snack. It's also good to relax in the evenings by the warm stove, munching on popcorn and eating apples from the autumn harvest.

Sewing is also on the list during these cold, dark winter evenings. A person would think the workload would lighten during the winter months, but it really doesn't, it just changes. There are so many projects to be completed before spring comes along. I want to cut out some shirts today to be sewn tomorrow. I also want to do the laundry today.

Last week, we were assisting Joe's (daughter Lovina) family in preparing for their church services, which they had this past Sunday. It was so nice the weather was warm enough they could have church services in their shed attached to their house.

Tables were set up in there to serve dinner and supper. It was nice this way to not have to re-arrange the furniture in the main house. Church services were announced to be at son Albert's soon, so I want to help them prepare for it.

Our Christmas cactus plant has been blooming for quite some time. It has around two dozen blooms on it now with many buds. It looks so beautiful, and our poinsettia from Jacob's family a year ago looks like it was bought over Christmas. Very beautiful!

Another poinsettia from son Amos' family two years ago is really perking up again. Without house plants, the winter would seem to have a dull appearance in our living room. Daughters Verena and Susan also have nice house-flower plants in their rooms and are blooming. I love to care for them all and to keep the flower plants alive.

DINNER SAUSAGE

1 pound pork sausage
1 small onion, chopped
1 10 3/4-ounce can cream of mushroom soup
1/2 cup milk
1 cup diced cheddar cheese
1 small (8-ounce) package of noodles

Fry crumbled sausage long enough to fry out fat but don't cook until crisp. Drain. Fry onion in a little oil until brown. Cook noodles as directed on package and drain. Mix all ingredients together in a 10- by 10-inch greased casserole dish and bake at 325 degrees for 30 minutes.

Serves 6 to 8.

JANUARY 2000

𝕴t is Monday morning, Jan. 17, at 8 a.m., and we are staying overnight in Greenville, Ill., as we arrived last evening. We want to attend the funeral tomorrow of my niece, who was killed on Friday.

She leaves her husband and a large family behind to mourn in Seymour, Mo. That is where we are headed. There is a large Amish community there. They moved from our area of Indiana to Seymour around a year ago. It was quite a shock to receive the sad news Friday evening. Death is so final. We will find out more details when we get there later today.

Ben is along with me, as is my daughter Verena, two of my sisters, their husbands, and a few others in our extended family.

The weather has been good to travel. Hope it stays this way as we travel back home, either tomorrow night or Wednesday morning. Glad for our van driver, as he seems good at the wheel.

One of my daughters (Liz) and family were to start out to Seymour Saturday evening. So we hope to see them when we arrive at the residence of my niece. Jacob's (daughter Emma) family is staying at our house while we are away to do our barn chores, etc. I reckon my daughter Susan is glad they are staying.

When we left yesterday from home on this sad-occasion trip, daughters Leah, son Albert, daughter Lovina, Emma and all their families were at our home for Sunday dinner.

So plenty of people were there to bid us good-bye. Son Amos' family was at our place Saturday evening also before we left. So we quick had sandwiches, chips, etc., put out before they went home. So it was good to see all our children and families before we left.

This will be our first visit to Seymour, Mo. Ben and I had plans to visit my niece and family some time this year, but didn't expect to make the trip this soon.

Noon, Monday, Jan. 17

Our family enjoyed the dinner today our children packed for us before we left. Son-in-law Joe barbecued chicken, ribs and ham on the grill, while us women prepared mashed potatoes, gravy, dressing, buttered corn, buttered peas and the list goes on. Thanks goes to Joe for barbecuing the meat.

We'll probably be at the viewing of my niece today. My niece was 18 years old when she lost her mother (my sister), and now again her oldest daughter is 18 and now she's gone to that Great Beyond. My niece leaves behind her husband and 13 children. The two oldest boys are married.

Monday evening

I'll quick write a note here and share more next week. But I found out this death could have been prevented. A motorist plowed into my niece's horse-drawn buggy. She was riding in the buggy with her son. Her son received only minor injuries, but the horse also was killed. It happened a short ways from their home. Every Friday she took her boy to a doctor to be treated to help with his muscular dystrophy. Oh! So shocking. She's my oldest niece on my side of the family.

But God makes no mistakes. Only "He" knows the purpose why she's in "His" care now. She is so badly needed with a large family.

I will get back to sharing recipes next week. I hope all you readers are doing well.

FEBRUARY 2000

Last week, I wrote about the untimely death of my niece, who was killed when a motorist struck her buggy outside Seymour, Mo. She leaves behind a husband and 13 children. We just got back from Missouri where we attended the funeral.

Our thoughts are for the bereaved husband and 13 children of my niece. She will be badly missed by her friends and relatives. She was a niece who always thought of us by sending a card and letter for Christmas each year and never forgot my birthday. My niece recently told her oldest daughter, age 18, "now you are the age I was when I lost my mother." History repeats itself. A total of

800 people attended the funeral. Sixty horse-drawn buggies led a procession to the graveyard. God is never wrong.

I want to answer some reader mail now. To the Greensburg, Pa., reader who wants the recipe of sugar cookies:

SUGAR COOKIES

4 cups white sugar
4 tablespoons baking powder
2 cups lard
2 tablespoons lemon juice
3 eggs
1 teaspoon vanilla
3 cups buttermilk
2 tablespoons baking soda
1/2 teaspoon salt
Enough flour to make a soft dough (9 to 10 cups)

Mix all of the above ingredients together in a big bowl. Chill dough a few hours or overnight. Drop by teaspoonfuls onto a lightly greased cookie sheet and bake at 350 degrees until golden. Sour milk can be substituted for buttermilk.

To the Madisonville, Ky., reader and all the others who write asking about a cookbook: It is not available yet, but we are in the process of completing it (Editor's note: It will be available in the spring of 2001. Watch future columns for details)

To the Middletown, Ind., reader who visited Shipshewana, Ind., and had a cookie called "Black-Eyed Susans." Sorry, I never heard of such a cookie.

To the Middle Grantsville, N.Y. reader: Sorry, I don't have a recipe for what you called "cheese biscuits," with filling that is made with cottage cheese.

I want to thank the reader in Manitowoc, Wis., who sent me 11 packets of garden seeds. Just looking at them makes me feel like spring is close.

We are having what you'd call real winter weather the past few weeks. The horse-drawn sleighs are in use now. The white stuff just hangs right in here with the cold. So it is taking more fuel to keep the stoves in gear.

We were to Levi's and Liz's on Monday evening, Jan. 24, as my daughter Liz turned another year older. How these years slip by. Quite a few others from our family were there also. A delicious meal was served.

It is now Wednesday evening, and Liz, Levi, Emma and Jacob have arrived here for supper. Who knows, some more of the family might come. They all know there's always a "welcome" sign to come for a meal -- anytime. I am always glad to see the children come home.

Time goes on as you know, time doesn't wait. See you next week, hopefully, in the newspaper. You great readers out there, thank you for sending the encouraging letters and recipes.

FEBRUARY 2000

This month, on Feb.17, my husband will be another year older. S'pose he will dread to see this being written. Life goes on. Time goes on and there is no way of stopping it.Time, time, time.

Daughters Lovina and Emma were here to spend the day today, also their loving children. Daughter Verena went to get Emma and children with the horse-drawn sleigh, which can be in great use on these snow-covered roads.

Today, the girls decided to cut out a coat, so the material and lining was brought forth and was cut out and sewn. Emma did a good job. She sewed till the coat was done. We need to cut out and sew several more coats for the girls. The project just kept getting delayed. No use to complain as why we didn't get these coats done before, we just have so much to be thankful for.

Monday, my husband and I assisted son Albert, or I should say, his wife and children, as he was working. We helped her cut-up two quarters of beef.

Sons Amos and Albert butchered beef Saturday. We put up 53 quarts of chunk beef and the rest will be ground into hamburger. We visited daughter Leah Monday morning before we went to Albert's, as her son, Paul Jr., can't go out very well in this cold weather. Lots of colds and flu in the area still. Hopefully people are keeping their doors locked from it in this household.

We went to Jacob's (daughter Emma) for Sunday dinner (noon meal) yesterday. While we were at Jacob's, son Albert's came here with intentions to stay for dinner. Discovering we weren't home, they followed our sleigh tracks to Jacob's. We had a nice noon meal and a wonderful day spent with family. It was then decided to go to Albert's for a rare beef supper in the evening. So Jacob's and this household headed to Albert's, taking leftovers from dinner with us. Joe and Lovina joined us there.

You readers out there may wonder what "rare beef" is? It's thinly sliced cooked beef. Lard is pre-heated in a skillet so it is very hot. The thinly sliced beef is well-seasoned with salt and pepper and then put into the skillet and stirred a couple of times and turned over and out of the skillet. This was a great favorite of my father years ago, so it is a family tradition.

I still think of the bereaved family of my niece, Leah Graber, of Seymour, MO. Leah, who passed away in a buggy accident a couple of weeks ago, leaves behind a husband and 13 children. I wish we could visit them more often, but being 600 miles away isn't so easy to travel. We traveled to Seymour for the funeral two weeks ago. God had a purpose to take this dear mother in "His" care, where there's no pain, no worry, only peace. She's greatly missed, but not forgotten, and all the reader letters and cards of encouragement have been wonderful.

Now to some other mail:

To the Indianapolis Star reader about the "haystacks." Haystacks are simple layered meals we make by frying hamburger with taco seasoning. Then cut and dice up lettuce, tomatoes, sweet peppers, onions, cooked spaghetti. We layer each ingredient on top of one another in a casserole and top with melted cheese. You can add anything to it such as rice, raisins, celery, mushrooms, etc.

To the Battle Creek, Mich. reader: I don't know the recipe for lemon poppy bread. Sorry!

To the Luray, Va. reader, you asked for marinated carrots.

I use 4 cups of sliced, cooked carrots, 1 medium onion, sliced thin; 1 green pepper, chopped; 1 small can of tomato soup, 1 cup of sugar, 1/2 cup salad oil, 3/4 cup vinegar, 1 teaspoon prepared mustard, 1 teaspoon salt, 1 teaspoon pepper.

Mix carrots, onions, and pepper lightly. Mix rest of ingredients and combine with carrot mixture. Refrigerate at least 12 hours.

To the Ryland Heights, Ky. reader: Sorry, I haven't a recipe for diabetic sugar-free peanut butter fudge.

To the Sumner, Ill. reader who asked me for a corn bread recipe. I can tell you how I make mine, it doesn't require any yeast and turns out yellow

in color.

I use 2 eggs, 1 cup milk, 1/4 cup melted shortening, 3/4 cup

yellow corn meal, 1 cup flour, 1 teaspoon salt, 3 teaspoons baking powder and 2 tablespoons sugar.

Beat all ingredients until smooth. Bake in a greased pan at 400 degrees for about 20 minutes. Good luck!

We always like ham and beans with corn bread and some like it with milk.

A reader in Harrison, Ohio, asked if I had a spaghetti pie recipe. Here is a favorite one around this household:

HOMEMADE SPAGHETTI PIE

6 ounces of spaghetti, cooked and drained
2 eggs, well-beaten
1 / 3 cup of grated Parmesan cheese
2 tablespoons of butter, melted
1 any-sized jar of homemade or store-bought spaghetti sauce (16 - 24 ounce)
1 - 2 cups of cottage cheese

Mix together spaghetti, eggs, cheese and butter. Put about 1/2 cup spaghetti sauce in bottom of a greased casserole dish (about 9 x 6 inch). Pour spaghetti on top of sauce. Spread 1 - 2 cups cottage cheese on top of spaghetti. Pour rest of sauce on. Cover. Bake 25 minutes at 350 degrees. Serves about six.

FEBRUARY 2000

It is 3 a.m. as I write this on a Thursday morning.

I feel like I need to get this task of writing done and on its way today. It must get in the mail.

I was going to get up early anyway as we want to get an early start with the cutting up of beef at Joe and Lovina's. We will then put the beef in jars and process it with pressure cookers. So it looks like a full day.

The rest of my daughters will be assisting, except Leah, as her son, Ben, (my grandson) received a broken ankle on Friday evening. He endured a lot of pain and had surgery on it Tuesday evening at Parkview Hospital in Fort Wayne, Ind. So Ben, who is 17, will be laid up for some time. He gets around with the aid of crutches now. Accidents do happen but some could be prevented. Having a break nowadays is quite expensive, and now Ben cannot work. We gave him a visit last night.

The temperature is 37 degrees now. We've had some cold days already and plenty of snow. There were huge drifts at places so our horse-drawn sleigh was put to use. The snow is melting fast, and you can see ground again. I reckon Tuesday evening was our last sleigh ride for a while unless we get more snow before spring.

To the Williamsport, Ohio, reader: Cookbooks aren't available now, but we're in the process of having one in the future (spring 2001). Hope this does it for all the other readers who write asking about it.

I want to thank all the readers out there for their nice sympathy cards of losing my great niece in Seymour, Mo. I was surprised to receive so many, also for the encouraging letters received. Hopefully, I can do better at answering more mail this year. Last year seemed stressful. Yet we have so much to be thankful for.

February means my husband, Ben, will be one year older. My brother's birthday is also on that same day. They are one year apart in age. We have three grandchildren who have birthdays this month.

Was glad we could hang the laundry out on the clothesline Monday and again Wednesday. It dried very good. In the cold weather, it's sometimes more of a hassle to get clothing dried. Most of the time, we hang wet clothing in the basement on clothes racks by the stove. It seems to get the job done. You see, our electricity isn't in working order. Ha!

Some readers have requested where we get those 1,000-piece Amish country jigsaw puzzles. Not sure about cost, but Lovina got them from: Doyle Yoder Publishing, P.O. Box 424, Berlin, Ohio 44610.

A reader in Hammond, Ind., requested an oatmeal pie recipe. She said she had not heard of such a pie, but it is a favorite around here.

OATMEAL PIE

> 8 eggs, slightly beaten
> 3 cups packed brown sugar
> 1 pound margarine, melted
> 3 cups light corn syrup
> 3 cups rolled oats
> 2 cups walnut meats, chopped

Cream sugar, margarine and eggs together until smooth. Add corn syrup, and mix well. Stir in oatmeal and nuts until blended. Pour into 4 8- or 9-inch unbaked pie shells. Bake in a 300-degree oven for 55 to 60 minutes or until set.

FEBRUARY 2000

Butchering of beef and pork seems to make its rounds at this time of year.

Butchering our meat is a tough job, but it allows the family to be together for a day of good, hard work. And it provides us with our meat for a long time. It was a time of busy butchering this past week.

We helped our daughter Lovina with cutting up four quarters of beef Thursday. In all, 81 quarts of beef were processed, and the rest was put

through the grinder for hamburger. Fresh beef can be used for so many things around here. I like to make a beef stew with those leftover bones. It makes such a good stew. The processed beef is great to use for dishes like "beef and noodles" or "beef and gravy." Also, I like to chop up the beef real fine, add ketchup to it, and heat it. This makes such good sandwiches. We like to just heat up the beef chunks for the evening meal with potatoes. It seems a soothing meat, so fresh.

On Saturday, it was pork. We helped our son Albert butcher three hogs with the help of other family members. The men do the cutting, and the women do the cleaning. We used to scald the hogs but now we skin them. By skinning them, there is no water to be heated in the butchering tank.

The hogs are hung on scaffolding and cut wide open to the stomach. It becomes a mess if the intestines are accidentally cut, which then requires washing off the area with water. The women like to see clean intestines, as they will be stuffed with sausage later. The women also cleaned the stomachs, tongues and brains. Nothing goes to waste.

Rendering lard afterwards, we have those "cracklings." Some are so fond of. (Cracklings are the crisp part remaining after the lard has been removed from hog fat by frying).

Liver pudding, produced from the head meat of a hog, is also made. This meat is cooked soft in a big iron kettle. We took the meat off the bones and put it through the grinder. Liver pudding has a good taste; many like it for breakfast.

Then the last of the butchering to be done in the iron kettle is "pon hoss" as we call it. This is made with the juice from the bones that are cooked in the kettle. It is made with a thickening to the juice and some liver pudding added to it. We also season it with salt and pepper. We usually use flour but some use cornmeal.

After it is cooked and thickened in the iron kettle, it is put into loaf pans to chill. When chilled, cut slices and fry in a skillet. At times, a little lard is added if it's not greasy, but at times no lard is added. Fry 'til golden brown. We like ours sliced on the thin side to fry. There are some who put it into jars and process to open later.

The hams, bacon, pork chops, ribs and tenderloins are taken care of afterward the "pon hoss." Some are processed and some sugar-cured. After all the mess is completed, the iron kettles, saws, knives, sausage stuffer and grinder are washed clean.

Everyone is then rewarded for their work with a delicious, noon meal. After the hog butchering was completed, the menfolk came to the residence to butcher a bull as we had son Amos' bull here, and also, put Joe's beef through a grinder as their grinder was not in working order. So this was a long, full day of working together. Son Amos and Albert's will go half with the beef. So they will both have lots of beef to care for this week.

Today, Feb. 17, my husband is 3,588 weeks old. Ha! I like to see him when he reads this!

Monday, we attended the funeral of an aged friend. In the afternoon, when we arrived back home, I quick got the laundry done. We had some snowy, icy roads which were very treacherous on the way to the funeral, but by the way back it had improved.

My grandson Ben, age 16, son of Paul and Leah Shetler, is continuing to recover from his broken ankle. This accident could have been prevented. He has endured a lot of pain since. He will be laid up for some time. His younger brother, Paul Jr., seems to be doing well.

Yesterday morning, we had six of our grandchildren here while their mothers went into town. All of them are under age 5. I reckon that's what these grandmothers are for: to help these young mothers. They enjoy it here, especially mealtime. Ha!

Some have written requesting a good homemade cake recipe for a birthday. Here is one:

CHOCOLATE CHIP CAKE

    1 3/4 cups sifted flour
    1 teaspoon baking soda
    1 teaspoon salt
    2 tablespoons cocoa
    1 cup shortening
    1 cup sugar
    1 teaspoon vanilla
    2 eggs, beaten

1 cup boiling water
6 ounces chocolate chips

Sift together flour, cocoa, salt and baking soda. Set aside. Cream shortening and sugar together in large mixing bowl. Add eggs and vanilla to shortening mixture. Beat thoroughly. Add water and flour mixture alternately, mixing batter until smooth after each addition. Spoon and spread into greased 13- by 9-inch plan. Sprinkle top with chocolate chips. Bake at 350 degrees for 45 minutes. Serves about 20.

FEBRUARY 2000

We're receiving some warmer weather the last couple of days. The sun is shining brightly, and it's 9 a.m. with a temperature of 51 degrees as I write this.

The snow drifts are gradually melting away, leaving a muddy mess on our gravel roads. The fields and yards look a dirty brown color with the trees being bare of those colorful leaves. Good to see spring come up again, but then there's lots of duties to be done as another winter ends. Why complain about growing older, though, as long as a person stays in good health?

Last week, my husband Ben turned another year older, and so did my brother-in-law. Most of the family was here for my husband's birthday Feb. 17. Daughter Verena barbecued pork chops and hamburgers on the grill.

Our two oldest children and their families, Leah and Paul and Amos and Nancy, were not present. Paul's son Ben couldn't go out with his crutches, as he is still laid up from a broken ankle. And Amos' family couldn't come because of these muddy road conditions. So they'll come on a later day for my husband's occasion. Everyone else had a very nice evening together here.

Grandson Ben had his second cast removed Monday and the third put on from his broken ankle. The doctor said it looks as if it's healing well. We and some of the family were at Paul and Leah's home for Sunday supper. Ben keeps himself in good spirits and hopefully he won't make a mis-move with his foot 'til it's fully healed.

My husband has two bird feeders hung on trees outside this winter. He says those birds need something to eat. So he keeps them filled. It's remarkable how those birds of all kinds come at those feeders. Those little creatures find their food day to day. Just looking out the window as I write this column, it is somewhat interesting to watch the birds.

Well, I must hurry along as time rolls right on. Time has a way of slipping by and just never waits. Right?

Before I go, some mailbag stuff:

To the Ludlow, Ky., reader: Those garden seeds you sent were greatly appreciated. Thank you!

To the Shallowater, Texas, reader: I want to thank you for the gift of hand-made stationary sent to us.

To the Marshfield, Mo., reader: It was good to hear you knew my niece and family of Seymour, Mo. God makes no mistakes as to take her into "His" care. Thank you all for the nice, comforting letters.

MARCH 2000

I've got the laundry ready to go onto the clothesline. So hopefully it will dry out nicely, as I want to iron today. I hope everyone out there is in good health.

This past Sunday was spent at Joe and Lovina's. Lovina prepared a good noon meal with grilled steak on the menu. Others there were Paul and Leah's family, son Albert's family, and Emma and Jacob's family.

Their evening meal guests were son Amos' family, Levi's family, Jacob's family, Ben and I and our daughters. It was another good meal. Son Amos' and Levi's had come to our house for supper and discovered that we were not home. So they went to Joe and Lovina's and found us all gathered there. In fact, Joe's family had all our family there on Sunday at one meal or the other.

Grandson Ben, son of Paul's family, gets around with the aid of crutches after having his ankle broken Feb. 4. He had surgery on Feb. 8. I am glad he could be at Joe and Lovina's on Sunday.

Saturday evening, son Albert's family had quite a scare with a chimney fire. Chimney fires are a danger this time of year, as creosote builds up after a long winter. Neighbors had called out the fire department, but the call was canceled as they quickly got it under control. A couple of their neighbors came to their rescue. Some items were already being carried from the house in preparation for fire. Their basement and breezeway got the smoke. But how lucky the house still stands and the smoke mess can be cleaned.

The crocuses have found their way through the ground. A beautiful scene to see that yellow color in the brown-dirty ground. The weather has turned so warm; we were out in the yard without shoes on. It felt so good to be out in that warm air. We took advantage of it and did a huge laundry.

It's amazing how many sympathy cards we have received from readers after the loss of my niece in Seymour, Mo. I want to thank all you readers out there for sending and taking your time to write. Also a thank you to the readers who have been sending recipes.

A Dunkirk, Ind., reader asked me how we make our homemade ice cream. It's never the same as store-bought. You have to have a six-quart freezer to make the ice cream. I use 12 cups of milk with 2 or 3 cups of cream included. At times more cream, like 3 cups cream and 9 cups milk, seven eggs, 3 1/2 cups sugar, 1 teaspoon salt and 4 teaspoons vanilla. Try it. You'll like it. The more cream -- the better! Good luck!

To the Keechobee, Fla., reader (Where is Keechobee?): I have never heard of "Flan with a caramel-flavored juice in the bottom." Sorry!

To the Homosassa, Fla., reader who requested a green tomato pie recipe: I make mine using the following ingredients: 6 green tomatoes, sliced; 1 apple, thinly sliced; 1 cup sugar; 3/4 teaspoon cinnamon; 1 tablespoon lemon juice. Arrange half of the fruit in the pie crust. In a separate bowl, mix ingredients. Then sprinkle over the fruit in the pie crust. Add the rest of the fruit. Put top of the pie crust on. Bake at 400 degrees for 35 minutes. Makes one pie.

To David in Indianapolis about how I make my chili. I put 1 quart or more of canned sausage in a 4-quart kettle and 1 large onion and fry together until golden brown. Then I add 1 pint water and, in a separate bowl, make a thickening of 3 tablespoons flour with water. Add it to the kettle.

Add tomato juice and kidney beans as you prefer. Season with salt, pepper and chili powder to your taste. I also add 1 tablespoon or so of brown sugar. Don't really have a recipe for it. I just sort of make it the way I know how. Everyone in the family seems to eat it very well. They like it with crackers. I like to use the canned sausage better than the hamburger. Good luck!

A lot of readers sent in their recipes for "brown-eyed Susans" in answer to a request from a reader. A reader in Hays sent in this good recipe:

BROWN EYES SUSANS

1 cup margarine, softened
1/4 cup sugar
1/2 teaspoon almond extract
Whole almonds
2 cups flour
1/2 teaspoon salt
Chocolate frosting

Cream margarine and sugar until light and fluffy. Blend in extract. Add flour and salt. Mix well. Shape rounded teaspoonfuls of dough into balls. Place on ungreased cookie sheet. Flatten slightly. Bake at 350 degrees for 10 to 12 minutes. Cool. Frost with chocolate frosting. Top with almonds, if you wish.

Chocolate frosting: Combine 1 cup sifted confectioners sugar and 2 tablespoons cocoa. Add 1 tablespoon hot water and 1/2 teaspoon vanilla. Mix well.

MARCH 2000

This is such a beautiful Monday morning. It's the first Monday of March, and the temperature is 52.

It's 8:30 a.m. now, and the laundry is hanging out there on the clothesline. It should dry well. It feels so good to hang the laundry outside again. During the cold wetness of winter, we often have to hang our clothing to dry in the basement on clothes-racks. It takes so much longer that way. It is just lots more work to try to hang the clothes outside during the winter; you almost freeze your fingers when hanging it outdoors in January. But one season comes and soon goes. I love a morning like this as spring is appearing on the calendar. It looks like Easter is late this year.

Son Amos and wife Nancy and daughter Lovina, along with her husband Joe, assisted us in hauling out manure from the barn. So our team of Belgian horses and the manure spreader was put into use for use in the fields. Plans were made Friday evening when they were here for supper.

Jacob's family (daughter Emma) also came on Saturday, not knowing this was going on. Just a quick plan because of the nice weather. So Jacob joined in to help.

I want to do some raking around the yard today, especially where those spring flowers are peeping through. The ground is dry enough for raking. Also I would like to put some seeds in the garden today after it is spaded. I'll probably put little radishes and lettuce in the ground. Some have their garden out already, which is unusual this early. I also want to put seeds in pots for plants.

During the spring, we used to raise and sell plants when we were young. We sold vegetable and flower plants. At that time, we sold a dozen for 10 cents. Some of the flowers were sold at the same price but the perennial plants were 5 cents each. They look a lot of care. We had six large beds to start off the early plants, and by April 1 we put out the late stuff on the open land. I'd hate to try selling plants now. Nothing frosted on us back then. The weather must be different now. At the end, to get rid of the plants, we'd sell them two dozen for 15 cents.

We had our first meal of those dandelion greens last night. The dandelions can usually be found nestled in lawns, gardens, pastures and roadways. Some take them for weeds, but the sight of those early dandelion greens delights us. They taste better early in the season when they are most tender. We use them as a salad with hard-boiled eggs added to it. Some wilt them, but I prefer the salad. Dandelions made in a salad for the evening meal really seems to relax a person for a good night's rest.

They sure were a delight on our table last night with cooked potatoes. Fried chicken was also on the menu with other vegetables, fruits, cheese and homemade cookies that daughter Verena baked last week. I'm glad Susan gathered the dandelions. I guess I am not that patient to gather them. Joe's and Jacob's families also joined us with supper and enjoyed the dandelions. Any kind of fried meat goes good with dandelions.

My husband is trimming our fruit trees now after he repaired three kerosene lanterns this morning. Glad he got them in working order. I want to join him outdoors to do some raking now. Just too nice out there to be working indoors.

A reader from Harrison, Ohio, asked for a homemade coffee cake recipe. Here is one that goes good around here:

SWISS COFFEE CAKE

3/4 cup warm water (about 105 degrees F)
1 package dry yeast
1/4 cup sugar
1 teaspoon salt
2 1/4 cups all-purpose flour, divided use
1 egg
1/4 cup lard
2 teaspoons margarine
Brown sugar, cinnamon for topping

Dissolve yeast in warm water. Let stand a few minutes, then stir. Stir in sugar, salt and 1 cup of the flour. Beat the eggs, add lard (softened) and the egg to the flour mixture. Beat in the remaining flour until mixture is smooth.

Drop by spoonfuls into a greased shallow baking pan. Let rise in a warm place until dough is nearly doubled. Dot top of dough with tiny bits of margarine, then sprinkle with brown sugar and cinnamon.

Bake 30 minutes at 350 degrees.

MARCH 2000

This seems a quiet Sunday evening, March 12, with none of the family here for supper.

Son Albert's, Joe's and Jacob's families were our dinner (noon meal) guests. They all left for their houses later in the afternoon.

We had the ground covered with that white stuff this morning in a late winter snow. It started to snow yesterday afternoon, and for a while it was like a blizzard. It makes a nice winter-like scene outside.

The grandchildren were having a nice, enjoyable time out there in the snow. Snowman after snowman was being made. All kinds of shapes. It was enjoyable to watch them play in the snow.

Yesterday, March 11, 42 years ago, my husband and I started up a home of our own. Lots of memories in these by-gone years. So many new homes have been built everywhere in this area since then. The one-mile road we used to live on when still at home with my parents only had two farm homes on it.

We then built a set of buildings, which made the third set of buildings on that road. Now there's more than a dozen families living along that road. There's just lots more people and reckon everyone likes a home of their home.

The Easter lilies were blooming nicely the other day, but they looked droopy this morning. I don't think the small amount of garden stuff will grow now.

I just took a try to put a few radishes, carrots and lettuce in the ground during a warm spell before the snow. So it'll be hit or miss now. Time will tell if we had bad luck with it. Suppose there are many others who got that spring fever to plant when the weather was so warm.

To the Blue Springs, Mo., reader for the sympathy card, letter and especially memorial gift in regard to my niece who passed away: Words just can't express the great appreciation. Thank you to everyone who sends such nice letters and cards.

I will finish this letter now.

It is now Tuesday evening. Daughters Liz, Lovina and Emma, and all their children spent the day here. Joe's and Jacob's families came in the evening.

Paul's family was here for supper. Liz and children left for their home towards evening.

So this seemed a long, enjoyable work-day together. It is always good to see the children arrive here. Jacob did the finishing touches of trimming our three apple trees at the top of the trees. My husband had been trimming the trees also. The snow is all melted away now. No trace of snowmen in the yard anymore. The snow made some moisture on the ground as it was beginning to be very dry. It was a nice day, and the grandchildren were playing outside, but this time no snow in sight.

A reader in Glens Falls, N.Y., asked about "dilly bread." Here is my recipe for that delicious bread:

DILLY BREAD

1 package yeast
1 /4 cup warm water
2 tablespoons sugar
1 tablespoon dry onion flakes
1 tablespoon butter
1 teaspoon salt
1 cup small curd cottage cheese
1 tablespoon dill seed
1 /4 teaspoon soda
1 egg
2 1/ 2 cups flour

Dissolve yeast in water in a large bowl. Add the rest of the ingredients except flour. Mix well. Add flour slowly, beating after each addition. Cover with cloth. Let rise in warm place until double, about 1 hour. Stir down and form into a loaf or shape into 12 buns. Place rolls on greased cookie sheet or bread in loaf pan, cover and let rise until light -- 30 to 45 minutes. Bake rolls in 350-degree oven for 12 minutes or until golden brown, 40 to 45 minutes for a loaf. Remove from pans, and brush with lard or margarine.

MARCH 2000

It is Monday, March 20, and spring of 2000 has appeared on the calendar. What does this tell us?

Yes, there will be the garden to sow and then comes more to do when those seeds have sprouted and are ready for hoeing and weeding. We put hours in to keep the garden free of weeds, which seems always to be quite a task. On those summer days, the hot sun is on our backs and the work seems to get tiresome. But then we think: "Why complain when we are in good enough health to work in the garden?" It feels so good to go to the garden and pick those vegetables to prepare a meal. So much easier when all kinds of salads, cooked vegetables, soups and sandwiches can be made with the fresh garden goodies.

Spring also means there is also the lawn to be mowed, and those beautiful flowers have such a good scent in the spring air. Spring is the best on my list of the four seasons.

Let me answer a few letters here:

To the Sugar Creek, Mo., reader: Those garden seeds you sent to me were greatly appreciated. Hopefully they'll be in the ground soon. Thank you!

To the reader of Rockford, Ohio, but who winters in Aiken, S. C., sorry, I have no recipe for the recipe of "Whities," as opposed to "brownies" and "blonde brownies." It's a cookie bar with white chocolate. Maybe someone out there has it.

To the Chicago reader: The cookbook will be ready to sell by the year of 2001. We'll let you know when it goes on sale.

To the Albridge, Ohio, reader: I never have heard of buying Pon Hoss in stores. We make it fresh on butchering day only.

To the Mitchell, Ind., reader who wrote about the brine for the shredded cabbage in pepper: Make it from vinegar, pickling spice, sugar and salt. Make the amount you prefer and to your taste.

To the Williamsburg, Kan., reader: Your lengthy letter and recipes about your family were interesting. Thanks for your time.

This has been a long day it seems. But it has been enjoyable. Daughter Verena baked 72 chocolate chip cookies before heading off to work this morning.

After the morning household chores were completed, I made a potato salad and baked a cake, which later, one box of Jello was poured over the cake and Cool Whip to top it.

Daughter Emma and children, and also Lovina and children came to help prepare and join in the dinner at noon. We were having some company from Ohio. Apple crisps and fresh cooked apples were done also.

Daughter Leah and family also showed up for dinner after they came back from the hospital. Their Ben had his cast removed from his ankle. Guess he can expect some pain from it yet.

After the noon dinner, everyone enjoyed visiting, singing and yodeling. Naturally the dinner dishes had all been washed by my daughters.

WASHDAY CASSEROLE

3 pounds hamburger
3 onions, chopped
3 cups potatoes, peeled and diced
3 cups celery, diced
3 cups cooked spaghetti
2 (10 3/4-ounce) cans cream of mushroom soup
9 slices bacon
1 (32-ounce) quart tomato juice
1 pound Cheddar cheese, grated

Brown crumbled hamburger and onions in a pan. Drain and pour hamburger mix into large casserole or deep 9- by 13-inch baking pan. Add potatoes, celery and spaghetti to casserole, and mix lightly with hamburger. Pour mushroom soup on top and spread evenly. Fry bacon and lay on top. Pour tomato juice over this. Add cheese over that. Bake 1 1/2 hours in 350-degree oven. Serves 10 to 12.

APRIL 2000

It was rainy-like this morning but has changed to colder. We've had snow, rain and sleet sweeping across the surrounding fields this evening. So it was a good, cozy time to be indoors around the warm stove.

One of my sisters had a quilting bee today for her family. So my brother and his wife and four of my sisters attended (we only had one brother in our family, with seven sisters). It was an enjoyable day together quilting. It's not too often we get together. So there was no dull moment. Singing took place.

At noon, my sister and daughters prepared a good noon dinner for us all. Too many calories in a day like this.

A quilt has its many duties. Lots of work to sew the material together, and mark off what design you prefer. Then put it in the frame, and there goes those many stitches on the quilt. A batting is put between the material also.

There's needles and thread to be bought. Lots to quilt preparation. My parents gave us children three quilts when we left their household. One was a diamond pattern, the other was a four-leaf clover, and another had tulip designs.

We had a different-type of breakfast this morning. Verena made those "breakfast burritos." She fries eggs, bacon and crumbles cheese on top. She then puts it all on a flour tortilla and rolls it up and then bakes it in the oven. They are quick and easy to make. We like our hot, homemade salsa to go with it.

I didn't get this all written last night like I had hoped, so I will try to finish this now and get it on its way.

We're having another meal of those dandelion greens on the menu tonight, with green onions, potatoes and ham (our own pork). I see some of the dandelions growing outside already have blooms.

We had an enjoyable day on Friday when Paul's family (daughter Leah) asked us to go out visiting the sick and shut-ins. The day just wasn't long enough. We appreciate good health that much more when you see others who can't get out and go.

To the Harrodsburg, Ky., reader whose chocolate pudding pie doesn't turn out. It sounds like you are making your chocolate pudding too thin. I make my chocolate pie filling with:

> 1 quart milk, scalded
> 1 /2 cup cornstarch
> 1 /3 cup cocoa
> 1 3 /4 cup sugar
> 1 cup cold milk
> 1 teaspoon and pinch of salt

Mix cornstarch, cocoa, sugar and cold milk. Pour in scalded milk. Stir constantly until thick. Remove from heat and let it cool some. Pour into baked pie crust. When cold, top with whipped topping.

Now, you great readers, try this recipe for a homemade peach-custard pie. It goes good around here.

SWISS CUSTARD PEACH PIE

> 6 fresh peaches or 1 1/4 pint sliced peaches, drained
> 2 eggs
> 1/2 cup sugar
> 1 /4 teaspoon salt
> 2 tablespoons melted butter
> 1 1/4 cups condensed milk

Places peaches in unbaked 8- or 9-inch pie crust. Mix eggs with butter, sugar and salt. Beat a few minutes, then add the milk. Beat once more 'til well blended. Pour the mixture on the peaches in the shell. Bake for 15 minutes at 375 degrees. Reduce heat to 300 until custard is firm, about 40 minutes longer. Serves 6 to 8.

APRIL 2000

As I write this, it is April 5. This day brings back memories of my mother who has gone to that Great Beyond. She'd be 95 years old today.

The temperature was at 25 degrees this morning before turning warmer later.

Today, my daughter Verena and I attended another quilting bee at my brother Chris'. Last week, I also wrote about attending a quilting bee. At this one, there were around 30 women and girls there to help quilt, plus a lot of children. There were three quilts in the frames today.

We gathered at my brother's place early. Coffee and a variety of cookies were passed around in the morning (our coffee break). At noon, a delicious dinner was served to all. The dinner consisted of 40 pounds of barbecued chicken and lots of other good stuff. The tables had been set up for us women and girls to be seated to eat. We had chicken, pie and cake; it was a delicious meal.

It seemed an enjoyable time with what goes on a day like this. Gossiping, singing and yodeling are enjoyed by all the women who are quilting. Time goes too fast on a day like this. Different kinds of pop and a variety of candy were passed around in the afternoon for a break.

They'll have some more women and girls coming tomorrow. Lots of quilting to be done yet in that family. We got most of our quilts done in a winter when the girls were still home.

Joe's and Jacob's families came here this evening to start "forming" in front of our tool shed. We want to cement the ground in front of our shed. Son Albert dug it out for us in the evening. The area has to be dug out before it can be cemented. Right now, it is just our dirt driveway that goes up to the shed.

If the outside of the shed is cemented, it will make it easier to get the horse-drawn buggies in and out.

I must hike off to bed where the rest are in a peaceful sleep. Tomorrow has its many duties again.

Another day has started and this morning, the temperature was 54 degrees.

Quite a change from yesterday morning. I want to finish this task of writing so I can get to the garden. I want to put a couple of pounds of onion sets in the ground. The ground has already been spaded.

The radishes, onions, lettuce and carrots seem to be up and growing. I haven't put too much out yet since it is so early in the season.

This morning, we had cornmeal mush for breakfast. Some may wonder how we make this. We cook our cornmeal mush the evening before and put in a loaf pan to give it shape. By morning, it is chilled. In the morning, we slice either thick or thin, however you prefer. Then put it slice by slice in a skillet with lard and fry 'til golden brown. Some use vegetable oil or bacon fat to fry it.

It can be served with syrup or whatever you prefer. We put molasses, honey or apple butter on top of the fried mush. It's very nourishing! This meal isn't always just for breakfast. I can remember how my mother used to cook the mush for the evening meal. She liked to have a cup of milk in one hand, and by spoon, she'd dip the mush in the milk and eat it. I didn't care for the cooked mush that way but liked it when fried in the morning. It's a good way to remember her this birthday.

CORN MUSH

4 cups water
1 cup cornmeal
1 teaspoon salt

Bring 3 cups of water to a boil. In a bowl, make a thickening with the cornmeal, salt and 1 cup of water. Add this mix to the boiling water. Stir mixture until it has reached the boiling point, then stir occasionally. Cook for 15 to 20 minutes, then pour into a deep baking dish. Cool, then slice and fry until brown.

APRIL 2000

The rhubarbs have really advanced within the last week. I reckon the ground is well soaked, and warmer weather will make them grow even more.

Rhubarbs are used in so many ways around here, as in jams, coffeecakes, shortcakes, pies, crunches, cobbler, desserts. We like our rhubarbs in so many ways. Also, some make a juice with it.

The green winter onions are a delight on the menu right now with their taste. We eat them along with the fresh dandelion greens this time of year. The dandelions are going into blooms, which means they are past their peak. They taste best when they are young and tender shoots. There are still some outside to be picked and put into a salad. Some people around here make a jelly with the yellow blossoms, but I never have. I have recipes for it, but our favorite jelly or jam around here is in rhubarb.

Daughter Liz and children spent the day here yesterday. In the afternoon, our long-time friend, Elda, and her sister came for a visit. She is 86 -- hard to believe; she gets around well.

In the evening, our son Albert and our daughter Lovina and family came for supper. Soon we'll have lots of goodies from the garden on the table every night. That's why spring is such a wonderful time -- my favorite season.

Here's a poem I read once but only remember part of it; it captures my love of the season: "First comes asparagus, lettuce and peas - Oh! How good taste all of these. Strawberries, onions, radishes, and string beans, carrots, limas, and turnip greens. Corn, potatoes, and cabbage for kraut -- much of this we'll have this summer, no doubt. Tomatoes, red beets and pickles, also some dill -- all of these help my garden to fill."

Well, I must finish this task of writing, as I need to get to the laundry this afternoon. So many duties to do. Always plenty of laundry and then there's that big stack of ironing. My daughter Susan has arrived home from work and is hanging it out on the clothesline now. She is also going to gather some dandelion greens for supper, which a sour cream sauce has been prepared. We are also having spaghetti and meatballs for supper tonight. Homemade apple crisp and Jell-O cake is on the menu for dessert.

GARDEN RHUBARB BREAD

1 1/2 cups brown sugar
2/3 cup of oil
1 egg
1 cup sour milk
2 3/4 cups flour
1 teaspoon salt
1 teaspoon baking soda
1 teaspoon vanilla
1 1/2 cups fresh, diced rhubarb

Glaze: 1/2 cup sugar, 1 teaspoon butter, 1 teaspoon cinnamon

Mix bread ingredients in order given. Pour into two greased loaf pans and bake at 350 degrees for 45 minutes. Brush on glaze and let cool. Delicious!

$\mathfrak{I}$ am writing this column on Palm Sunday, April 16. This day brings back memories of the evening of Palm Sunday, April 11, 1964.

That was the day a tornado swept through this area. Never before had it been recorded in this part of Indiana. It was a hot and sultry day. We had attended church services that day, and some families were at one of my sister's houses for supper. As the evening went on, we hadn't expected storms. Later, though, some of us stood out in the yard watching those dark clouds above us. There must be a bad storm about 10 miles from here, we thought. So we all left for our homes. As I entered the dining room, I said, "What's different?" Something seemed different in the air, a stillness, a darkness. But we didn't think much of it and went to bed. All was quiet here.

The next morning, we completed the chores as usual, ate breakfast, and my husband prepared for work. But the one who usually hauled him to and from work did not show up. He soon found out why: A tornado had passed through the nearest town, downing a big furniture store, grocery store and surrounding homes.

I have a sister who lives in that tornado-hit area. So we felt we just had to go check on her and her property. So my parents and my husband, I and our three children we had at the time went to see how it was at my sister's farm. The only thing the tornado had done was blow out a storm door. How lucky to see it didn't do more.

Their neighbor just to the north reported the storm sounded like a freight train, and there were vibrations like those of a passing train. Luckily, my sister and family were not home at the time the tornado passed. The farm building just south of their house was downed, which were well-kept buildings. Such a sad look to see it down. Even today, there's still tin in trees where the wind drove it in like a hammer.

Tornadoes are such a display of the mighty hand of God. If we concede this great point, then we should be concerned what lessons He wants us to learn from them? Was He speaking only to others? Or just to the people hit? It is human to point out how someone else might profit from a lesson or two.

After seeing my sister's place was generally OK, we then traveled around in that area to see what had taken place. Going down this one road, I'll never forget the sight. Where nice farm buildings once stood, there was nothing but flattened rubble. And nearby a surreal field of broken dreams: Freezers, refrigerators, bath tubs, stoves, lavatories and furniture were all scattered across this field. There were clothes hanging off of tree branches and lots of treasures of all kinds from what a house holds. Some cows were sitting there, so dirty and stunned, and some dead. What a feeling one must endure at such a time. It must've been quite a feeling to see all your buildings leveled.

It was a day well-spent to help those tornado victims. There's always plenty of people who will help at such a time. It's like starting new again.

There's a book about the tornado called "The Mighty Whirlwind" by David Wagler. It is quite touching to read. So many farm homes leveled and the losing of loved ones. This disaster was painful to all in our community, yet most of the victims grew from the experience. Their faith in God was strengthened. They feel they have a better knowledge of God, who holds life and death in "His" hand, whose plans are not without purpose. Some were glad to share their stories in this book.

One of Ben's cousins of northern Indiana also had all his buildings leveled.

MAY 2000

It is the last Thursday of April, and it seems to be a nice, sunshiny day so far.

Daughters Lovina and children, and Emma and children, are spending the day here. Yesterday evening, we washed off walls inside and scrubbed the board fence outside. The start of repainting that fence took place. Daughters Liz and Emma and their children spent the day yesterday. Also, we sewed some dresses, and aprons were next on the list. It was a very busy day.

So Emma and Verena are painting the rest of the board fence today, which will make for a better appearance. We had it painted around eight years ago. It must have been good paint as it still didn't look bad as yet.

Lovina is doing some sewing for me now. Lovina and her husband Joe came here after supper last night. Lovina and Joe's three girls fell asleep while they were here, and also Jacob's two oldest girls fell asleep in the evening.

So instead of carrying them to the buggy and going home, we decided we would tuck them five girls into bed here. It was cute to see those little girls in a peaceful sleep. They all slept well, being at Grandma and Grandpa's. Everyone enjoyed a good breakfast in the morning.

Daughter Susan went to work today at the factory in the nearby town. Glad she is back to work as she had a bad 1999 with her broken ankle. She enjoys the work at her place of being employed.

Easter was late this year. Easter was always a time to think of coloring eggs with the children. But that is a thing of the past now that our children are grown, although I took a notion to color some with the help of Susan this year. We did it for the grandchildren.

Good Friday was spent at Levi's (daughter Liz) home, so I helped their children with the coloring of eggs. They were so thrilled to color those eggs. Thought we'd color some in case some of the married children would come home for meals over Easter time.

Memories linger of when Mother would fry eggs with the meals when company came on Easter Day. She'd fry eggs for whoever could eat the most, when us children were all at home.

The twins, Arlene and Marlene, daughters of son Amos, turned 7 years old this past week. Time has a way of slipping by. I remember well what an exciting morning to receive word to have a set of twins in the family.

Last night, son Albert's and three sons with three of their school buddies took a hike through the woods and came here for a while. It is about one mile across the fields and woods between our houses. They came here for an evening meal, stayed the night and headed back in the morning. Reminded me when our children went to school and at times brought some overnighters from school.

Ham is popular at Easter time. Here is a simple, delicious recipe for baked ham.

BAKED HAM

3 /4 cup flour
1/4 teaspoon powdered mustard
1/4 cup brown sugar
3 to 4 pounds of ham
1 cup coffee cream

Slice ham. Mix flour, sugar and mustard well. Roll ham in mixture of flour, brown sugar and mustard. Place in baking dish. Pour cream over meat and bake at 350 degrees until done.

MAY 2000

This has been such a beautiful day. The day started off with plenty to do.

My daughter Verena cleaned all the windows in and out. Susan and I did a big laundry of plenty of bed blankets, all the curtains, five rocking chair covers, bed sheets, pillow cases and you name it. Being such a drying, sunshiny day outside, we really took advantage of it. We had a late dinner because we were trying to do all we could before noon, and the time just didn't wait on us. Time went on.

In the afternoon, curtains were hung back up, which made for such a good appearance again. The rocking chairs and couch covers were put back on. What a clean feeling to see everything back in its place. Also, the beds were all made, with sheets smelling so crisp and fresh. Some winter coats were washed and will be back in place 'til next winter. The lanterns were given a good washing this morning, which takes some work. And our screens were washed and put on the windows. There are so many spring duties to be done. It seems endless but how can one complain when in such good health?

It's around 4 p.m. as I write this, and we're going to Joe's as they're putting up a fence. So we must get on the road. Will write more later. It's time to go.

This is Thursday morning now and soon the mailman will be here and I must finish this so I can beat the mailman to the box. Daughter Liz and children arrived this morning, so it has been nice having them here for a visit.

Daughter Lovina and her kids also stopped by. Verena took Lovina's horse-drawn buggy to go after daughter Emma and children, to bring them here for a visit. But, it so happened about a half-mile from here the wheel broke from the axle of the buggy, which keeps the horse under control and the buggy hooked to a pole. It was scary for her. Lucky we have people out there to be helpful at such a time. She was shook up afterwards of the ordeal. She came back home and took daughter Liz's buggy then to get Emma. Glad it didn't happen when Lovina and the children were in the buggy on their way here. It was so good to see that nobody got hurt. The incident disturbed the morning

hours, but sewing is taking place now and the sprouts took over with the winter potatoes, so the girls will take care of that project.

Breakfast was served to daughters Liz and Lovina and all their children. It consisted of fried eggs, potatoes, bacon, cereal, toast, cheese, sliced tomatoes and coffee. The children also always enjoy their soft ice cream, which wasn't all eaten last night, being held in the ice-chest overnight.

I will share more about happenings here next week; I hope all you readers are healthy and happy. For all those who have written asking about rhubarb recipes, here's one:

RHUBARB BUTTER CRUNCH

3 cups fresh, finely chopped rhubarb
1 cup sugar
3 tablespoons flour

Topping:

1 cup brown sugar
1 cup raw rolled oats
1 1 /2 cups of flour
1/4 cup butter or shortening.

Mix rhubarb, sugar and flour well and place in a greased baking dish. Combine the topping ingredients and sprinkle it over the rhubarb mixture. Bake at 370 degrees for 40 minutes. Serve warm with milk or cream. Delicious!

MAY 2000

Editor's note: My name is Kevin Williams, and I am Elizabeth's editor. Elizabeth was puzzled when I first brought up the idea of creating an Amish Cook Web site. She had never seen the Internet and certainly had not used e-mail before. Elizabeth's world is far-removed from the dot.coms, computers and cars that clutter most of our lives and, as her editor, I make every attempt to keep it that way.

The Internet, however, will provide readers with a place to go to learn more about Elizabeth, see photos of her farm, archive old columns and recipes, read gardening tips and household hints and even ask her questions.

Elizabeth began to warm up to the idea of the Internet when I told her that we could post some of her most requested recipes on her site, which might cut down on the number of letters from readers asking for the same thing. I will maintain the site, but the material will all be supplied by Elizabeth. On my frequent visits to the Coblentz farm, I'll be taking your e-mail with me and gathering material for the site. Readers can visit Elizabeth on the Web now at www.oasisnewsfeatures.com. And, of course, snail mail will continue to be an option:

As I look out the window and see those red tulips blooming, my mind goes back to those years gone by when several of my daughters were spending the day here. In the morning, I noticed something red on the lawn, and I said, "What's that red?"

Upon going outside and discovering it, I found the red was from the blooms of the red tulips laid so nice in a row. It was in the spot where my granddaughter Mary had been outside before she passed on to that Great Beyond. Who laid those tulips there? Granddaughter Mary passed away two years ago. Memories linger on.

Yesterday was an enjoyable and busy day. We hoed in the garden in the morning. It's good to have those fresh eats from the garden on the menu. Susan spent the day at her place of work and Verena done a huge stack of ironing. I am always glad to have that completed.

Around 11 a.m., daughter Leah and children came and we all headed into town. There, we met Susan for lunch. At that lunch, Susan's "secret pal" revealed herself. It was quite a surprise, as the "secret pal" turned out to be Susan's niece, Elizabeth Shetler.

Susan was guessing all year who it could be but never gave a thought of her niece. Each year, someone in the family has a "secret pal" who sends nice notes, cheery cards and gifts. The one receiving the items has fun guessing all year who is sending the items. It's all in good fun.

The noon meal was enjoyed by all present, and Susan was returned to her place of work. It was Susan's birthday today, so the lunch was a treat. Then in the evening, all the family gathered here in honor of Susan's birthday and also for my husband's belated birthday. The whole family was present for the evening meal. All the children came with a covered dish and more so there was plenty of food. Homemade ice cream, cake and strawberries always seem to finish a meal well. There was plenty of singing, yodeling and fun afterwards. There is no such thing as an evening that is too long when all the family is together.

Last night was so enjoyable. Today is a more tranquil day. Verena has evening cleaned and mopped around here and we have done laundry, which always seems plentiful. I reckon you readers who have large families know how laundry piles up. Try this easy, but delicious, chicken casserole dish.

CHICKEN CASSEROLE

1 pint chicken
2 cups macaroni
1 pint milk
2 cans cream of mushroom soup
1 medium onion, chopped
1 /2 pound Velveeta cheese, cut into pieces

Mix all together. Put into casserole. Let stand overnight in refrigerator. Bake 1 hour or until done.

MAY 2000

BY KEVIN WILLIAMS

𝕭enjamin A. "Ben" Coblentz, 69, passed suddenly from this earth Saturday. Ben's wife, Elizabeth, who pens this weekly column, is still coping with the shock and grief.

I was 19 years old in 1991, when I first pulled into Elizabeth's driveway one warm July afternoon. From that chance encounter, The Amish Cook column was born. I've been Elizabeth's editor ever since, and during that time, the Coblentzes have become practically family. I share in their weddings, births and, sadly, deaths.

During my years of visiting the Coblentzes, I've been blessed to know Ben. Rare is the couple who remains affectionate and loving after 43 years of marriage. But Ben and Elizabeth were that living rarity. Ben would affectionately tease Elizabeth (he called her "Lizzie") at the dinner table, and Elizabeth would give back as good as she got. Ben was Elizabeth's calm center. Elizabeth is the emotional one, but she was balanced by Ben's pragmatic peace. They were the perfect balance.

With a long white beard and weathered hands from decades of working as a carpenter, Ben was ever the supportive spouse. In a busy household of children and grandchildren, Ben would sit quietly in his rocker, with a soft smile and gentle demeanor watching it all.

Ben and I were from two different worlds, yet I felt very close to him. I don't milk cows or cultivate the craft of carpentry as he did. I'm a city boy, more comfortable in my world of computers and cars. Yet we always found things to talk about. We could talk about baseball. We were both avid Cincinnati Reds baseball fans. I would visit with the latest news of trades or home runs and a smile would flicker across his face.

He would show me his purple martin houses or patiently let me follow him into the barn as he did the afternoon chores. It's hard to measure how much any one person impacts our lives. A life is a portrait comprised of brushstrokes from the many people we pass. I look back at the still incomplete portrait of my life, and some of what I am, are the brushstrokes of Ben. For that, I'll always be grateful.

Ben helped teach me to savor simplicity: the pleasure of a purple martin, the quiet calm of sitting on a rocker by a flickering fire or scanning the starlit sky on a crisp, clear January night. In our increasingly material 21st century society,

171

people measure their happiness by tangible things they can touch. For Ben, happiness could be found in the intangibles, in what he could not touch: a bird in flight, a grandchild's innocent heart.

Ben also was my secret ally. Editors often have trouble getting their writers to adhere to deadlines, and, Elizabeth is no different from any other columnist. I like for Elizabeth to send her columns to me on Thursdays. If Thursday morning came, and the column had not been sent, Ben would be nudging Elizabeth out of bed early, envelope and stamp in hand, reminding her to write. Ben was very proud of Elizabeth's column.

The Coblentz farm is my retreat, a place I go to escape the noise of the sometimes rude world we live in. I stand on their porch and savor the pastoral peace of a landscape unbroken by power-poles and listen to the rhythmic cadence of a passing horse's hooves. The peace seems to lend itself to infinity, an unchanging land, frozen in another century. If forever exists, it would be found on an Amish farm, where change is glacial.

But even on an Amish farm, things change. Quickly.

The Coblentz family has been plunged into sudden sadness with the unexpected passing of Ben from a heart attack. The heart attack followed a small stroke the week before.

Adding insult to injury, Elizabeth, her eight children, and some spouses, were riding in a van to the hospital, following the ambulance, when another van turned into their path. The impact totaled the van and sent Elizabeth into the windshield. Fortunately, no one was seriously injured. Elizabeth is now nursing a broken heart and some bruised ribs.

Ben's gentle soul lives in his sons, Amos and Albert. If the legacy a loved one leaves is his or her children, then Ben can look down from Heaven with happiness. All of his eight children are wonderful. In the baseball terms he loved, he's eight for eight. That's the best average one can ask for.

MAY 2000

𝕴 turned on the emergency flashers and slowed to a crawl. A column of charcoal black horse-drawn buggies clattered on the road in front of me, moving slowly and solemnly.

It was the surreal union of two worlds, as my car joined the funeral procession of buggies. I was honored and deeply touched to be invited to the private cemetery ceremony where Ben A. Coblentz was laid to rest Tuesday, May

23, 2000.

On any other day, I would be tapping my fingers impatiently on the dashboard, waiting for the slow-moving vehicle to get out of my way so I could speed to my destination. Instead, I was forced to take a deep breath and watch the peaceful, pastoral Indiana countryside move by like a slow-motion movie. Century-old barns, gently burbling creeks and well-manicured meadows were a reminder there was once another time: a time when things were simpler, were quieter. But it's still there. We just never look.

I originally wanted to write more detail about Ben's funeral. But as I stood in the cemetery, watching the Coblentzes grieve and dealing with my own sadness, it seemed to me these were intensely private moments. It's privacy and anonymity that have helped the Old Order Amish keep the hands of time turned back to a simpler society. So I'll leave the details, if she wishes to share, to Elizabeth when she returns to writing this column.

There was a visitation Monday, May 22, and a funeral Tuesday. My parents came with me to the visitation, as they too have grown close to Elizabeth and Ben through the years. I also brought my girlfriend. I was happy to have company, as this would have been a lonely journey without them.

Hundreds of people filed past Ben's open casket, a testimony to how many he touched with his gentle spirit. When the crowd had cleared Monday night, I turned back to say goodbye to Elizabeth one more time and, not watching where I was going, tripped over a chair. Uninjured, but embarrassed, I looked back and saw Elizabeth laugh. It was nice to see her smile. The Coblentzes are accustomed to my clumsiness.

Ben and Elizabeth were inseparable. After 43 years of marriage, I was in awe of their playful affection and genuine love for one another. Ben delighted in recalling the day they first met on a crowded buggy ride. They both always said how fast those years seem to fly. To them, their wedding seemed like it was last year.

I found the announcement Elizabeth wrote about her own wedding, in her usual simple no-frills style. The following appeared in an Amish newspaper in 1957:

Oct. 21, 1957: Nice and cool weather. Lots of flu and colds are around. Different schools are closed on account of the flu. Thursday, Oct. 17, was the wedding day of Ben A. Coblentz and Elizabeth Graber (the writer). They were married by Bishop Mose M. Miller from Indiana.

Now it is a funeral being written about.

The funeral service was spoken all in German, so I didn't understand much.

Still, it was moving just the same. The crowd was so large that two separate services had to be conducted, one in the Coblentz's home, the other in a shed outside. Elizabeth seemed to be doing very well, surrounded by the support of her family.

I sometimes lie awake at night, wondering what life means, wondering why we are put here on this earth, only to have it one day abruptly end. But I think 43 years of love and devotion that burns as brightly at the end as it did at the beginning may be much of the meaning. It's one of the best answers I can come up with.

On the way to the visitation, a storm lashed my windshield with driving rains and a wind-whipped westerly. But as the city melted away in my rearview mirror, shafts of sunlight poked through the clouds bathing the surrounding fields in a golden light. Approaching the Coblentz farm, a sea of buggies greeted the eye. Ben would have been amazed. A colorful rainbow arced across the eastern sky. Somewhere, I'm sure, Ben was smiling.

JUNE 2000

This is a very beautiful, sunshiny Thursday morning, and I guess I should get this column in the mail today.

Daughters Leah, Lovina, Emma, and their lovely children, came for the day today. Now the garden is getting a good weeding. What would I do without my family for support, especially as I write this letter with tear-stained eyes? It's so hard to put this into words, but we must keep our faith from our Heavenly Father above. "He" will help us in such a time of our great loss, very great loss. It just doesn't seem this has taken place with my dear, beloved, calm, patient husband, Ben. Ben's gentle soul lives on in our broken hearts. Such a wonderful, supportive husband and father to all of us.

Lots of memories linger on, as we have to go on. Some readers, who lost spouses, told me in their letters to keep on going: don't sit and think. What would I do without the support of my two daughters, Verena and Susan, here at home? Verena takes over the chores, unless some of our married children are here. Our married children also have been so supportive.

Daughter Liz and her children spent the day here yesterday, and son Albert's family was here for supper yesterday. Joe's (daughter Lovina) family came later in the evening and stayed for the night. So we're never alone, as it seems we're overnight someplace or someone in the family stays here overnight. How supportive!

174

I am so glad Ben didn't have to suffer long. God's ways aren't our ways. He's the "One" who never made or makes a mistake. "He" had a purpose to take Ben away from pain and especially, worries, in this troublesome world we have to live in.

On Sunday, May 14, we got up early to start the day off. Ben did the morning chores as usual. And he then got the horse harnessed and hitched up to our new buggy, which he had purchased not too long ago, had breakfast, and then we went on to church services.

At lunch after services, Verena came and said: "Dad doesn't feel too good."

So I got up and went to the table of men where he was seated. I asked, "Ben, aren't you feeling good?" And he just mumbled something and we saw right away there was something wrong. Our son Albert and son-in-law Paul got up from the table and carried Ben in a blanket into the yard. Someone else ran to a phone to call for help. Ben was admitted to a hospital, where they determined he had a stroke. But Ben's recovery was quick, and he was able to go home after an overnight stay. He came home and seemed alert.

He walked out to the barn on Wednesday morning and again on Thursday morning and was always worried to see that the cow got milked. He was always the one who, at 4 a.m., got out of bed to milk the cow. Such a nice week that God spared with us, that final week. Because on Saturday morning, May 20, I fed him two eggs, toast, two cups of homemade garden tea and some applesauce. He seemed OK. But all at once, he began to breath hard.

EMS was called again, but life had fled him before they came. So peaceful to see his eyes set on me and feel he was gone. Such a terrible feeling to lose a good husband. So many memories linger on. We had many good days together since we were married on Oct. 17, 1957. Born to this union were eight lovable children: two sons: Amos and Albert; and six daughters: Mrs. Paul (Leah) Shelter, Mrs. Levi (Liz) Wengerd, Mrs. Joe (Lovina) Eicher, Mrs. Jacob (Emma) Schwartz Jr., and Verena and Susan at home with me. How thankful to have them with me.

God has a purpose for it all. We must adjust to a different life. It sure has been different. Can't explain what it's like without my dear husband, Ben. Also, we have 29 grandchildren. We had 30, but dear little Mary left at 5 years old for a better home.

The funeral for Ben was on Tuesday, May 23, with around 700 people attending. Everyone was invited for a noon lunch as usual. There were 12 tables set up for the lunch at noon in our tool shed. I feel we had so much good help from friends and relatives over this time for the loss of Ben. Thanks goes out to them who helped in our time of great loss.

I should thank all the readers out there for all the cards and gifts since the death of my dear husband, Ben. Words can't express the appreciation to you great readers out there.

On Sunday, this column's editor, Kevin Williams, and his mother brought over 1,000 e-mails plus a 32-gallon tub full of cards. The gifts will help with the hospital bills. Thank you all to be so supportive. I won't be able to write everyone to express my appreciation. But I hope this does it.

Good luck to all out there, 'til next time. We never know what the future holds. God only knows.

JUNE 2000

$\mathfrak{I}$ am writing this letter at 4:30 a.m. June 15 here at the desk of Joe's (daughter Lovina's husband) family as the girls and I spent the night here.

Five years ago this morning, we were busy with the wedding of Jacob and my daughter Emma. Today is their anniversary. They are blessed with two little girls and one son. Church services will be in their home June 25. So we've been assisting Emma in getting ready for it. Lots of cleaning to do at such a time.

Last night, it was so stormy. Tornadoes were predicted, and I guess we felt best to go someplace else, which is why we stayed the night at Joe and Lovina's. By staying here, we also got in on Joe's daughter's (little Elizabeth) birthday cake as she turned 6 yesterday. Can't imagine her going to school this coming fall.

Seems impossible I will have four grandchildren entering school in September. The twins, Arlene and Marlene, daughters of son Amos and wife Nancy, and Elizabeth, daughter of Liz and Levi, also will be entering school. How these years slip away.

So glad for my eight children and 29 grandchildren who have been so supportive to me, especially since the passing of my dear husband, Ben, last month. Lots of memories linger on. Only those who experience the loss of a life partner know the grief one goes through in this time of sorrow. Friends and relatives have been supportive, and also you readers out there. I want to thank you, and I won't be able to thank you all personally, so I hope this will do. Words can't express the appreciation for all those many cards. My editor has brought two 32-gallon tubs full of mail and more than 1,000 e-mail letters.

I feel so unworthy to receive all this. Maybe someday I'll be able to go through them all again and thank more people. But I must go on and not sit and think. Death is so final, but Ben can now rest, with no more worry, pain, only peace, which he deserved.

Part of getting back to normal is writing this column, and that means recipes. For those who saw my oatmeal pie recipe last month, a Mansfield, Ohio, reader wrote in saying she had run short on the corn syrup the recipe requested, so she substituted half for maple syrup. She said it turned out great. Also, the rhubarb is advancing in places now. Here is a simple rhubarb recipe.

RHUBARB PIE

1 beaten egg
1 cup sugar
1 teaspoon vanilla
2 cups rhubarb
2 tablespoons flour
Dash salt

Mix all of the above ingredients, and pour into unbaked pie shell.

Topping:

3 /4 cup flour
1/3 cup margarine
1/2 cup brown sugar

Mix topping ingredients, and sprinkle over the rhubarb mixture. Bake pie at 400 degrees for 10 minutes, then at 350 degrees for 30 minutes.

JUNE 2000

It is a Sunday and such a dreary day.

Jacob (daughter Emma) and family were here overnight. Breakfast was prepared for us all. They then left in the morning to go to his folks for noon dinner.

We also had a nice noon dinner. The potatoes were peeled and cut up as for the noon meal. Meatloaf was done, also. So we had a head start for dinner.

Son Albert and family and Joe (daughter Lovina) and family were our dinner guests. One empty chair remained, without my dear husband Ben. It's not the same, but we must learn to go on in our lives without him. I, at times, do not understand, but God has a purpose for it all. Again, once more, thanks to all you readers out there for all those nice cards and gifts. I feel so unworthy for it all. You readers have been so thoughtful during this time of sorrow. Ben was such a great husband and father, always supportive to all the family.

God's ways aren't our ways. "He" had a purpose to take Ben in his care. So glad Ben didn't suffer at all. Doctor said he fought to live. How lucky God spared him with us for almost a week after his stroke. Only those with experience know how it is to lose a loved one. Glad he could go before me, as he so relied on me. But it took both of us to go on in life. Death is so final.

I must manage to keep looking up. Our children are so supportive. What would I do without my daughters, Verena and Susan, who still live with me at home?

Sunday evening, my sister, who also lost her husband last year, her daughter and family came for a visit. They stayed for supper. Then her other two daughters and families came. My children then began arriving.

Paul's (daughter Leah) family, son Albert and family, Levi (daughter Liz) and family, Joe (daughter Lovina) and family and Jacob (daughter Emma) and family all came here for Sunday supper. So we had around 60 here.

Mashed potatoes, gravy, steak, meatloaf, buttered corn, buttered peas, spaghetti and meatballs, lettuce and egg salad, cheese, radishes, carrots, onion greens, cookies and other baked goods were on the menu.

There was more on the menu, but I can't think of what it was right now. Was good to have them all here, but two were missing: my dear husband and my brother-in-law. They were so badly needed in this troublesome world we have to live in. God, help us in our sorrowing time.

A reader in Ulysses asked for a potato pattie recipe.

POTATO PATTIES

1 1/4 cups flour
1/4 teaspoon salt
1 egg
1 cup milk
3 to 4 potatoes, sliced

Dry potatoes on paper towels. Mix flour and salt in a bowl. Add egg and milk, and beat until smooth. Dip slices into batter one at a time and drop into hot fat. Fry until golden brown.

JULY 2000

$\mathfrak{I}$t is 2:30 a.m. on a Thursday morning as I write this column. I forgot it had to be in the mail today. I must get this written and on its way.

I'm going to be gone most of the day today, accompanying my daughter Emma and her husband Jacob on errands, as he is off this week on vacation.

Some brighter happenings this week as new life came into the family. The highlight of July 1 was another grandchild being born. Joe's (daughter Lovina) family welcomed a new member named Loretta. She was born at 6:28 a.m., weighing 6 pounds 10 ounces and is 19 inches long. Lots of beautiful black hair. She joins three sisters, Elizabeth, Susan and Verena, and one brother, Benjamin. My daughter Verena is now there to assist with the household duties while Lovina tends to the new baby. This makes 30 living grandchildren.

Jacob, Emma and family are staying here tonight. They came over in the evening to assist with some household chores. I have church services coming up in this home later this month, so there's lots to do to get ready.

Daughter-in-law Sarah Irene (son Albert) and family also came for the day yesterday. So Albert's and Jacob's families were here for supper. What would I do without family? Life must go on without my dear, beloved husband, Ben.

We've had so many rains lately. The garden is doing great, as are the

surrounding fields of crops, hay and pastures. Some places it is too wet. My garden isn't completed as yet. I need to put more plants in the garden. Weeds have taken over through this wet weather, but I shouldn't complain. I just need to re-plant again. There's plenty of garden goodies out there; I just need to get out and weed. Working in the garden is peaceful, and it brings back happy memories of Ben and I putting out the garden together.

Well, maybe I can get some shut-eye now. I can't neglect this writing. Time goes on and life goes on. We must look up to the future. God makes no mistakes. Good luck to all you great readers out there. Your encouragement has meant so much.

Meanwhile, a reader in Newport, Ark., wrote asking how I make stuffed baked potatoes. It's easy and delicious!

STUFFED BAKED POTATOES

8 medium potatoes
5 tablespoons margarine
Salt and pepper
1/2 cup milk

1 cup grated cheese

Cut off tops of potatoes after they have baked in the oven for about an hour at 350 degrees. Scoop out insides and mix with rest of ingredients. Fill potato shells and bake 20 minutes longer.

JULY 2000

It is a nice, sunshiny Wednesday morning in July as I write this.

July is a month full of birthdays in this family. New granddaughter Loretta (born July 1) is doing fine and so is her mother, Lovina.

Lovina's son, Benjamin, has a birthday July 14. My son Albert and grandson Albert Jr. both have birthdays July 15. Mine is on July 18, and my daughter Emma's is on July 19. Son-in-law Paul's is on the 31st. So it is a busy month of birthdays!

Speaking of Paul, we were over to look at Paul's (daughter Leah) garden Sunday afternoon. Their sweet corn measured 9 1/2 feet tall. Some are having corn to eat, but ours is not quite ready. Some also are eating their tomatoes. Again, ours just need a little bit to go. The garden will be plentiful this year.

The rain has been so plentiful that farmers around here are having problems getting their hay baled. Our garden is doing great, except the rain also has let the unwanted weeds show up. I've been trying to keep ahead. Lots of hoeing needed.

We went to view a good, long-time friend who died suddenly Saturday evening. His funeral is today. They had just visited me two weeks ago. He was my late husband's boss for many years. So it was quite a shock.

Church services will be held here July 23. (Editor's note: Amish church services are in the homes of church members on a rotating basis. There is no formal church building.) There's plenty to do at this time. Seems so much different these days without my husband, but we must go on. God is always above. We can never forget that.

Well, I must get busy, as my daughter Verena is cleaning around here. She is giving this house a good cleaning. I can at least give her a little help. Lovina and children also are here visiting for the day. Loretta is such a sweet little bundle.

Paul's (daughter Leah) family had church services in their home last Sunday, so I will share a recipe of a dessert that Leah had made for the evening meal:

CINNAMON PUDDING

Step 1:
 2 cups brown sugar
 1 1 /2 cups water
 2 tablespoons margarine
 Mix and let come to a boil.

Step 2:
 1 cup white sugar
 2 tablespoons margarine
 2 teaspoons baking powder
 1 cup milk
 2 teaspoons cinnamon
 Enough flour to make a batter

Mix all the ingredients in step two together well and spread into the bottom of a greased pan. Pour step 1 over it and sprinkle with nuts. Bake 45 minutes at 350 degrees. Serve with whipped cream.

JULY 2000

It's a cool, sunshiny Thursday evening. The work of the day took off at an early start.

Jacob's (daughter Emma) family was here for the night. Jacob left for work, and Emma started to wash off walls at 6 a.m. I really didn't think the walls needed to be washed off again, only the ceilings and woodwork, but she went ahead. Daughter Lovina and Emma were washing off the walls of the dining room and kitchen the day before my dear husband passed away. The day after the funeral, which was May 24, the living room, bedroom and spare bedroom walls were all washed off before the furniture was put back in place. What a relief when everything feels clean again.

Visiting us today were daughters Leah and Emma. Daughter-in-law Sarah Irene and two boys came in the morning and left after our noon dinner.

Everything is clean now: the bedroom, living room, dining room, kitchen, enclosed porch and our wash-house. The kerosene lamps and dishes look sparkling again. We had the curtains washed and windows cleaned before the death of my husband, so that was one job less to do over the funeral. But then I decided to wash them again, as church services are being conducted here this Sunday. So the curtains and windows again look clean now also.

My three grandsons Levi, Ben, and Joseph were set to work by weeding my garden today. The weeds had taken over, but that, too, looks nice again. So it was a work-day around here. Daughter Verena has been a good help around here. She finally went back to work, where she cleans rooms at a motel in town a couple of days a week. Sounds like they really missed her good work.

It seems different not to see a cow in the field and not to have to milk it mornings and evenings. It was always relied on Verena to do the job. This way, by getting rid of the cow, there's no hay to buy, no manure to haul, maybe no vet bill to pay. So it's been a relief not to care for the cow. But she gave a lot of milk, although we didn't use much at times. The cow is in good care, I'd say. A friend of ours bought it as he milks around 200 cows.

Will share some recipes with you great readers out there. A reader in Holmes Beach, Fla., wrote asking me for an apple fritter recipe. I have an easy one.

APPLE FRITTERS

1 cup flour
1 1 /2 teaspoons baking powder
1 /2 teaspoon salt
2 tablespoons sugar
1 egg, beaten
1 /2 cup milk (reserve 1 tablespoon aside)
1 1/ 2 cups apples, chopped

Sift dry ingredients together. Beat egg and add milk. Pour into dry ingredients. Stir until the batter is smooth. Pare apples and dice or slice very thin. Add apples to batter and blend together. Drop by spoonfuls into deep, hot fat (370 to 375 degrees). Fry until golden brown on all sides.

Makes 12 to 15 fritters.

I wanted to share a favorite cookie recipe around here. It has Swiss origins, and many of the people around here have Swiss heritage.

SPRITZ

1 cup butter
2 /3 cup sugar
3 egg yolks
1 teaspoon vanilla
2 1/ 2 cups flour

Heat oven to 400 degrees. Mix the first four ingredients thoroughly.

Using one-fourth of dough at a time, force through cookie press on an ungreased baking sheet. Bake 7 to 10 minutes or until set but not brown. Bake at 350 degrees. Makes 6 dozen.

AUGUST 2000

𝔍t is 4:30 a.m. as I write this column on a clear Thursday morning.

We are in need of rain, but we take one day at a time. Even though we need the rain, the gardens have produced great yields this summer. Corn is growing very well in this area, and lots are selling vegetables and fruits.

I've been up for a while now doing writing. I also am a writer for The Budget. (Editor's note: The Budget is a newspaper distributed among the Amish-Mennonite community; it contains dispatches from Amish people throughout the country. The letters from writers known as "scribes" are more formal than this column, and contain news of area births, weddings and news. It's a way of communicating among the Amish, who use no phones, e-mail, etc.)

I've been writing for The Budget for some time now, and I also needed to write some for the cookbook that is coming out soon. So it's been write-write-write in this early morning hours. There's a gathering in Sugarcreek, Ohio, soon of all the Budget writers. I've attended in the past, but I do not think I will be able to this year. Too much to do around here.

My belated husband, Ben, would always encourage me to keep this "Amish Cook" column going. He'd ask me if I wrote it yet and if I was writing it, he'd come with an envelope and stamp to get it on its way.

We had church services here on Sunday, July 23. The services went smoothly, with many in attendance. My children were a big help in making sure church went well; these were the first services held in my home since the death of my dear husband two months ago. Time goes on. God has a purpose for everything.

The bench-wagon is sitting in our yard now. The bench-wagon carries the church benches from place to place wherever church is being held. It will head next to daughter Lovina's, where she will be holding services soon.

We've been helping Joe's (daughter Lovina) family as church services are to be in their home on Sunday, Aug. 6. She is busy caring for a small baby, Loretta, born July 1. Loretta is doing very well, with lots of thick, beautiful black hair. Her siblings have welcomed baby Loretta. Granddaughter Elizabeth, who will begin school in the fall, is always holding and caring for the new baby. The newborn in the family is welcome cheer at this time of year.

We have a wedding to attend in this community on Thursday, Aug. 3. I will be a cook on Tuesday, helping to prepare pies, dinners and everything else that is needed for the big occasion. My daughter Susan will be a table-waiter at the wedding, so that should keep us busy this week, plus preparing for Lovina's church services.

Speaking of preparing pies, some have written asking my recipe for pie crust. It's a simple, delicious recipe. I'll share it here. Thank you readers again so much for your support, cards, notes, etc.

PIE CRUST

3 cups flour
1 cup lard
1 tablespoon vinegar
1 egg
1/3 cup water
1 teaspoon salt

Mix lard, salt and flour as usual. Add to other ingredients and mix. Makes 3 pie crusts.

AUGUST 2000

We had a much-needed rain during the weekend. How thankful we are for the rain, as it was beginning to be dry. We are having fresh garden potatoes at meals. They are a delight to cook, with their jackets on.Garden goodies have perked up and so will the hay crops.

I'm writing this column at Jacob's (daughter Emma) home this Monday morning, July 31. Daughter Emma and Verena are doing barn chores, which included their cow to be milked before the milk hauler comes. I miss seeing our cow in our field. We sold it after Ben's death. While they are doing barn chores, I have been washing dishes and also the kerosene lamps. The glass globes that surround the flame need to be clean so the light is bright and clear. It's always an extra chore than to turn a switch for a light, right?

This weekend turned out different in so many ways. On Friday evening, Paul's (daughter Leah) family had all my family plus other families invited for supper. Such a delicious and plentiful meal!. We left for home, and it really began pouring rain, so son Amos and Nancy and family, and Joe's and Jacob's, all stayed at my house for the night. This allowed everyone to get out of the rain.

This also meant that Saturday morning, breakfast had to be prepared for 25 people. We enjoyed fried potatoes and eggs, bacon, toast, cheese, bananas and cookies. I always like to feed them good when they come home. Always enjoy seeing my children come. It seems any time will do. They all know that, I guess. Ha!

The girls and I had planned to spend Saturday night at Paul's (daughter Leah) home and go along with them to a nephew's for Sunday dinner. But plans changed when my son-in-law, Jacob (daughter Emma's husband) was taken to the hospital late Saturday. Jacob, who is a young man in his late 20s, had passed out. So glad he is home now, but is in bed still being so weak. Not sure what happened. S'pose we'll come here again tonight to help Emma with the chores.

The girls are in from the barn now. Our horse has to be harnessed up and hitched to our buggy so we can leave for home. Life goes on.

Here's a casserole recipe daughter Emma took to Paul's Friday night. It's good!

ZUCCHINI CASSEROLE

3 cups shredded, unpeeled zucchini
1 cup Bisquick
1 /2 cup cooking oil
1/4 cup onion
1/2 cup cheese
4 eggs
Parsley to taste
Salt and pepper

Beat eggs, oil and seasonings until well mixed. Add the rest, and stir. Pack into a casserole dish and bake at 350 degrees for 40 minutes. Delicious!

AUGUST 2000

We have been blessed with frequent rains. They were so badly needed as the ground was somewhat dry.

Our sweet corn was flattened by the wind, though, that came with the storms. Heard others around here had the same problem also. At least we could still pull the ears at Jacob's (daughter Emma) as we processed 29 quarts and 20 pints of corn and also 18 quarts of tomato juice.

We made a mild tomato juice, with mangoes, carrots, celery and onions. We are not putting hot peppers in the juice this year so that the grandchildren will be able to drink it this winter. It's so good to fill those jars for the coming winter.

Right now, it shows 2:30 a.m. on the clock; I woke up and thought I must get this written while the rest are in a peaceful sleep. We had an enjoyable evening as Ben's brother and family came for a good visit. They are here visiting in the area for several weeks.

Paul's (daughter Leah) and Jacob's families were here also. Jacob's are here for the night. So good to have them here. Makes life so much better when the children are here. It's such an empty place without my dear, beloved, patient husband, Ben. But we must go on.

We were helping Joe's (daughter Lovina) family with their baby Loretta during the weekend. Loretta is now five weeks old and a very happy, healthy baby. The weekend at Lovina's was spent preparing for church services and the large lunch served afterwards. For those new to this column, Amish services are not in a formal church house, but in homes of church members. Each church member takes a turn or two throughout the year to have the services in their home. Church services are every other week. Hundreds often show up for a service. Often people will go home on Sunday afternoon, but then return to the place where services were for an evening supper. Lovina served a taco-style supper to those who came back in the evening. Homemade ice cream was also on the list, plus many other goodies including baked pies and cakes. Son Albert's family and his wife Sarah Irene will take their turn next for church services. So we must help them prepare for it. Was so good to have all our eight children present on Sunday at Joe's for church and the evening meal. Everyone cleared out a bit early from the evening meal as a storm was approaching.

We were glad to attend the Thursday wedding of my niece. It was largely attended. I was a cook, and my youngest daughter, Susan, was a tablewaiter. It was an enjoyable day. It was good to meet far-off friends.

Well, I guess I have written enough for now. I want to get some shut-eye, as it will be time to prepare breakfast before I know it. Bacon and eggs is a favorite around here for breakfast; will share a recipe for it.

SCRAMBLED EGG AND BACON BAKE

1/4 pound bacon
8 eggs
1 cup milk
3/4 teaspoon salt
1/8 cup of butter, melted

Fry bacon; drain and crumble. Put eggs in a bowl. Beat lightly. Add milk, salt and butter. Add crumbled bacon last. Grease pan. Bake in a 12- by 9-inch pan at 425 degrees until knife comes out clean. Serves 10 to 12 people.

AUGUST 2000

𝕴t is 4:30 a.m. Thursday, Aug. 17, as I write this. It seems on the chilly side this morning.

It has been a busy week with Paul's (daughter Leah) family doing a lot of cementing Monday evening. We had some cement work that needed done outside.

On Tuesday morning, I helped my daughter Emma put 44 quarts of homemade V-8 tomato juice in jars. Afterward, daughter Verena and I came home and went to my son Albert's to assist in getting ready for their church services, which are to be in their home this Sunday. We took some of their children home with us during the day as they had to enroll several of their children for school. So son Albert returned in the evening to pick them up, and Jacob's family came also, so we had two of our children home for the evening meal.

Processing of tomato juice has been on the list lately. We processed 24 quarts yesterday afternoon. We made the juice milder this year, with plenty of onions, sweet peppers, carrots and celery. Good drinking for those cold winter months ahead. Hopefully my garden-grown hot peppers will be far enough along by the time I make my next batch of tomato juice. We like hot peppers and plenty of it in our tomato juice. But for the grandchildren, it is good to make it mild. Those small ones will drink more of it that way.

I miss my departed husband Ben. He always put the hand-cranked juicer together and then turned it through while I put in jars to be processed. He also rinsed all the parts of the juicer at our water pump. He was helpful in so many ways. Ben put in hard-working days all our years of marriage. He suffered a lot of asthma and hay fever during summer and often with pneumonia during winter. Ben needed a lot of good care, and I was happy to give it to him. It's so hard for his parting, but God has a purpose for it all. He is the One who makes no mistakes.

Homemade Refrigerator Pickles

1 cup vinegar
1 tablespoon salt
2 cups white sugar
6 cups sliced cucumbers

1 cup sliced onions
1 cup sliced green peppers

Heat first three ingredients to boiling until sugar is dissolved. Pour mixture over cucumbers, onions and peppers. Put into covered container and refrigerate.

AUGUST 2000

I am writing this column late at night, still thinking of the enjoyment we had earlier this evening.

We had all my children and their families, plus some friends, here for evening supper in honor of my dear daughter Verena's birthday. She deserved such a celebration, as she's been such a help to me around the house the past few months since my husband passed away.

We had pork steak, chicken and hamburger patties on the grill. Then there were homemade mashed potatoes, gravy and you name it, on the menu. A lot of food was also brought in by family and friends. There was a table full of all kinds of goodies. It was a well-spent evening in the company of our family. The children know they are always welcome home.

Son Albert and his wife, Sarah Irene, had church services in their home this past Sunday. Quite a few returned to their house in the evening for supper. A good lunch was also served after church.

It is now Thursday morning, Aug. 24, and I have just returned home from a restful night's sleep at my daughter Emma's. I must get this written and in the mail, as this needs to be sent out yet, and I have not completed it.

Susan is at her job right now, and Verena and I returned home from Jacob's and daughter Emma's. We spent the night there and this morning made a double-batch of homemade salsa, thick and chunky, before we left. She has her hands full with their young ones, so the help was welcome.

I can describe how we make our salsa. The ingredients we use are:

SALSA

14 pounds tomatoes, scalded, peeled and cut up
10 green peppers, chopped
5 cups onions, chopped
1 cup vinegar
2 ounces hot peppers, chopped
1/2 cup brown sugar

1 /4 cup salt
2 teaspoons oregano flakes
3 teaspoons cumin
3 teaspoons chili powder
1 teaspoon garlic powder
10 teaspoons Clear Jel

I mix all of the above ingredients, except for the Clear Jel. Everything is cooked on the stove-top for 45 minutes; then I add the Clear-Jel. After that is added, I cold pack it for 20 minutes. Delicious! Homemade salsas really go good around here.

The weather around here has been great, with frequent rains. The garden goodies are bountiful, so there has been a lot of canning going on here. Green beans are a really good crop this year, so there are lots of those being home canned.

Son-in-law Jacob took our horse to have him re-shod. So good to have family to do it for me. So we're on the road again. Ha!

Must get in mail before mailman comes.

GARDEN GREEN BEANS

3 tablespoons butter
3 tablespoons flour
2 cups milk
3 hard-boiled eggs
1 /4 pound of your favorite cheese, sliced
3 to 5 slices toasted bread
Green beans from the garden (1 quart)

Cook your green beans until tender. Drain them and place in a casserole. In a saucepan, melt the butter, flour, milk and cheese together. Pour over the green beans. Slice 3 hard-boiled eggs over the mix and crumble several slices of toasted bread over the mixture. Cover with cheese slices, and cook at 350 degrees until cheese slices melt.

SEPTEMBER 2000

Lately, with the aid of frequent rains and plenty of sunshine, the garden has done well and so have the weeds. The weeds have taken over in the garden. We need to spend some time soon getting rid of those weeds.

Some of the children were here Saturday to put a new roof on the south part of our barn. The shingles were blowing off from the wind. So it was in a bad state of repair. What would I do without family?

Today, tomato juice was processed, which will taste good when the cold winter months come. It's good to open all kinds of fresh fruits and vegetables during the depths of winter. It provides a splash of cheer to brighten those dreary days. I also hope to process a lot of grape juice this fall. We have a lot of yellow tomatoes this fall, which also need to be harvested. They are ones that Ben and I planted earlier this year. I prefer the red tomatoes, but Ben thought he wanted to try a yellow tomato for this fall.

On Sunday, some of the children were here visiting and of all things my 2-year-old granddaughter, Verena, daughter of Joe and Lovina, had to be rushed to the hospital. She was badly dehydrated. So while Joe and and Lovina were keeping vigil at the hospital, my daughter Verena (who turned 34 last week) went over there to take over their household chores and watch over Joe and Lovina's four other children. What would we do without Verena? Everything appears to be OK with little Verena now, just a bad dehydration.

A reader from Fort Wayne, Ind., wrote to ask me how I can corn. I usually cut the corn off the cob and put it in quart glass jars. I then put in 1 teaspoon of salt in for quart jars and fill the jar with water before processing. The same reader also asked how I can tomatoes. I wash the tomatoes and cut them up into chunks. We then put them through a strainer for juice. Put tomatoes in glass jars and add 1 teaspoon salt to a quart. Process for 25 minutes. Same time length applies to corn.

Some have also written me asking about how to prepare corn relish. This is a favorite around here.

CORN RELISH

4 quarts fresh corn
3 green bell peppers, chopped fine
1 bunch celery
1 red bell pepper, chopped fine
1 tablespoon turmeric powder
1 tablespoon mustard
1 heaping tablespoon flour, mixed with a little vinegar
1 tablespoon celery seed
1 teaspoon salt
1 quart white vinegar
1 cup sugar

Mix turmeric, mustard, flour, celery seed, salt, vinegar and sugar. Mix well. Pour over vegetables and cook on low heat on a stove-top pot for about 30 minutes. Cold pack for 5 to 10 minutes following proper canning procedures.

SEPTEMBER 2000

This is a nice, sunshiny Thursday morning with my daughters Leah, Liz, Lovina and Emma, and their children here today.

Lovina's sweet little girl, Verena, appears to be nicely on the mend from her hospitalization for dehydration a couple of weeks ago. Grandchildren really add life around here. The school-age grandchildren are now in school for the year. Some of the children around here attend public schools, some the one-room Amish schools, and others are home-schooled. My children all attended public schools. It just depends on what the parents prefer.

We processed thick and chunky salsa this morning. Many people have written to me asking about what ingredients go into our homemade salsa, which is very popular this time of year with all the vegetables in the garden ripening.

Salsas can be used in so many different ways and in so many different dishes. Our salsa takes 14 pounds of tomatoes (scalded, peeled and cut up), five cups of onions (chopped), 10 green peppers (chopped), two ounces or more jalapeno peppers (chopped), one cup vinegar, 1/ 2 cup brown sugar, 1/4 cup salt, two teaspoons oregano flakes, three teaspoon cumin, three teaspoons chili power, one teaspoon garlic powder and 10 teaspoons of Clear-Jel (a thickening sold in most supermarkets). (Editor's note: Elizabeth's salsa canning instructions are being omitted this week. An agricultural extension agent in Indiana raised concerns about the safety of Elizabeth's canning methods, which do not follow USDA guidelines. The Purdue University Agricultural Extension Department will test some of Elizabeth's salsa as a public service. Results of the testing will appear in this column, with details posted at the Web site, www.theamishcook.com.)

Yesterday afternoon, we had tomatoes here to be used up before they spoil. I hate to see tomatoes go to waste. Thought I had processed enough for the year 2000, but yet we processed 33 1 /2 quarts of V-8 tomato juice, which will be good to open when those cold winter months come along. I put in four different colored tomatoes, along with celery, carrots, sweet peppers, banana peppers, jalapeno peppers and plenty of onions.

How relaxing to see my daughter Liz and her husband Levi drive in with their horse-drawn buggy last night while in the midst of making tomato juice. Liz stepped in to help me finishing process the tomato juice. It is hard work to do such processing. What a surprise to have them stay for the night. It's so good to have family. What would I do without family?

Our drains, which drain away waste water, started to not be in working order so our son Albert came yesterday and what a mess to go through but was just glad to see those drains in good working order. Again, it is so nice to have children who come around and are helpful.

On Sept. 4, my son-in-law Joe and my daughter Lovina were here, and with the help of my daughter Verena, the old roof from our barn, which was just replaced, was cleared away. A good meal was served to all after that hard work. The old roof pilings had just been lying on the ground around the barn. The wood had really rotted from the century-old barn roof. It looks very nice with a brand new roof sparkling in the sunshine. The menfolk in our family recently put on the new roof. Now our straw-shed where we keep our straw needs to be painted next.

Well, I must close with best regards as there is work, work, work to be done around here.

As we approach the holidays, this is a wonderful, delicious and easy recipe for all to enjoy. Hope you readers like this recipe for banana nut bread.

Here is a good recipe for the upcoming holidays:

BANANA NUT BREAD

1 cup sugar
2 tablespoons margarine
1 egg
3 teaspoons thick, sour milk
1 teaspoon baking soda
2 cups flour
1/2 cup nut meats
1 cup mashed bananas

Mix sugar, margarine, egg, milk and soda very well in a large bowl. Then sift in the flour, nut meats and bananas. Mix very well. Pour into lightly greased loaf pan and bake at 350 degrees for 1 hour.

SEPTEMBER 2000

It is Monday, Sept. 11, and another day has dawned.

We had two inches of rain Saturday night and Sunday morning. We've had our frequent rains all summer. But in our garden, the weeds have taken over, although we still get those good home-grown vegetables from it. When I should've been in the garden pulling weeds, my dear, beloved husband, Ben, had to be taken good care of at the time, and afterwards I really didn't care for anything to be done in the garden. Still doesn't seem real that I'll never hear his voice again. But our Heavenly Father will always help us if we keep our trust in him.

It was Ben who gave me as a gift the treadle Singer sewing machine. Must be around 46 years old, before our marriage. So lots of sewing has taken place on that Singer. It's a good sewing machine and still in good working order.

The sewing machine is on my mind this morning, as it has been in use over the past few days. Our caps (covering for our heads) are of black material in this area. In some Amish communities, they have the white coverings (caps, as we call them). My daughter Emma sewed two coverings for me when they were here as I was in need for new ones.

My daughter Verena was saying this morning we need to see where our buggy blankets and buggy robes are as the cold days of autumn and winter will probably arrive soon. They were put away somewhere during the funeral for Ben, so we could clear room in the shed for visitors.

So Verena and I went out to the tool shed to discover where they might be. Verena crawled up to the loft, and the blankets were on our two sleighs where mice were enjoying their good nest. Ugh! They were making holes through those blankets. Guess I'll have to stitch some of those blankets now. Well, those eight blankets got a thorough washing, and they are dried nice now on this lovely, sunshine-filled day. After the hustle and bustle with those blankets, they are now clean for the cold days ahead. Will be nice to have them on our buggy to help keep warm during the winter. An umbrella also helps during those cold winter days to shield us from rain, wind and snow.

After our deal of those blankets, Verena and I done a huge laundry, and Verena took over the ironing, which was more than plenty of it. So glad we are caught up with that huge stack of ironing now. What a relief! The children have been a great help around here. Also, thanks to you great readers for your encouragement and nice notes and the e-mails my editor brings to me. That's something new. Meanwhile, a reader in Tacoma, Wash., requested a good molasses cookie recipe. This is a favorite around here:

AMISH MOLASSES COOKIES

5 cups sugar
2 1/2 cups lard
4 eggs
1 cup molasses

1 cup hot water
3 tablespoons baking soda
1 teaspoon baking powder
1 teaspoon salt
2 teaspoons vanilla
12 to 15 cups flour

Cream first four ingredients. Dissolve soda in hot water. Add to creamy mixture. Add vanilla and flour. Make small balls and bake on greased cookie sheet at 350 degrees.

SEPTEMBER 2000

$\mathfrak{A}$s I relax for this Thursday night, my mind wanders to my cousins in Missouri. My cousins, the David R. Graber family, had moved to Seymour, Mo., from this area a while back.

I just found out their 20-year-old son, Jonas, was recently killed when a pick-up truck slammed into their horse-drawn buggy at 55 miles per hour. Jonas and the horse were killed instantly. Christian L. Graber, 19, was treated for a concussion and released. They are the sons of my niece, Mrs. Amos (Leah) Graber, who was killed in January by a logging truck who passed in a no-passing zone about five miles from Seymour when she was taking her son with muscular dystrophy to the doctor. Those roads are becoming more and more dangerous as fast-moving cars and trucks compete with horse-drawn buggies for space on once quiet roads.

Lots of tragedy to that one family this year. Buggy accidents are not uncommon. My sister Lydia was killed in one, leaving 10 children behind. The baby she was carrying lived and was delivered the next day.

My son Amos also was in a buggy accident, six years after my sister died in one. He entered the hospital with an eight-inch gash on his head that required 50 stitches. At the hospital he lost at least three pints of blood, besides what he lost before entering the hospital, which was a lot. The doctor said that Amos being a strong, well-built boy helped him survive losing so much blood.

My daughter Liz, my daughter Emma and their children spent the day here today. The laundry was done and hung out on the clothesline. It was somewhat dreary in the morning, but the sun came out. So the laundry is not all dry.

Meanwhile, Emma dug out our potatoes that my husband, Ben, and I had put in the ground this spring. They are big ones! Surprising. This year must've been good for potatoes. Liz's 6-year-old son, Levi, assisted Emma putting those potatoes in buckets and carrying them to be put in those potato crates. Emma's 4-year-old, Elizabeth, tried to help a while. She turned 4 years old Sept. 12. It was a cute scene.

In the evening, Liz's husband, Levi, came here. He had ingredients along to prepare a chili soup, as it was requested at the factory where he works to bring a soup. (Editor's note: As farming becomes less and less common among the Amish, it is not unusual for the men to take factory or carpentry jobs).

Their place of work was having a carry-in dinner tomorrow. So he was a chief cook in the kitchen here, chopping up onions and hot peppers. He also browned the hamburger, then added onions, hot peppers, chili beans, stewed tomatoes, tomato juice and I don't know what all he added of spices, etc.

Anyway, it was good and hot chili soup. Such a good taste. I had cooked red beets from the garden earlier in the day. I peel them, slice them and then fry them in butter, also adding salt and pepper to it. Sliced tomatoes, mangoes, hot peppers, chicken, sausage and Jell-O was also on the menu for our family meal this evening.

After dinner, we all washed and cut up rhubarbs for rhubarb jam for Emma. It was enough to make four batches. I can't recall I ever had rhubarbs so nice in the middle of September. Probably from our frequent rains. We had two inches from Saturday night until noon Sunday. Since then, we have received two-tenths of an inch. So the garden feels wet. The grass also has stayed so green this summer. We have so much to be thankful for.

Here is a recipe of a casserole we had the other night to you great readers out there.

DAIRY CASSEROLE

8 ounces noodles
1 pound hamburger, fried
2 cups corn, cooked
8 ounces cream cheese
1 cup milk
1 can cream of celery soup
Onion salt, salt and pepper to your taste

Combine all ingredients. Bake for 30 minutes at 350 degrees.

And these are nice with soup or to help round out a casserole main dish:

HOMESTYLE BISCUIT MUFFINS

2 1/2 cups flour
1/4 cup sugar
1 1/2 tablespoon baking powder
3 /4 cup cold butter or margarine
1 cup cold milk

Combine dry ingredients. Cut in butter or margarine until mixture resembles coarse crumbs. Stir in milk just until moistened. Spoon into greased muffin tins. Bake at 400 degrees for 20 minutes. Makes 1 dozen.

OCTOBER 2000

The weekend of Sept. 23 started out with Joe's (daughter Lovina) family coming here with chicken and charcoal to have it grilled. So Joe took over with the barbecued chicken. We soon had an easy Friday evening meal. Jacob (daughter Emma) and family were here also. Best of all, they all stayed for the night. The next morning, everyone had a Saturday breakfast together, which is always enjoyable.

Jacob started to clean the mess away from our recent new barn roof, and Joe and grandson Ben assisted later. Now we could turn our horses loose in the other field since all those nails, boards, etc. were hauled away. What a relief! The horses can now graze in those places where there's plenty of pasture. What would we do without family who are always willing workers?

Then on Saturday night, my daughters Verena, Susan and I went to Paul's (daughter Leah) family for the night as their daughter Elizabeth had girls from this area around her age invited for the night, and their parents and families came then for Sunday dinner. Joe's and Jacob's families were included also.

A good noon meal was served to all in attendance, with 94 barbecued hamburgers on the grill. Joe's and Jacob's families and us stayed to help eat those good leftovers. We stayed at Paul's for Sunday night as they wanted us to stay and beings none of the girls had to work Monday, we decided to stay.

On Monday morning, the dishes were put back in order and the floors were all mopped at Leah's, and we left and headed for Jacob's as I knew my daughter Emmae had homemade tomato juice to process. With little children, I knew she would appreciate help. So we processed 24 gallons of juice. No laundry was done Monday morning with it being rainy. But Tuesday was a very nice day to hang the laundry on the line, and the ironing was also completed. It's good for grandmothers to help these young women with small children. Good health means so much.

This is now Wednesday, Sept. 27, and my cousin and his wife from Milroy, Ind., took a van load for some of us area widows, plus family of theirs to go shopping and out for a meal. Words can't express the appreciation for such an enjoyable day. It happened it was also my cousin's birthday from Milroy and glad the restaurant where we ate gave him a free piece of pie for his day. He deserved that. So thoughtful of my cousin John to take us out for the day.

Well, I must go as Jacob's family is here now. A reader in Bloomsburg, Pa., requested a homemade peanut butter cookie recipe. Here is our favorite:

HOMEMADE PEANUT BUTTER COOKIES

1/2 teaspoon salt	1 cup shortening
2 eggs	1/ 2 teaspoon soda
1 1 /2 cups white sugar	1 teaspoon vanilla
2 1 /2 cups flour	1 cup peanut butter

Drop by teaspoonfuls on cookie sheet. Bake at 370 degrees for 12 minutes. Makes 50 cookies.

OCTOBER 2000

We're now well into October 2000, and the first chills are in the air. Life goes on.

On Thursday, all our four married daughters were home for the day, and all four families were here for supper. It was a wonderful day together, but it feels a lonely feeling after everyone has left for their homes at night. What would I do without family during this time as my husband lies in a peaceful sleep, never to return?

Grape time has arrived here. On Monday, we processed our grapes into juice. We worked up 98 quarts of homemade grape juice Monday evening. Since the weather was nice, everything was done outside on the picnic table. Finally, the lantern had to be lit as darkness came upon us. We didn't get all the jars we wanted processed that evening. We took the grapes from their stems and washed them and put them in clean, sterilized canning jars.

We process our grape juice for 20 minutes, adding two cups grapes and one-fourth cup sugar to a quart and then three cups grapes and half cup sugar to a half-gallon jar. I suppose when we open the jars this winter we can dilute it with some water.

I didn't like to add too much sugar to the jars because of blood sugar worries. Sugar can always be added later for the ones with sugar problems. We processed 132 quarts in all. It'll be a good wintertime breakfast drinking and healthy. So I must clear space for all those jars to be stored in the cellar.

Daughter Emma found a recipe in a cookbook for grape juice, so she made it that way. That recipe called for five heaping cups of washed grapes and 12 cups of hot water. Let it boil for 45 minutes. Put through a strainer. Put juice on stove and add two and a half cups sugar. Let juice come to a boil, and then put in jars and seal. So I guess I'll see how hers tastes to take a try for another year.

Daughter Lovina and children spent the day here, yesterday, and they were all here for supper. We babysat for daughter Emma's two oldest (Elizabeth and Emma) in the afternoon, while Jacob and Emma went to Riley's Children's Hospital in Indianapolis to visit a close relative.

So I prepared a fresh vegetable soup for all. I peeled and cut up potatoes and onions and added carrots, corn, peas and tomato juice, and I got a mango and celery in from the garden to add. I had a big kettle on the stove. I added one quart of our home-canned chunk beef, which made it taste delicious. Everyone seemed to enjoy the soup. That's the way I like to have a fresh soup of garden goodies. We still have tomatoes, sweet peppers, red beets, hot peppers and celery from the garden as of Oct. 5.

To the readers in Independence, Mo., and Speedway, Ind., and all others

who have asked: No, my house is not open to the public for tours or visits. We just try to live private (Editor's note: In celebration of the 10-year anniversary of Elizabeth's column next spring, Elizabeth's editor will choose one reader and a guest to join him for dinner, at Oasis Newsfeatures expense, at Elizabeth's home. The dinner guest will be selected from people who purchase one of Elizabeth's 40-page Christmas "cookbook-lets" by Dec. 15. The booklet is filled with holiday recipes and stories. The cost is $19.95 to Oasis Newsfeatures, P.O. Box 2144, Middletown, Ohio 45042. Please include a short note as to why you would like to visit with Elizabeth.)

Here is the recipe for a homemade vegetable soup from the garden. You readers have a good week!

HOMEMADE VEGETABLE SOUP

2 tablespoons butter	1 cup potatoes, diced
2 cups tomato juice	2 cups milk
1 /4 cup flour	1 onion, chopped
1 /2 cup celery, chopped	1 cup diced carrots
1 1 /2 teaspoons salt	1 pound hamburger

Brown meat and onion in butter. Drain grease. Add remaining ingredients, but reserve the milk and flour. Cook vegetables until they are nice, soft and done. Mix the milk and flour, and stir until smooth.

Add to soup and cook until thickened.

OCTOBER 2000

It is 9 a.m. on this Tuesday, Oct. 17, 2000. This is the time of day that wedding services started off when my husband Ben and I were united into marriage in 1957. Lots of memories linger, and who thought a year ago that Ben would not be here for our 43rd anniversary? Only God knows the reason why he is not here.

I can remember that day so clearly:

At 4 a.m., my sister and I were hard at it frying chicken, which was to be served for the noon meal after our wedding. Many invited guests couldn't attend because of the Asian flu at the time. As I have written about in the past, I also had a severe case of the Asian flu at the time. The week before our wedding, my temperature was up to 105. Being 21 years of age, it seemed high enough. Most of our family was down with flu, but everyone was OK, only feeling weak by the wedding day. We caught the flu by visiting someone who had it. It was so catching, but we hadn't realized it. My father, Ben and one of my sisters never caught it. My mother was still in bed on the Tuesday before our wedding day, which was on a Thursday.

Some women came over on that Tuesday to help bake the pies and make those "nothings" (a traditional Amish wedding pastry; recipe is at www.theamishcook.com), which most weddings around here you'll see them on the wedding tables.

Some serve the cakes from sheet cakes on trays, have layer cakes on the cake stands and are cut on the wedding day. It's usually a variety of cakes. The single girls arrive Wednesday to help peel and cut potatoes. Celery also is washed and vegetables diced up for the dressing.

On Thursday, the day of the wedding, carrot salad is made and potato salad is prepared if it is on the menu. In some places, chicken is cut up to be fried on the wedding morning. There are many cooks helping, and the tables are set. Lots of work goes into preparing for a wedding day. With plenty of women for cooks, it makes it easier for everyone. The waiters are single boys and girls who make sure everyone has enough food. We had seven single couples as waiters at our wedding; some have many more.

There are lots of dishes, kettles, silverware and pans to get washed for both meals. There is a noon meal right after the wedding and an evening supper for those who stay all day. It always seemed easier to get those dishes out of the cupboards than to put them back in order.

Ben and I then moved onto our current farm March 11, 1958. What a change it made in life. Now we have six girls and two boys and 30 grandchildren (31, counting Mary Shelter who passed away). How time flies.

As I look out my window now, the leaves are falling from the trees. They are such beautiful colors of all kinds -- beautiful fall weather.

Later in the evening: daughters Liz and children and Emma and children spent the day here. Their husbands joined them here for supper. Son Albert and sons gave me a visit also toward evening. Joe, Lovina and family also came for supper. Guess what? After supper, dishes were washed by Levi (Liz's husband), with help from Joe and Jacob, who wiped the dishes dry. They were singing while doing it, as the girls put away the food. I guess that was a rare occasion for the men to seen helping in the kitchen. Ha! What would I do without family?

Ironing was on the list to do today and also canning of green tomato pickles.

Never thought I would get those canned as it's such good eating from those jars. A friend of Liz shared the recipe, and now it's in our family to help fill those canning jars for the long winter ahead.

I will share a recipe used for the dressing I mentioned earlier, served at weddings. It also would be good for those upcoming Thanksgiving meals.

SIMPLE DRESSING

1 whole loaf bread	3 eggs, well-beaten
2 tablespoons butter	3 cups chicken broth
4 tablespoons chopped celery	1 medium onion
1/2 teaspoon poultry seasoning	
Salt and pepper to taste	

Toast bread, cut in cubes. Combine celery, onion and seasonings. Bring broth to a boil and add to bread and celery. Add eggs last and stir well. Put into casserole dish and bake 1 hour at 350 degrees. Delicious!

OCTOBER 2000

It is a very foggy Thursday morning. It was foggy yesterday morning also. Looks as though the sun will come out. It would be good if it does to dry the laundry, which is hanging out on the line.

My daughters Lovina and Emma, and their children are here for the day while Verena and Susan are away at their jobs. This is the second day in a row I've spent with family. Daughter Liz wanted to spend the day here yesterday, but I was helping Lovina at her place. So we had an enjoyable day working together at Lovina's. Always cleaning and chores that need to be done in a household.

Daughter Leah and children were here on Tuesday. It is always good to see family come home. Such a different life without a husband now. But we must accept life and go on.

Last week was a busy week processing those green tomato pickles. Several of my daughters had green tomato pickles to process, so I was around helping them. We also processed red beets. I should also process ours as I pulled them from the ground. Not much in the garden anymore; it's history for 2000. But those weeds survive. Ugh!

Sunday morning, my children and myself went to the graveyard to look at Ben's grave for the first time since he passed away. This is also where granddaughter Mary is and my folks, sister, and lots of other relatives are buried. Difficult to visit.

We then had a picnic at a nearby park. We had barbecue chicken on the grills and a variety of other food. Albert's family stayed overnight Saturday, so on Sunday morning we had a delicious breakfast casserole, homemade apple crisps and other goodies.

Looks like local schools are canceled this morning because of the fog. My granddaughter Elizabeth (of Joe's and Lovina's) won't have to go to school today. She is in kindergarten. Seems different to see her around here today.

The red maple tree, a gift from son Amos, is in its beautiful red leaves this time of year.

NOVEMBER 2000

𝕴 am writing this column in the first week of November, and it's just hard to believe that the year 2000 is almost over. We just passed a memorable anniversary in my life.

On Oct. 29, 1963, Ben and I moved onto this farm with only two children: Leah and Amos, at the time. Leah was 4 years old, and Amos was 2 years old the next day. He couldn't understand why we don't go back home, but they finally adjusted to their different home. Thinking back, land wasn't selling high as it is now. The wages were low, and it was hard to find a job at the time. I guess we learned to save. Being without a job was tough, especially having bought a farm and those farm payments came along. But somehow there was always a way. Not to say we never worried, but why worry if we can pray?

I guess it's not what you earn, it's what you save. It's a good thing my mother taught us how to save. Mother was a good housekeeper. Lots of memories linger.

Some of the family reminded son Amos Monday evening he was another year older. Granddaughter Rosa (Liz and Levi) also had her third birthday Monday.

We had some trick or treaters last night (Halloween). No tricks, only treats for them little ones. Ha!

It looks like a fall day out there. Daughters Verena and Susan are at work, and I'm waiting to get a ride to attend a Tupperware party at my niece's, and tomorrow my daughter Leah is having a Stanley party.

Well, it is now Thursday, Nov. 2, and I am here at Jacob's (daughter Emma). Some of the family reminded Jacob he is turning another year older, by having a supper last night for the occasion. The girls have left for work, and we're getting ready to attend Leah's party today.

So we'll have dinner there also. On the breakfast menu here at Jacob's were homemade breakfast sandwiches using shredded potatoes, cheese, scrambled eggs and home-canned sausage in them and then baked. Home-canned salsa goes good with these sandwiches, plus Emma's home-processed grape juice. She also baked cinnamon rolls and Long John Rolls (see www.theamishcook for Long John Roll recipe) for Jacob's birthday treat at his place of work.

To the readers who asked about Clear-Jel, it can be bought at food stores. It is used as a thickening in pies. Good luck!

Here is our recipe for homemade cinnamon rolls that Emma fixed this morning.

CINNAMON ROLLS

1 1/2 cups milk
1/2 cup sugar
2 packages dry, active yeast
1/2 cup warm water
6 cups flour
3 eggs

2 teaspoons salt
1/2 cup butter

Scald 1 1/2 cups milk. Add 2 teaspoons of salt, 1/2 cup sugar and 1/2 cup butter or margarine. Add 2 packages of yeast to 1/2 cup of warm water, and let stand 5 minutes. Add to above mixture. Add 3 beaten eggs and then 3 cups of flour. Mix. Add 3 cups more flour. Let raise to double bulk. Roll out, and spread with melted margarine. Sprinkle brown sugar on top and then cinnamon. Roll up. Cut up about 3/4- to 1-inch width. Let rise. Bake in hot oven (about 350 degrees), 5 to 7 minutes. Frosting can be added.

NOVEMBER 2000

We are relaxing on this Monday evening, Nov. 6, after eating a delicious supper.

Homemade potato soup was on the menu. So now it is just a cozy night around the stove on a chilly night. Looking around the house, what a relief that the windows are once again cleaned and the curtains were washed. We got a lot done today. What a huge laundry that dried so nice today. We took care of curtains, bedding, covers of all kinds and plus all the rest.

What would I do without my good helper today, daughter Verena? Susan was at work on her job while Verena and I were home working, but Susan had plenty of work yet to do when she returned home.

I guess we should appreciate the nice days. Outside, it is 30 degrees. Should get my celery out of the garden. That's the last remaining to be picked. But those weeds remain. Ugh!

The nearby woods looked an autumn splendor today. There are colors of all kinds, but the leaves are falling fast from the trees. The grass looks a green color as yet. We must enjoy this nice weather while we have it. Our fall harvest in the fields has been completed.

Hopefully, our garden will be plowed yet this fall for the forthcoming spring. It's so good to open those jars now that were processed from the summer, full of still-fresh home-canned vegetables, fruits and meats.

The stoves must get in good working order before we use them too much. I'm always afraid of those chimney fires. More work in the wintertime. We have to carry in fuel and empty the ash pans from the stove. I dread to think of these cold days and nights approaching without Ben. It can be so lonely. But we must go on.

Joe's and Jacob's families were here for Sunday dinner. Joe barbecued chicken and steak for the meals. Plenty left.

Daughter Leah had her Stanley party Thursday with such a good turn-out. She served a good dinner at noon for whoever came. Very delicious! The party was in the afternoon. The women of all my married children were in attendance. Leah had made more than 100 long John rolls and 75 chocolate chip cookies to serve for the party, plus lots of other goodies, cold drinks and coffee. There were many women and children to be who enjoyed Leah's good treats in the afternoon.

Son Amos and his family were our supper guests Thursday night. A skillet casserole was on the menu.

Here is the recipe for homemade potato soup we enjoyed this evening. You readers have a happy, healthy Thanksgiving!

(Editor's note: The recipes for the skillet casserole and long John rolls, plus a selection of Elizabeth's Thanksgiving recipes can be found on the Internet at www.theamishcook.com.)

PLAIN POTATO SOUP

3 or 4 large potatoes, cut up
1 medium onion
2 tablespoons margarine
1 quart milk
Salt and pepper to taste

Cut up potatoes and onion in water and cook together until done (potatoes are slightly soft). Remove potatoes and onions from water, place into a bowl and mash with a potato masher. Add seasonings of salt and pepper to your taste. Then add margarine and milk. Put back on medium heat and cook until potatoes are fully tender. Serve with crackers. Delicious hearty soup on a winter night. Variation: Some people add noodles to this soup.

NOVEMBER 2000

It is Sunday, Nov. 12, as I write this. The day had a lot going on. We spent Saturday night at son Albert's. On Sunday morning, we all left to attend church services nearby, which started at 9 a.m. Then a noon lunch was served and visiting took place.

We left for our residence in the afternoon. We enjoyed taking in another area on our way home through places we used to travel years ago going to church services. So many changes as of now: families who have moved to other states and then who God took in "His" care. Gone but not forgotten.

Our evening supper guests were Paul's, Joe's and son Albert's families. On the menu were tomatoes from a "discovery." Daughter Verena discovered a couple of tomato plants last week in our woods with lots of red and green tomatoes on them. The red tomatoes weighed one pound and are so good. The green ones I should make some more green tomato pickles (picture and recipe at www.theamishcook.com). It's such a good recipe with green tomatoes and onions.

I am so glad our chimneys are in good working order. Once again, Joe and Jacob cleaned out both chimneys last Thursday evening; we needed the heat in those stoves. Our dining room's new stove hasn't been put in use as yet. We must read instructions first. If Ben would only be here, but family will give good help. What would we do without family?

I dread to think of these winter months when you have to keep those home fires burning. Lots more work it seems, although no garden to care for like during the spring and summer. I guess all seasons have their plenty of duties. Right?

We had our first snow Nov. 14, and this is now Friday morning, Nov. 17. I must get this letter completed as it goes on its way today. The snow flurries are falling with the temperature at 30 degrees. Winter is on its way. As I look out the window, the trees look bare except the apple trees still have their leaves.

As I am writing this, my daughter Verena is finishing up reading her book of "New Dawn on Rocky Ridge," part of the many Laura Ingalls Wilder series that are so popular around here. I must hurry as time has no way to wait. Too much work to do. Glad I have the health to do it.

We're invited to a wedding on Wednesday, Nov. 22, at La Grange, Ind., for the daughter of my niece. I'm to help bake pies, etc., on Monday and help cook at the wedding. Time will tell if we go.

You readers might enjoy a Christmas recipe as the holidays are coming forth.

Thanks to you great readers who keep sending sympathy cards, etc. I just can't answer each one personally. Words can't express the appreciation, so thanks again. The following cookie recipe goes good around here.

DECEMBER 2000

It was so good to have a lot of wood cut up from our woods. It was cut, hauled up, split and stacked in our shed by son Albert, son-in-law Paul and his son, Ben, Joe and Jacob. What a relief to have it done and a supply of wood for the winter. In the afternoon, our garden was plowed and other odds and ends jobs, which had to be done, were done. How good to have helpful family. It was a quick plan to do all of this, and I guess the weather was for it. Our Belgian team of horses did the work in the garden; they are so easy to handle and do such good work.

Thanksgiving Day: I am now writing this on Thanksgiving Day. It's been a

long day. Myself, daughters Susan and Verena and Lovina and Joe's spent the day at his sister's home in Centerville, Mich. Was an enjoyable day, with turkey being on the menu. Let us be thankful of the plentiful food. Those Pilgrims must have had many struggles long ago. Guess we'll never know the terrors they braved years and years ago. So much to be thankful for.

Thanksgiving morning we had breakfast at a restaurant in Howe, Ind. It was a full house with all those deer hunters eating in there also. We waited for an hour in there until we could eat. It was a busy place. It was a long day to get to Michigan.

We had such a bounteous harvest this year as the weather really cooperated for the crops. So we spent Thanksgiving Day being very thankful. I now must get to bed and get some shut-eye.

This is now Sunday evening, Nov. 26, and and I want to get this letter completed. We went to church this nasty morning -- rain all day. Ugh.

We came home from church in the evening. What a surprise to have all six married children and their families here for supper. It hardly ever happens this way on a Sunday evening, because of all the different places people have to go. We had lots of good food and laughter. Nothing like having all the family here for the evening; the evening just isn't long enough then.

Try this hearty casserole for quick company. A reader in Bloomsburg, Pa., asked about a hamburger casserole recipe; this is a good one:

HAMBURGER DINNER

2 pounds ground beef
2 tablespoons oil
1 1/2 cups chopped, fresh onion
1 1/2 cup chopped celery
1 can drained bean sprouts
2 (10 1/2-ounce) cans cream of mushroom soup
1 1/2 cups warm water
1/2 cup rice (not instant)
1/4 cup soy sauce

Brown beef in oil. Drain off fat. Combine beef with rest of ingredients in a large bowl. Mix well and pour into a 9- by 13-inch baking dish. Cover and bake at 350 degrees for 1 hour, or until vegetables are done.

DECEMBER 2000

December of 2000 is halfway over, as we enter Christmastime. This is the special holiday of the year for family gatherings and spreading of cheer.

We usually have our family gathering on New Year's Day. This year will be quite different without my beloved husband, Ben. A sad holiday. But God has a purpose for it all. The "One" who never makes a mistake. We must go on. It's snowing tonight with temperatures at 13 degrees on this cold Wednesday.

Daughter Verena made a pizza for dinner as we had my editor visiting from out of state. She used this pizza dough, which took 2 cups flour, 2 teaspoons baking powder, 1/2 teaspoon salt, 2 1/4 cups milk and 6 tablespoons salad oil. Heat oven to 350 degrees. Measure flour, baking powder, salt, milk and salad oil into a bowl. Stir vigorously until mixture leaves the side of bowl. Gather dough together and press into a ball. Knead dough in bowl 10 times to make smooth. Place in pizza pan or baking sheet. Turn up edge 1/2 inch and punch or pleat. Brush the pizza pan with oil. Top with any kind of meat, pizza sauce, mushrooms, cheese and onions, whatever you prefer. Bake at 350 degrees until done. Delicious pizza!

Well, this is now Thursday morning, and I must get this column written. The ground is covered with snow, and I can still see those snow flurries falling. What a nice winter scene. Maybe soon we can put our horse-drawn sleigh into use. But I dread to think of keeping both stoves in gear. Always afraid of house fires. So many duties to do during the winter to keep the home fires burning.

The holiday season of Christmas is coming too fast. There are gifts to be bought or made for the children and grandchildren for our upcoming family gathering. I haven't decided when to have our Christmas gathering this year.

We have six married children and 30 grandchildren to get gifts for. While that's a lot to get gifts for, it's not like what my grandparents had every Christmas.

It was always enjoyable to go to our Grandpa's, usually on New Year's Day. The grandchildren would receive a sack of candy, which included a hanky or a water glass of some kind. This was for more than 100 grandchildren and great-grandchildren. These gifts are special remembrances to this day.

There also was always plenty of food to eat and songs to sing. The frying of chicken for the gathering took all morning, almost until noon, which the chicken had been butchered fresh a day or two before. Grandpa's had 14 living children at that time. I remember when I used to help Grandpa for that great day.

Here are some good recipes to prepare for this holiday season:

CHURCH WINDOWS

12 ounces semi-sweet chocolate

1 stick margarine
1 package colored marshmallows
1 cup nut meats

Melt chocolate and margarine together until creamy. Fold in one
package of colored marshmallows. Spread 1 cup of chopped nut meats
on wax paper. Cover with marshmallow-chocolate mixture. Roll up like
a jelly roll. Refrigerate or chill until solid. Slice and serve.

CARAMEL CORN

2 cups brown sugar
2 sticks of margarine
2 gallons popped popcorn
1/2 cup light or dark corn syrup
1 teaspoon baking soda

Mix and cook for 3 to 4 minutes on a high burner, stirring constantly.
Remove from burner and add baking soda. Stir well, but quickly, until
baking soda is blended in -- about 2 more minutes. Pour over popped
corn. Mix very well. This will coat 2 gallons of popped corn.

JANUARY 2001

Happy holidays to you all great readers out there -- far and near. Winter has come upon
us with three degrees above zero. Brrrrr. But we have to accept the weather as it comes.
Guess we can't be the judge for the weather. Good for our stoves that keep us warm but always
afraid of those chimney fires. Taking care of those stoves is always a hassle -- keeping them
home fires burning and keeping them in good order.
It's snowing and blowing out there. Drifts are covering the roads; some roads might close yet.
School bus passed this morning.
We done a laundry this morning and hung the laundry on our inside racks by our stoves to dry.
Too cold to hang out on our clothesline, which would be so nice to do, to hang it outside. But
one season comes and one goes. It doesn't seem possible at this time of year, December, as cold
as its been, that we still have leaves hanging on our apple trees.
I don't know when our Christmas family gathering will be this year as we are waiting on some
family members; hope they can all be present for breakfast, dinner, etc. It will be different
without my beloved Ben. But I guess life must go on in this sad world of ours. Right?
Sunday was spent at Paul's (daughter Leah), also, son Albert's, Joe's and Jacob's families were
there with a delicious dinner with fried chicken on the menu, plus mush. Good to be together!
We all left for our homes in the p.m. It was cold!
This is now, Friday, Dec. 22 ,and it's three below zero. Seems the cold weather won't give up on
us. Hoping for warmer temperatures. Takes a lot of fuel during weather like this. The ground is
still covered with those huge snowdrifts at various places. Traffic has been slow, and the school
bus didn't

pass. Many schools are having their holiday vacations this week until Jan. 2. Lots of happy faces!

Should be making some holiday treats, but I'm not in the holiday spirit this year, it seems. We always made candy, cookies, popcorn balls, etc. when the children were in our care. Such as our main candy was peanut butter balls and peanut butter cups. Also fruit cakes.

PEANUT BUTTER CUPS

1 pound margarine
2 pounds peanut butter
3 pounds powdered sugar
1 pound melted semi-sweet or milk chocolate, whichever is preferred

Mix margarine and peanut butter. Work in powdered sugar. Shape into balls, the size of big marbles. Dip in melted chocolate.

PEANUT BUTTER BALLS

2 cups crunchy peanut butter
3 cups Rice Krispies
1 pound powdered sugar
1/4 pound margarine
1 pound melted semi-sweet or milk chocolate, whichever is preferred
Mix and make size of walnuts and dip in melted chocolate. You can put raisins in the chocolate also.

JANUARY 2001

Looking out the window on this cold morning, it's a winter scene with the snow-covered ground, and the trees are a Christmasy white. How beautiful!

We've had several mornings of fog. New Year's Day was very bad to drive through that fog. But we got home safely from Levi's, (daughter Liz), being there in the assistance of their new arrival, Suzanne. Then a friend of ours took us to son Amos' to spend New Year's Day. They were butchering hogs when daughters Verena and Susan and I arrived. We assisted them with the butchering.

Three hogs were butchered and mostly all cut up, and sausage was made. It was an enjoyable New Year's Day at son Amos'. We left for home around 5 'o clock. A delicious noon meal was served while we were at Amos'.

I still admire my blooming Christmas cactus and two poinsettias, which seem so nice. Three years ago, son Amos' gave us one, and two years ago, Jacob's gave us one. They're still such hardy plants. I love flowers but seems I have too many indoors during the wintertime.

I can see out my window birds gathering in the snow to eat. The birds enjoy when someone throws feed out for them. That's something Ben always tried to throw feed out for the birds. He always was a bird watcher at all times. He is still missed, and an empty chair was at the table New Year's Day. Doesn't seem the same.

We've had a cold winter thus far. Hoping for warmer weather. The cold and snowy just hangs in here. Sleigh-riding goes good on these snow-covered roads. It's taking a lot of fuel to keep these home fires burning.

We spent Christmas Day at Joe's (daughter Lovina) with other family members present. Enjoyable day with plenty of food for the meals. What would I do without family?
I'm processing meat in those pressure cookers now. Verena hitched the horse to the buggy and left for Jacob's (daughter Emma) to see about their steak to be sliced up for the freezer,and Susan is wrapping gifts for her nieces and nephews. We're just having a late Christmas family gathering this year, Jan. 14. Glad all can be present, hopefully. God only knows what the future holds for 2001.
We'll have lots of delicious desserts and plenty of food at our Jan. 14 family gathering. This is one of the sweet treats that may be on the menu. Try it, and enjoy those calories!

NO BAKE PEANUT BUTTER DROPS

1 /2 cup brown sugar
1 /4 cup evaporated milk
1 /2 cup chunky peanut butter (creamy can be used if you prefer)
2 1 /2 cups Rice Krispies cereal (or whatever cereal you prefer)
Stir together milk, sugar and peanut butter in a saucepan. Bring to boil and stir until melted. Remove. Stir in cereal. Drop by teaspoonfuls onto waxed paper. Cool until firm.

BUTTERMILK PIE

1 /2 cup butter
1 cup buttermilk
3 eggs
1 1/ 2 cups sugar
1 tablespoon flour
Beat together ingredients, and pour into unbaked pie shell. Sprinkle with nutmeg. Bake at 350 degrees for 35 minutes. Delicious!

JANUARY 2001

As I get up this cold morning, it's good to have the stoves in gear. It's also a nice feeling to have plenty of fuel, which has taken a lot since December.

Just hope for no house fires. More duties with stoves at this time of year. The calendar shows we're in January of 2001. We've had cold weather with plenty of snow. We have to expect the weather whatever this time of year.

My daughters Susan and Verena, and I spent Saturday night at Joe's (daughter Lovina). Lovina's daughter, Verena, wasn't feeling her best. Verena and Susan attended church services Sunday at one of my niece's and family.

In the evening, we went to Jacob's (daughter Emma) for the night to assist Emma with the rest of their beef butchering. Steaks were sliced up on Monday; they were trimmed up for beef chunks. We processed seven quarts and 10 pints of beef chunks, which can be cooked every which way. Noodles, gravy, soups, etc. can all be cooked with the beef. Steaks were bagged and put in the ice chest. Now their beef is taken care of for the rest of the winter.

Jacob's folks, his sister and family were there for Sunday supper, also, so we made "rare beef." It was the first time they had tasted such. My father always made "rare beef." It's beef sliced very thin and seasoned with salt and pepper and, I tell you, father had it well peppered. You make the lard real hot in a skillet and drop in the rare beef by pieces. With a fork, stir around the beef a couple of times, turn it over and do the same and out it goes into a bowl. In the wintertime when beef was butchered, we'd have lots of rare beef. Especially for the evening meals with cooked potatoes (jackets) and sour cream.

Son Albert and sons were here last night to get their summer sausage as they have been smoking in what you'd call our smokehouse. Ben had fixed it up to smoke our summer sausage years ago, and it's just an old stand. We made the Canadian summer sausage, which took the ingredients of 60 pounds of ground beef, 33 pounds of ground pork, 4 pounds salt, 5 pounds white sugar, 1/3 pound pepper and 2 ounces saltpeter. Mix as you would sausage and stuff tightly in muslin sacks or you can buy those store-bought sacks. Hang in cellar for one to two weeks and then smoke with hickory wood.

After smoking has been completed, let dry for six to eight weeks before using. This used to be so handy to slice when visitors came. We slice and serve it with crackers. Also when working in the garden and wanting to come in for a lunch break, a summer sausage sandwich is quick and easy to prepare.

Well, I should help daughter Verena with breakfast. She's preparing burritos with potatoes, scrambled eggs, bacon and shredded cheese.

I can't neglect this job of writing. First job on list and now laundry has to be done. Ironing is also on the list. Plenty of it.

Done my last shopping yesterday for my family gathering, which will be on Sunday, Jan. 14. What a relief when it's over with, Ben not being with us. But life must go on.

Try this delicious coffeecake, which we may serve at the family gathering this weekend:

GERMAN COFFEECAKE

3/4 cup warm water (about 105 degrees F)
1 package dry yeast
1/3 cup sugar
1 teaspoon salt
2 1/4 cups all-purpose flour, divided for use
1 egg
1/4 cup lard (or shortening)

About 2 teaspoons margarine
Brown sugar and cinnamon for topping
Yield: 1 coffeecake

Dissolve yeast in warm water. Let stand a few minutes, then stir. Stir in sugar, salt and 1 cup of the flour.
Beat the egg, add lard (softened or melted and cooled) and the egg to the flour mixture. Beat in the remaining flour until mixture is smooth. Drop by spoonfuls into a greased shallow baking pan. Let rise in a warm place until dough is nearly doubled. Dot top of dough with tiny slivers of margarine, then sprinkle with brown sugar and cinnamon. Bake 30 minutes at 375 degrees. Delicious

JANUARY 2001

This seems to be a nice Wednesday evening. The days come and go. Had plenty of cold days and still snow on the ground.
Takes plenty of fuel for the home fires this time of year. Daughters Lovina and Emma and children spent the day here. They came last night so got them to stay for the overnight.
Both daughters took each of their husbands, Joe and Jacob, home early in the morning as to do their chores and be ready to leave for work at 5:30 a.m. Joe and Jacob both work at the same place.
Then Lovina and Emma returned, and a breakfast was served. Joe's 6-year-old Elizabeth then headed for school, being a kindergartner. Looks so cute to see her go to school with her school bag on her back. Emma and Lovina stayed all day, and Joe and Jacob met them here after work. Daughters were glad to not drive home alone in this cold weather.
I must write about what happened in the morning. Three flaps of eggs had been delivered, so daughter Lovina was going to make a run to her house with horse and buggy to take the eggs home. Verena went outside for a moment with Lovina to help with the buggy. When Verena went back in the house, she discovered Lovina's little 18-month-old Benjamin having a ball with those eggs. He had thrown 14 eggs to the floor and 1-year-old Jacob Jr. was playing in it, as he still crawls around. But the mess was soon taken care of. Benjamin climbed on the step stool and on the sink to the eggs. Lucky he didn't get them all as he'd had 90 eggs to toss. Ha! Sweet little boy.
This week is going fast. Daughter Leah and children stopped in and had dinner here with us Monday evening.
Saturday night was spent at son Albert's, so on Sunday morning we attended church services with them. Was glad our horse was harnessed and hitched to the buggy so the girls didn't have to do that, as Albert did the duty. Son Albert's, Joe's and Jacob's families were our Sunday supper guests.
Today, 32 years ago, a daughter named Elizabeth was born to Ben and me and goes by the name today of Wengerd (Levi) now. She has three daughters and one son. A baby, Suzanne, was born on Dec. 26, 2000. Her oldest is in first grade in school.
Didn't get to see son Amos over the weekend.

Word came that my Dad's step-sister, my step-aunt, Elda, died, and the funeral was Friday morning. I still remember as a young girl she took me along to school one day as a little visitor. I recall that day with her sitting at her desk at a public country school. I will remember her as a great step-aunt.

Brings back memories of those times. I'm so glad to have some of my Dad's mom's stainless steel cookware. She took good care of it. I got the cookware through the children's sale of my deceased folks' belongings. Lots of memories. I remember when dad's mom took us as young ones to babysit for us when my folks went to town for only a short while. Grandma would place a cardboard box upside down and put pretzels, etc., on it, and we'd kneel around the box and enjoy the treats. What a treat at that time. She was a great grandma.

Well, I must get back to work.

FEBRUARY 2001

We entered another month today: February. The day looks dreary and damp.
Had lots of rain the last couple days. Many were glad for the rain to have water in their cisterns. Some cisterns had gone dry. We have had plenty of snow this winter but no rain. We have a big cistern and seems we don't run out. We used to use the cistern water when Joe's (daughter Lovina) family lived in the trailer home across our driveway and Jacob's (daughter Emma) family lived with us in this household after they married. Took a lot of cistern (soft water) to do laundry, etc.
The highlight of Tuesday, Jan. 30, was another grandchild for me. A baby girl, Leanna, was born to son Albert and Sarah Irene at 1:05 p.m. weighing 7 pounds, 9 ounces. She joins Elizabeth, Ben, Joseph, Albert Jr., Irene, Emma and Marvin.
So we had all of Albert and Sarah's children in our care until all was over with the baby. They enjoy coming to Grandma's.
Daughter Lovina and children were here also that day. So it was a full house. Joe's and Levi's families were here for supper also. Son Amos' family spent Saturday here to see what needs to be done, as church services will be here in the near future.
Then Sunday morning, I told Jacob's (daughter Emma) family to drop in for breakfast on their way to his folks' for church. This way, daughter Emma didn't have to mess around for their breakfast. So dishes were washed and the next was rest and then think of dinner. So Albert's and Joe's (daughter Lovina) families were here for Sunday dinner. Joe's family went after pizza in a nearby town. So pizza was on the menu. We got plenty, just in case some other family members would drop in for dinner. We never know but always glad to see them come. I suppose they all know they are welcome.
This morning, the girls made omelets but made them a different way. They took five eggs, 1 heaping tablespoon of flour, 1 teaspoon salt, pinch of pepper or to your taste and 2 cups milk, and added shredded cooked potatoes (jackets) and put it in a hot, buttered covered skillet on medium heat. Turn it over and add cheese on top. It was good this way for a change.
Daughters Emma and children are here today. She's helping me with cleaning for church. She's washing off walls, ceilings, etc. It's been a big cleaning day thus far. So glad it's being done.
Again, Emma's small daughters Elizabeth and Emma want to write also so I gave them paper and pencil to write. They think they're probably helping me with this column. Ha!
Here's a recipe that a reader in Hammond, Ind., asked for:

HOMEMADE CORNBREAD

1 cup flour	1 cup cornmeal
1 egg, beaten	1 tablespoon baking powder
1 /4 cup oil	1 cup milk
1/ 4 cup sugar	

Beat just until mixed. Put into 9-inch pan and bake at 350 degrees for 20 minutes. It goes good with ham, beans or milk.

FEBRUARY 2001

This is a nice, sunshiny day with a temperature at 54 degrees on Feb. 8.
Remarkable how the weather has been. So much fuel it has taken in the cold weather all winter. Was wondering how the winter will hold out with those stoves, but so far so good. I am always afraid of fires with stoves burning all winter.
Tonight, a wedding supper is to be nearby, and I'm to help be a cook for the wedding. They have two tents up for it outside in the yard and tables in the house for the people to be seated and eat. This is the time of year we never know how the weather will be. It's been a nice day so far.
Daughter Lovina and children are here today, which makes life go on. We are in the process of getting ready for church services to be here soon.
(Editor's note: For those new to the column, Amish families have church services in the homes of church members on a rotating basis. There is no formal church building. Church services are every other Sunday.)
Church services will be at our house this Sunday for son-in-law Jacob and again March 4 for my turn. So it's been clean, clean, clean around here. We want everything to be looking clean and in order for all the people who attend the service. Everything, including the walls and ceilings, is being cleaned for the upcoming church services. The curtains and windows need to be cleaned also. I just hope the curtains can be done and the laundry hung outside instead of drying on racks inside. Clothes that dry outside always have such a refreshing smell.
Daughter Emma and children were here Tuesday when her husband Jacob returned from work. He took the wall mop and started to help wash off our kitchen walls. Ha! The kitchen was soon cleaned. Those wall mops are so handy to wash off walls and ceilings.
The snow has melted away after our nice snow this week. So the yard and fields look a dirty brown. Looks like a couple hundred birds are in the yard now. They find their food from day to day. Ben would always fill those bird feeders all winter long. So many kinds of birds would be eating at those feeders. I must say it was interesting to watch those birds, how they tried to take food or whatever from each other on the yard. As cold and windy as it has been this winter, there's still some leaves on the trees.
We enjoyed three van-loads of Amish people recently from our area who were visiting shut-ins and widows, etc. for the day. They just visit for a while and go to the next place. Today, my sister, her husband and their six married daughters were out to visit the shut-ins and widows. I was on the list for them. Hard to believe I am now on the list. But we must go on. God makes no mistakes.
Now this is Friday evening, and we've had a lot of rain today. Daughters Leah and Emma and their children were assisting us with the cleaning and my floor-to-ceiling wall cupboard dishes

were washed, which was plenty of dishes to wash and dry. The dishes now look so sparkling. What a relief!

It is now Sunday evening and we had dinner at son Albert's to see Leanna (their newborn). Some other family members were also dinner guests. I must also add Levi's (daughter Liz) little Suzanne is a growing and healthy baby. She has lots of black hair.

I want to thank you great readers out there for all the encouraging notes and letters. It makes me feel so unworthy for it all. Wish I could answer everyone. So I hope a "thank you" here helps. With all the cleaning and washing around here, this is a good casserole for a busy wash-day.

FEBRUARY 2001

Here are some recent reader mail questions submitted by mail and e-mail. I hope this does the duty to catch up a bit.

A Pendleton, Indiana reader wrote asking about my recipe for homemade noodles. There are many different recipes for noodles. Many of the recipes are passed down from parent to children. Each family has their own distinct recipe. Unfortunately, it's a tradition that is not as common as it used to be. When I was a little girl, all the mothers fixed homemade noodles, rolling them out and letting them dry on racks. It would always be an exciting day when mother would fix noodles. That's where I learned to make noodles. This is a recipe that goes good around here and is easy to make:

NOODLES

9 eggs
6 cups flour or more
1 teaspoon salt
1/2 cup water

Mix together well. Knead until nice and smooth. Dough should not be sticky. Roll out and cut into width of noodles desired. Let set all day, and you'll have dried noodles. A hand-cranked noodle maker is so handy to do noodles.

Linda in Newton, N.J., wrote: In a recent recipe for banana bread, you called for "sour milk." What do you mean by that? Please explain. Thank you. We use sour milk in breads, rolls, etc. Let milk sour, and if not on hand, you can add a small amount (tablespoon per cup) of vinegar to the milk to get the same taste. Adding vinegar will sour the milk.

Sour milk makes a good taste in some breads; it gets thick and makes them moist. When I was still living at home, mother would let the milk sour and skim the cream off the top for a homemade sour cream. Some weren't fond of that. Never drink sour milk, but it's good for baking. Hope this helps!

Pat in Bainbridge, Ind., asked if I have a recipe for church peanut butter. Yes, we make a peanut butter spread for church. Mix equal parts corn syrup, marshmallow creme and peanut butter. Some spread it on a slice of bread to eat, while others make a sandwich out of it. Hope this is what you were looking for!

Netra in Tacoma, Wash., wrote asking about the proper way to freeze garden-grown vegetables. We only freeze certain items; others just don't freeze well. Strawberries, raspberries and cherries freeze well. We roll them in sugar and seal them in empty 2- to 3-quart plastic ice cream containers. These seal well. Other fruits don't freeze so well. Vegetables, such as radishes and hot peppers, just don't seem to freeze well, but green beans and corn keep nicely in the ice-box. We steam green beans and corn first in a kettle, let them cool, and then seal and freeze them. These are good ways to keep certain fruits and vegetables, but for most of our produce, we home-can it, not freeze it. It keeps this way much longer, and fresher. Jennifer in Big Rapids, Mich., asked: "When you find blood in your raw eggs, what does that mean and should you use it in cooking?" I never use the eggs if they have blood in them.

Do you have a recipe for oatmeal raisin cookies? (Mary, Bloomsburg, Pa.) Is this the recipe you want?

OATMEAL RAISIN COOKIES

3 cups lard
6 cups brown sugar
1 /2 tablespoons vanilla
2 cups oatmeal
1 tablespoon salt

6 eggs
2 tablespoons soda
6 cups whole wheat flour
1 cup raisins

Mix together, put into rolls and chill overnight. Cut 1/8-inch thick, and bake about 10 minutes in preheated 350-degree oven until golden. Delicious!

MARCH 2001

𝔄nother cold morning as we enter the month of March.

We have experienced a cold winter already, and it takes a lot of fuel to get through these months. There are stoves to care for as to keep wood and coal in them. Always glad when we don't have the stoves in gear. Hope we get through the winter without any chimney fires.

We were helping Joe's (daughter Lovina) family Monday with canning their beef of hamburger and packing for the ice-chests. Now their beef chunks are in jars also.

I like to cook those beef bones off and make stew with it, adding cubed potatoes, onions, cabbage and carrots. Whatever you wish. We are getting ready for church services on Sunday to be here at this residence. So it's clean, clean, clean.

Had church services here two weeks ago for Jacob's(daughter Emma) family. Lots to look after to see that we have enough food for the Sunday noon lunch for all who attend the services. Seems so much more work without my husband, Ben. What would I do without family?

It's always nice when warmer weather comes and services can be outside in a cleaned-out shed. No furniture to rearrange in the house. (Editor's note: Many letters were received inquiring about the wall-mop Elizabeth uses to clean her walls and ceilings prior to church services. Information about this will be in an upcoming column.)

Daughter Susan had her Amish pen pal Lorraine here from a farther off area over the weekend. It was exciting to meet someone who she had just known through letters.

They had been corresponding for quite some time now, and this was the first time they had met each other in person. They are about the same age and have a lot of common interests. The day was very enjoyable.

Other family members of ours got in on the day, which passed too quickly. The weather seems warmed up some so maybe we can get our windows cleaned again from the outside. Inside, it's no problem to clean windows.

Hard to believe it will be time to make the garden again soon. A reader from Madisonville, Ky., wrote to ask about garden-planning and how to keep Mexican bean beetles from the garden. Does Elizabeth have any suggestions on how to control Mexican bean beetles? I always like to grow marigold flowers in my garden. Keeps a lot of stuff out. They just don't like the marigolds. I put rows through my garden. My daughter Leah puts rows through her garden and then plants them surrounding the outside border of her whole garden. Seems to keep all kinds of pests away. I hope this helps.

A reader in Delphos, Ohio, asked if I have a recipe for onion pie. Following is the recipe:

ONION PIE

4 thick slices of bacon, diced	2 cups peeled and chopped yellow onion
2 eggs, beaten	1 cup sour cream
1 tablespoon flour	1/2 teaspoon salt
1/4 teaspoon fresh ground black pepper	9-inch pie shell, unbaked

Preheat oven to 425 degrees. Saute onion until clear, and pour cooked onion into a large mixing bowl. Place bacon in a large, deep skillet. Cook over medium high heat until evenly brown. Drain, chop and add to onion; mix well. Stir in sour cream. Beat eggs enough to break up yolks, then mix in to pie mixture. Add flour to thicken mixture (onions will create a lot of water); then add salt. Mix well and pour mixture into prepared pan. Sprinkle top with caraway seed, if desired. Bake in preheated oven for about 1 hour, or until onions start to turn golden brown on top.

MARCH 2001

On Friday, my sons Amos and Albert, his son Ben and my daughter Verena went to a horse sale in Shipshewana, Ind., to see my team of Belgian horses get sold.

So I guess they're history now. They were never worked too hard, but they were here when we or one of our children needed them. They would ably perform such tasks as hauling manure, plowing the garden and getting up wood from the woods. They were a tame team, but were now in their 20s. I really didn't need them many more, and they were an extra duty to do, to give them water and feed. So the fields behind our barn look empty without them.

We still have the horses that pull our buggy. Lots of changes have taken place the past year. Glad our church services are over for another turn; they were here Sunday. Lots of cleaning took place before. Was glad for the help of family and also, grandchildren, who pitched in to assist. Some barn repairs, etc., were done.

The Monday after church services, lots of cleaning also is done. We did a lot of laundry Monday. The Saturday before church services, my son Amos, wife Nancy and their eight children, plus my daughter Lovina, husband Joe, and their five children were all overnight guests. So it was a full house. Was good to have them here.

Everyone helped with Sunday morning breakfast and then got dressed for church and got everything in order before the first people showed up. Everything was ready in time. Home-baked cookies and crackers were served to the small children in the morning as a treat.

And, as usual, a good noon lunch was served to all in attendance at church. We had coffee, ham, two kinds of cheese, lettuce, hot peppers, red beets, pickles, rhubarb jam, margarine, peanut butter mixture (equal parts peanut butter, corn syrup and marshmallow creme), home-baked bread, milk, etc. A hot milk soup and crackers was served for the little ones for lunch.

It is now Thursday morning, and I must get this in the mail. Were to Jacob's for supper last night for barbecued pork ribs and stayed for the night. So I am back home now and have completed the chores around here; now I want to help daughter Leah as Paul's have the next church services in their home.

So you readers stay healthy. Try this good casserole if you have to feed people in a hurry! A reader in Devils Lake, N.D., asked about a recipe called pizza cookies. It's a recipe we used to fix around here all the time; it's a delicious cookie. Try them!

PIZZA COOKIES

1/2 cup sugar	1/3 cup brown sugar
1/2 stick margarine	1 egg
1/2 cup peanut butter	1 teaspoon vanilla

Topping: 1 cup chocolate chips and 2 cups mini-marshmallows

Mix all the ingredients together except for the topping. Add 1 1/2 cups of flour. Press or roll dough on a pizza pan (15-inch size). Roll dough to edge of pan. Bake at 375 degrees for 10 minutes. Remove from oven. Add chips and marshmallows. Return to oven for 5 to 8 minutes. Cut when cold. Good luck

MARCH 2001

This is March 15, and, hopefully, the laundry will dry on the clothesline.

Daughter Liz and children are here today. Little Suzanne seems to be growing. Joe's and Jacob's families were our last night's supper guests. My daughter Verena was working while daughter Susan and I assisted daughter Leah in cleaning for their upcoming church services.

On Tuesday, Verena, Susan and I assisted Lovina to start to prepare for their church services coming up in the near future. As I look out the window, it seems I should see Ben out by the apple trees, pruning them. He always gave those trees a good pruning this time of year.

Last year, son-in-law Jacob pruned the top of the trees, and Ben was giving Jacob instructions on how to prune the trees. So I don't know how or what about these trees now. I used to help Ben prune those trees the last couple of years. He showed me which branches to prune.

A sad feeling as this will be a thing of the past. But I often think how nice we have it now, to think how my great-great grandfather from Santiglet, Department Dauchs, France, came to America on account of his conscientious objection to compulsory military training in France. This was behind his decision to immigrate to the New World, America. It sure must've been sad to leave their families, friends, loved ones, their neighbors and all the scenes of their childhood, never to see them again to a land unknown to them more than 3,000 miles away across the wild and stormy deep.

They made the trip in five months; it could now be made in hours by airplane. It was a different life in Europe. Their cooking was quite simple compared to ours now. Lots of their food was dried. When they boarded the ship, they didn't step onto a luxurious ocean liner as we see them today.

Conditions aboard the ship were anything but agreeable. The edibles taken on board were not very good and not any too plentiful. Meat was salted and packed in barrels, and even some of it spoiled en route. Many kegs of drinking water were taken aboard. Bread kept best after it was double-toasted. A few dried fruits were then quite unknown. Living quarters became extremely crowded, and sleeping conditions were very poor as well as rather unhealthful. They did not have the proper food and sanitation facilities, so sickness became prevalent. It would not be unusual if 10 percent of the people on board a ship from Europe to America would die. When their ship encountered storms at sea, their ship tossed and rolled furiously, but there was a railing all around the deck to guard passengers from falling into the sea. These storms sometimes lasted two or three days causing plenty of confusion, anxiety, suffering and seasickness.

It was always impossible to walk the boat when such storms occurred, and it often upset tables and rolled the seasick passengers from their berths. The massive sails were often tossed about like a feather, masts broken and sails torn, which were repaired before the ship could continue on its hazardous journey.

There wasn't a weather bureau like today, which could've aided the sailors to steer clear of storms. Nor aids to carry the messages to the ship.

Coming to this wooded new land, America, was a lot of work. Axes being used to chop down those trees to build their new homes. Homes were built not as being built now-a-days. Had to work hard to make a living.

Well, I must get back to work. Wish I had more time to answer all mail, but thanks to you great readers who take time to write.

MARCH 2001

Spring has arrived this Tuesday morning, March 20. So it makes one feel like doing outdoor cleaning once again. Makes one think of planting a garden when it gets warmer.

Was surprised, though, to see the snow-covered ground Friday morning and blowing snow. What a winter scene with everything snow-covered. Quite a few from this area left to attend the viewing or for the funeral at Kalona, Iowa, of my deceased first cousin's wife, which was held Friday.

Travel was bad for some on their way home, Saturday, as Iowa had more snow than in this area. They saw many cars, semis, etc. that had slid off the road.

My column is in a newspaper in Kalona and other nearby towns, and relatives got good comments about the column. Glad you great readers out there in Kalona, Iowa, are enjoying my worthless letters in your newspaper. We attended church at Paul's (daughter Leah) Sunday. Next church will be at Joe's (daughter Lovina). So it's clean, clean, clean.

Last week, I talked about my ancestors on my father's side. Our ancestors on my mother's side also had a tough time. My ancestors on my mother's side were Mennonite fugitives from Bern, Switzerland. They went to Alsace, France, during the last half of the 17th century and established themselves in the county of Rebeau Pierre, near Santa-Marie-Aux-Mines. However, they were driven out from there in 1712 by the order of Louis XIV, King of France. They traveled northward and located in the township of Mont-be-Laird, which, at the time, was part of the Empire of Germany known as Duchide-Wartemburg. Our ancestors were among a group of Mennonite families who settled in that part of Germany in 1793. Our ancestors had purchased a large farm in Monte-pre-Voir Township of Nevier District of Monte-be-Laird. This ancestor was blessed with six sons and five daughters. Lots more could be written about my ancestors, but I have to sign off as it is almost mailman time, and I must get this on its way today. But I will continue another time.

Will share some recipes with you great readers out there. Thanks to all the Kalona, Iowa, readers for the great encouragement for my writings that friends and family told me about upon their return from the funeral. A reader in Battle Creek, Mich., asked for a good, crunchy cookie recipe. This ranger cookie recipe is a good, crunchy one and is a favorite around here. Enjoy!

RANGER COOKIES

1 cup brown sugar	1 cup sugar
1 cup lard	2 eggs
1 tablespoon vanilla	1/2 teaspoon salt
1/2 teaspoon soda	1 teaspoon baking soda
2 cups flour	2 cups Wheaties or Rice Krispies
2 cups rolled oats 1 cup coconut (optional)	1/2 cup nuts (optional)

Cream first 3 ingredients. Add beaten eggs and vanilla. Mix thoroughly. Add sifted dry ingredients. Stir in cereal and nuts. Roll in walnut-size balls or drop by scant tablespoonfuls on ungreased cookie sheet. Bake 10 minutes at 400 degrees. Makes 5 to 6 dozen.

APRIL 2001

This has been a very cold, snowy day March 25. It's not a spring-like day. It felt like a day in January or February. The ground is covered with white stuff. And visibility was poor at times because of the blowing snow.

Yesterday was a nice day. Some time ago, this area held a benefit auction for my nephew to help his family catch up on medical bills. I offered two breakfast meals. So yesterday morning, we gave breakfast for a total of 17 people, a family from our area. This is rare that I would have a group over for a meal like that, but it was for a good cause. It was an enjoyable breakfast, consisting of scrambled eggs, ham, smoked sausage, home-baked bread, which some like with rhubarb jam, hot pepper butter and margarine, brownies, peaches, Jello cake, coffee and orange juice.

My daughter Verena stirred together what we call "mystery biscuits." She made four batches of them, which was more than plenty. But I'd always rather have enough of everything as to run out of food at such a time. These

"mystery biscuits" are so easy to make and good eating with the sausage gravy. Don't know why they are called mystery biscuits. The recipe is at the end of the column.

To the 26 eggs we prepared for scrambled eggs, we added cheese and milk and put them in a buttered skillet to fry. Was glad for daughter Verena and Susan's help to clean up after the breakfast. What would I do without my girls? But I guess there'd always be a way.

Jacob's (daughter Emma) family was also here for breakfast, so Emma also got in on the dish washing. Was glad for her help.

Son Albert, wife Sarah Irene and family were here today as our dinner guests, and Joe's (daughter Lovina) family was my supper guests. Joe's family stayed for the night.

Well, this is Thursday morning now, and I must get this column completed to get it on its way. Don't want to delay this as it must get on its way. Where did this week go?

It was enjoyable to attend the musical play for young voices presented by the local school March 22. Levi's (daughter Liz) daughter Elizabeth was in the play. It was so interesting to see those first-graders doing such a good job. We met two other grandchildren there also: Joe's little Elizabeth, who is in kindergarten, and son Albert's son Albert Jr., who is in second grade. Brings back memories of when my eight children went through school and attending their programs. I never regret taking time out of my busy schedule to attend.

Levi's family came here for supper Tuesday evening and decided to stay for the night. Levi and Levi Jr. drove home in their horse-drawn buggy after breakfast, and we took Liz and daughters home afterwards.

Jacob's family came for supper Wednesday night, and their two little girls got sick, so they stayed for the night as to not take them out in that open buggy.

Night air isn't good. They act better this morning. Jacob left for home earlier so he could complete his morning chores and be ready for work. They just live a mile down the road.

Today we want to help daughter Lovina to do the finishing touches for her Sunday church services to be in her home. This morning, Emma and Verena made a breakfast casserole for our meal. It's baking now in the oven. It consists of six slices bread, six eggs, two cups milk, salt and pepper. They added one pint of sausage to it. We always use sausage. After it's about baked, top it with cheese and let it melt. We like it! It's easy to bake.

Daughter Susan is doing the morning cleaning, which needs to be done as always. I had best close this letter. Thanks to you great readers out there for your encouraging cards , letters, etc.

VERENA'S MYSTERY BISCUITS

2 cups sifted flour (although we never sift it)
1 tablespoon baking powder
1 teaspoon salt
1/4 cup mayonnaise
1 cup milk
1 teaspoon sugar

Sift flour, baking powder and salt. Add remaining ingredients. Mix until smooth and drop by tablespoonfuls on greased cookie sheet or fill 12 muffin tins 2/3 full. Bake 18 to 20 minutes at 375 degrees.

APRIL 2001

This leaves it Thursday, April 5, and brings back memories of my deceased mother's birthday who was born on this date in 1905.

The temperature today is at 68 degrees now at 11:30 a.m. with a sunshiny day. Very nice day!

Daughters Lovina and Emma and families are here today. Always good to have them here. Last night's supper guests were Paul's (daughter Leah) and family, Levi's (daughter Liz) and family, Joe's (daughter Lovina) and family and Jacob's (daughter Emma) and family. So pork steak was put on the grill with barbecue sauce on it, plus potatoes, fresh vegetables, soup, etc. Plenty of it all to eat. Was a good meal together.

Joe's family had church services in their home on Sunday, and son Albert's have it next time. we are trying to help everyone with cleaning, etc. Seems plenty of it.

The grandchildren are enjoying the day out on the trampoline as it was set up recently. The sandbox is also an enjoyable spot out there for the small grandchildren.

Hopefully the dandelion greens will soon appear on the menu. The first ones are the best. Makes a good salad with sour cream and hard-boiled eggs. Some are putting out gardens but mine is at a standstill as yet. Bought three pounds onion sets so I should put them in the ground, also lettuce and radishes.

Son Amos, Nancy and family were our Friday night supper guests. They stayed for the night. So we had Saturday morning breakfast together, and Amos trimmed one of our apple trees. All of my family knows there is always a "welcome" sign at the door for them. I am always glad to see them.

A reader in Tacoma, Wash., asked if I had a recipe for homemade wheat bread. This is a favorite around here. Slice it when warm and smear with butter or homemade jam. Yummy. Try this recipe!

APRIL 2001

This week has thus far been very stormy and rainy. Lots of water standing in the fields, yards, etc.

Some roads were flooded in the area. Glad my three apple trees got pruned. Son Amos did one tree and started another, and son-in-law Jacob finished it. Son-in-law Levi and daughter Susan carried away the branches. Then on Saturday, I started the third one, and Jacob did the rest. Son-in-law Joe carried all the branches away on a pile to be burned. It's wet enough to have it burned, but it's so windy. We're having plenty of high winds lately. Reminds me of tornado weather, which some areas have experienced this week.

Joe's (daughter Lovina) family was our supper guests tonight, so dandelion greens were on the menu. Had our first spring 2001 meal of dandelion greens Saturday. Had it for the evening meal and for Sunday dinner, which we spent Sunday dinner at Joe's. Joe and Lovina had a church singing in the afternoon, which was for our church district. Refreshments were served later to all in attendance.

The dandelions need a good rain and warmer weather to make them grow faster. The first younger ones always taste the best. We make a sour cream of vinegar, milk, salt and salad dressing and add the dandelion greens and hard-boiled eggs to it. Some put a hot gravy over the dandelions, but we prefer salad dressing. Dandelions go good with potatoes and some kind of meat. We prefer bacon or sugar-cured ham and ribs. Some make jelly with the dandelion greens.

Daughter Verena and Susan and I were assisting today in getting ready for a wedding supper for a couple in our area, which will be on Thursday evening. A lot of other women and girls also are assisting, which includes baking pies, peeling potatoes, washing and cutting celery sticks for the table decorations, and dicing up onions, celery and carrots for the dressing. (Editor's note: In

Elizabeth's area, cut and washed celery stalks serve as table decorations at weddings.) Always plenty to do at a time like this. I'm to be one of the cooks at the wedding, and my daughter Verena will be one of the tablewaiters.

Some have put out some garden but not in this household as yet. Still worried about a late freeze. Well, I want to write down some recipes for you great readers out there. I appreciate your thoughtful letters and cards out there. Nice of you readers to take the time to write.

To the Bloomsburg, Pa., reader who requested a macaroni and cheese recipe, try this!

BAKED MACARONI & CHEESE

8 ounces macaroni
1 egg, beaten
1 teaspoon dry mustard
1 cup milk

1 teaspoon butter, melted
1 teaspoon salt
1 tablespoon hot water
3 cups grated cheese

Heat oven to 350 degrees. Cook macaroni in boiling water until tender. Drain well. Stir in egg and butter. Mix salt and mustard with hot water. Add to milk. Add cheese to macaroni, reserving enough to sprinkle on top. Pour into buttered casserole dish. Add milk mixture. Sprinkle with reserved cheese. Bake 45 minutes, or until top is set.

GREEN BEAN SALAD

1 onion, thinly sliced in rings
1 can wax beans
1 cup kidney or great northern beans
3/4 cup vinegar
1 teaspoon salt

1 green pepper, thinly sliced in rings
1 cup green snap beans
1 cup sugar
1/2 cup oil
1/2 teaspoon pepper

Mix all together and refrigerate at least 12 hours.

APRIL 2001

We were surprised this morning, April 17, to see a layer of snow on the ground and the temperature at 30 degrees.

So it was good to have the stove in gear again. I'm ready for warmer weather. Good we can't judge the weather. The grass has now turned a beautiful green with the snow on top. Looked a great scene out there.

We had as supper guests last night: Levi's (daughter Liz), Joe's (daughter Lovina) and Jacob's (daughter Emma) families. So a vegetable soup was stirred up together, dicing peeled potatoes, 1 quart of canned beef, 1 quart of corn, 2 quarts of tomatoes, and 1 pint peas, onions, beans and fresh cut-up carrots to fill a large kettle. Vegetable soup was the main thing on the menu, which they all enjoyed. A fresh vegetable soup always tastes the best. I'm not too fond of canning vegetable soup. It just then has a different taste for me when processed. Ê

223

After a delicious dinner of soup, Joe's and Jacob's families decided to stay for the night. So it was a rushy morning the next morn when everyone was leaving for their jobs and Lovina's daughter Elizabeth leaving for school. Verena left also for her job.

After everyone left, daughter Lovina was washing off the walls and ceilings in the kitchen and dining room. Daughter Emma was doing some sewing for me as I want to give baby gifts for some of my family newborns.

In the evening, daughter Leah and children came this afternoon and brought a huge Easter gift, which came from my Secret Pal. The gift was dropped off at Leah's Sunday night. So I'll keep on guessing, guessing who is my Secret Pal this year. It sure was a nice Easter gift. Thanks for now if you may happen to be reading this, whoever it may concern.

Then Albert, Sarah Irene and family dropped in to be here for supper. So a casserole was the main thing on the menu. To prepare the casserole, I put 1 pound of hamburger in a skillet, diced up an onion on top and then added potatoes, which were put through a hand-cranked salad maker. The shredded potatoes are pressed down on top of everything in the skillet and add salt and pepper and top it with a can of cream of mushroom soup. Cover the skillet and simmer for 40 minutes. Top it with cheese and when melted its ready to serve. We all like this casserole.

It was a casserole that was prepared years ago from one who gave "stainless steel suppers" in homes. Daughter Leah and a niece went along with that man in the evening to keep his dishes washed. They enjoyed doing that. It was so tasty, the food he prepared in his stainless steel cookware. He furnished the food.

Well, this just about does it for Tuesday and ready to hike for bed. Cold out there but a comfortable stove to keep us warm.

It is now Wednesday, April 18, and still chilly. Daughters Susan, Verena and I had attended Communion services (Easter Sunday) at son Albert's.

We spent Saturday and Sunday night at Albert's. We helped them clean up on Monday morning from having church services. The highlight at the table Sunday after church was when a cake with re-lightable candles was presented to my oldest grandchild, Ben, son of Paul and daughter Leah, for his birthday. He finally had to give up to blow those candles out as they always re-lighted. Way to go, Ben!

This is now Wednesday, April 18, and the temperature was 28 degrees this morning. Brrrr. Felt like winter again. A huge laundry hangs out there on the clothesline. The house got a good cleaning, which always makes a good feeling. Well, it's time to see what is for dinner. I'll write more next week!

Amish Cook editor's note: Many readers have written asking about recent recipes for wheat bread and sugar cream pie. The original wheat bread recipe did not list the proper flour amount and the sugar cream pie had an ingredient omission. We apologize for any inconvenience. The correct recipe versions follow:

WHOLE WHEAT BREAD

1 cup milk
3 tablespoons butter
1 cake yeast
2 cups sifted flour

1 tablespoon salt
4 tablespoons honey or maple syrup
1 cup warm water
4 cups whole wheat flour

Scald milk. Add salt, syrup and 3/4 cup of warm water. Stir well. Let cool to lukewarm. In remaining 1/4 cup of water, dissolve the yeast; add to other mixture. Add flours gradually and knead into a smooth ball. Place in buttered bowl and brush top with soft butter. Let rise until double. Knead lightly and shape into a loaf and place into a pan. Brush with soft butter and let rise to double. Bake at 350 degrees for 50 to 60 minutes.

SUGAR CREAM PIE

1 cup white sugar	2/3 cup brown sugar
1/2 cup flour	1/2 teaspoon salt
1 cup boiling water	1 cup thin cream
1/2 teaspoon nutmeg	1 teaspoon vanilla

Combine dry ingredients. Add slowly the 1 cup boiling water. Then add cream, vanilla and nutmeg. Pour into unbaked pie shell. Bake at 425 degrees for 10 minutes. Reduce to 350 degrees and bake until done.

MAY 2001

𝕴t is very windy today with sunshine this Monday morning, April 23. Reminds me that today, daughter-in-law Nancy Jean is another year older. Ê
So happy birthday, Nancy Jean! Amos and Nancy's twins, Arlene and Marlene, will be 8 years old this week. How these years take way.
On Saturday night, we spent the night at Jacob's (daughter Emma) family, and plans were to have dinner on Sunday there. Joe's (daughter Lovina) family had the same intentions.
Amos and Nancy Jean were planning to stop by our place for Sunday dinner, but when they got here they found no one home. So they came to Jacob's, where all of us were. Amos had plans to show us how to "broast" chicken. Also, french fries were put in the hot baking oil. It looked so neat to see the stand with his iron bucket, kettle, or whatever you call it, and a fire was built under it. The chicken in the hot oil requires 15 minutes and it's ready. Son Albert's family also arrived for dinner. So at Jacob's were son Amos' and Albert's and families; Joe, Lovina and family; and Verena, Susan, and I.
Susan had gathered a lot of dandelion greens Friday. So that was put on the menu with hard-boiled eggs and a sour cream to it. The winter onions from Jacob's garden were good tasting, along with mashed potatoes and gravy and corn. Plenty of food on the table. Cake and ice cream did the finishing touch of the dinner. It was so nice -- folding tables and benches were set up on the lawn outside for this family dinner. Relaxing!
It was a nice Sunday, but usually as the saying goes, "Rain on Easter Sunday, it'll rain for seven Sundays afterwards." But it must've slipped this year as it was a nice Sunday, the first one after Easter Sunday. By the way, it also was my sister Leah's 66th birthday. Happy birthday, Leah!
In the afternoon, at Jacob's yesterday, daughters Verena and Susan wanted to go for a ride in our horse and buggy in this wonderful spring weather. Ê
Anyways, they ended up with 15 more going along. Most of their nieces, older and smaller ones, went along. Those small ones crawled on the buggy with smiles on their faces as to travel along. Good there were older girls along to hold those small ones. Guess they all enjoyed the ride.

While they were doing that, the men folks and boys went to hunt mushrooms in the woods behind our house. No mushrooms for the evening meal. No mushrooms to be seen. Too many mushroom hunters out there. It would sure be lots better if people would ask the property owner before entering the woods to hunt for those mushrooms. I'm not fond of the mushrooms, but some of the family like them.

Glad son Albert's church is over with as four of my children and I had church services during the last two and a half months. We all have to take our turns. So it was clean-clean here and there. When son Albert's family had it on Easter Sunday it was snow and rain and a cold wind. They all enjoyed the hot "one-kettle soup" with the rest of the church bunch. (One-kettle Soup is made with potatoes, canned beef chunks, spaghetti and onion cooked together). A soup like that goes good on a cold windy day.

Son Albert and boys were helping Verena one evening, so we could put our driving horse out in our pasture field where Verena and Susan had cleaned up and burned for it. At times, life seems dull to have some things done around here without my dear, beloved Ben. Everything always seems to work out, though, and get completed. What would I do without family? God always has a way, it seems.

We stayed at son Albert's home that Sunday evening when Albert had church so the next morning, Verena started to take over with the mopping of floors and Susan with the cleaning of windows. All the dishes and the laundry also were done at Albert's.

By 9:30 a.m., we were ready to leave for home again. It's always a relief when church services are held and the next day all is cleaned again.

A reader in Tralfagar, Ind., asked about "fried pies." I have not made those before. Does anyone out there have a recipe to share?

To the North Newton, Kan., reader, who wanted to know how long I was writing this column. I began in August of 1991 (Editor's note: In celebration of the 10-year anniversary of this column, a limited number of copies of "The Best of The Amish Cook, Vol. 1" are available at the Kansan office, 121 Sixth, Newton. The volume contains 200 of Elizabeth's columns in chronological order from the first one she ever wrote through 1996. A second volume from 1996 through 2001 will be released in the fall).

A reader in Decatur, Ind., asked about the recipe for knepfle; it's a soup my mother used to make. Very easy, delicious and hearty. Here is the recipe:

KNEPFLE

1 egg
2 cups flour
1 cup water
1/2 teaspoon salt
1/2 teaspoon baking powder
1 quart broth (any kind: vegetable, chicken, beef, whichever you prefer)

Put cup of water-egg mixture into dry ingredients bowl. It will form a crumbly dough (called knepfle). In a 3-quart kettle, bring broth to a boil. Hold the dough over the boiling water and drop the dough in as small pieces as you can with your spoon or with a knife. Dip the spoon or knife into the broth to prevent the dough from sticking. Let cook about 5 minutes at a boil. Serve.

(Variation: Some use water instead of broth and drain the soup in a colander. They then serve the knepfle in a bowl with browned butter over it).

MAY 2001

$\mathfrak{I}$t is Monday evening, and the house is clean again and back in order after having communion services here yesterday.

The church benches were set up Saturday evening and now are back in the bench wagon where they are stored. It will probably stay here another two weeks; we are having church here again, as it is Joe and Lovina's turn to have church at their place -- they live in a trailer across the driveway from us. This bench wagon goes from place to place.

We also serve a lunch before everyone leaves for home toward evening when we have communion. Our menu was beef and noodles, also ham, peanut butter, rhubarb jam, apple butter, sandwich spread, margarine, crackers, coffee, tea, red beets, cheese and cookies.

We ate early and the dishes washed, so we were able to have a nice, long relaxing Sunday evening with all our family here. A well-spent Sunday evening.

What a relief to think spring cleaning has been completed. Lots of painting took place, which makes everything have a better appearance. But that doesn't end the work.

Gardens are being made and will need a lot of care. Then comes canning. Plenty of sewing also has to be done. The early spring flowers have been blooming, which look so beautiful with the green grass.

Son Amos is to see his doctor next week, so hopefully, his ankle is mending. I guess we'll just have to take one day at a time.

To the Harrisonburg, Va., reader in answer to "what is Milnot?" It is a brand-name cream that comes in tin cans and is sold at stores. As with other liquid creams, we can beat it as a topping by adding sugar to it when whipped. Use as a coffee cream, as well.

To the Muncie, Ind., reader who wants the recipe of buttermilk pie. It takes 3 eggs, 1 cup buttermilk, 1 teaspoon vanilla (or rum flavoring), 3 rounded tablespoons flour, 1 3/4 cups sugar, 1/4 cup melted butter and 1 9-inch pie shell. Beat eggs well and add buttermilk and vanilla. Combine sugar and flour, and add to egg mixture. Add melted butter and mix well. Pour into unbaked pie shell; bake at 350 degrees until set. Good luck.

Thanks to all who take their time to write. Enjoy those encouraging letters and cards. Will share a few recipes with you great readers out there:

This is a family breakfast favorite:

MAY 2001

$\mathfrak{W}$e've entered another month, May 2, 2001. The farmers are busy putting out their crops, and gardens of all kinds are being planted. The vegetables in the gardens are so handy when it comes time to meal planning, soups, salads and sandwiches -- you name it. What would I do without a garden? Lots of work, though.

As I retire for the night, I am thinking, "What would I do without family?" My son-in-law Joe got the garden ready so I could plant. Daughter Lovina was here and onions (three pounds), plus the onions from last winter, were set out. Ê

Jacob's (daughter Emma) family came in the evening and planted more vegetable seeds out in the garden. Also, son Albert and family came, and Albert put up the purple martin houses, which the martins have been flying around for their houses this year. I couldn't put the martin houses up as it was always my deceased husband Ben's duties. He always kept those houses clean as long as the purple martins were around, and there were many sets of them. So many purple martins entered their houses tonight. Ê

It's a sad feeling to see the garden being put out as Ben and I put it out last year. Sometimes I can't even think about those good memories of our last year together when he was home from work a lot more. I thought it was time for him to stay home and relax after all our years of marriage. He was a good-hearted man to all who knew him. But God had a purpose to take him in "His" care. We can't question why, but I miss him more and more.

Albert noticed a drain wasn't right that led to our cistern, so Albert and Jacob were caring for that while Joe had the grill in gear to barbecue ribs for supper for all (Joe's, Albert's and Jacob's families). They all deserved a good evening meal. (For photos of Elizabeth's newly planted garden, go to www.theamishcook.com, scrapbook section).

Daughter Susan and I helped daughter Liz Tuesday in getting ready for church as its to be at her place Sunday. It's usually clean, clean, clean for church at such a time.

The trees are a beautiful color of leaves. Looking out at the woods its such a variety of colors. Also the variety of flowers have bloomed. How season from season changes.

I'm admiring the beautiful potted flower plant on my sewing machine, which was given to me by the Decatur Daily Democrat newspaper recently. The flower was greatly appreciated. Looks beautiful!

CINNAMON COFFEECAKE

1 tablespoon vegetable oil
1 cup sugar
1 cup milk
2 teaspoons baking powder
2 cups flour
Topping: 1/2 cup brown sugar, 1 teaspoon cinnamon, 4 tablespoons butter or margarine.
Stir together the first 5 ingredients until well moistened. Pour into greased and floured 9- by 9-inch pan. Sprinkle brown sugar over cake top with pats of butter and sprinkle with cinnamon. Bake at 350 degrees until toothpick inserted into cake comes out clean -- about 25 minutes.

MAY 2001

Daughters Verena, Susan and I, with several of Joe's (daughter Lovina) daughters, traveled to church this cool, sunshiny Sunday morning, May 13.

It so brought back sad memories of a year ago -- except it was Sunday, May 14 -- when my dear husband Ben and I rode to church, not thinking it would be our last Sunday to go to church in our horse-drawn buggy together. God had other plans and we can't question "why" when things happen that we don't understand. Only "He" knows why Ben was taken in "His" care. It's been a hard day to think of a year ago.

Today, though, is also Mother's Day, which is a happier occasion. Hope all of you mothers out there had an enjoyable day. Son Albert and family, plus Joe's (daughter Lovina) and Jacob's (daughter Emma) families were our Sunday supper guests. Joe barbecued pork chops and pork steak, and we also had mashed potatoes, gravy, baked beans and buttered corn as the main hot food. Ê

Rhubarb cake dessert is also on the menu. Rhubarb is on the list at present. It can be used in so many different ways: shortcakes, jams, pies, etc.

Talking about the garden, I wasn't thinking to put out much of a garden this year. But when you see the ground ready to plant and get in that good spirit to plant, I guess a person gets carried away. So I've put out lots of garden goodies. It's interesting to plant the garden once more and watch for the first sprouts to appear. So we need the rain and warm sunshine.

Then comes the hard work: weeding and hoeing. Without both, there would be no garden, crops or hay. We put some onion plants and sweet potato plants in the ground that a reader gave me. Was greatly appreciated!

On Saturday, I received a nice blooming plant from my "secret pal" for Mother's Day, along with a card containing $5. So I guess I'll keep guessing all year who it's coming from. It's a nice potted flower.

Levi's (daughter Liz) had church services in their home Sunday. Verena, Susan, Lovina and I helped clean their home Monday morning. Always feels good to get the house back in order after church. Levi's family was supper guests Monday night, so it was Levi's job to barbecue the pork and steak.

Mother's Day is worth writing about. Many of our mothers and grandmothers were considered good cooks and housekeepers, yet their cupboards didn't contain nearly as many convenient foods, soup bases and instant foods as ours do now. It used to be simple meals, although good and healthy. Maybe we are too wasteful at times. Love is the best gift on Mother's Day.

Here is the rhubarb cake dessert recipe that was on our menu. Enjoy!

RHUBARB CAKE

1 1/2 cups brown sugar	2 cups flour
1/2 cup shortening	1 cup buttermilk
1 egg	1/2 teaspoon baking soda
1 1/2 cups fresh rhubarb	1/2 teaspoon salt

Combine shortening, sugar and egg. Beat until light and fluffy. Combine soda, salt and flour together. Add to shortening mixture. Alternately with buttermilk, fold in the rhubarb. Mix well. Pour into a greased 9- by 13-inch pan, and bake at 350 degrees for 30 to 40 minutes. Top with whipped cream if desired.

JUNE 2001

This leaves it a Sunday evening, May 20, 2001. It's a year ago now that my dear husband, Ben, was taken to that Heavenly Home. He's in a place where there's no more worry and pain, only peace. But I must go on.

Was glad to see daughter Emma and Jacob and family coming here last evening, Saturday, as it just made a better feeling to have someone come. They stayed for the night. So this morning we had breakfast together.

Didn't know if some other family members would show up for dinner, so we waited to start a dinner.

Paul's (daughter Leah); Joe's (daughter Lovina) and Jacob's (daughter Emma) and all their children were our dinner guests. They had dinner here and stayed all day, leaving in the evening. It was a day well-spent together with family. Then to my surprise, Ben's sister and husband drove in and gave a visit.

Daughter Lovina will never forget her 29th birthday last year, May 22, as the funeral of Ben was the next day. So this was a quieter birthday this year.

Now the news of this evening: at 8:30 p.m. a daughter named Laura was born to son Amos and Nancy Jean, weighing 9 pounds, eight ounces, and 22 and 1/4 inch in length.

She joins one brother, Ben, and seven sisters: Susan, Elizabeth, Mary Jane, twins Arlene and Marlene, Lovina and Lisa. I suppose Amos's Ben would have been proud for a brother, but the baby is happy and healthy and that is all that matters. This makes 33 grandchildren living, one, Mary Shetler, deceased.

Now it looks a stormy Monday morning and the laundry was hung out on the clothesline early, only to bring the clothes back in because of the rain.

I don't like to leave it hang when a storm comes up. It really rained and rained and then quit, so, again, the laundry was hung out and this time it all dried. Doesn't look like the rain is over with, though.

We were having plenty of rain lately. Had two inches of rain by noon.

Verena went over the property she owns to do some cleaning up and my youngest daughter Susan had been weeding flowers and wherever it needs it. Spring brings many tasks. What would we do without family?

A couple of readers recently have asked for recipes for "Apricot Pie." Following is a good recipe:

APRICOT PIE

2 cups dried apricots
1/2 cup sugar
Pinch of salt
Pastry for 2-crust pie.

2 cups water
1 1/2 tablespoons cornstarch
3 tablespoons butter

In a saucepan bring apricots and water to a boil. Cook for 10 minutes. Add sugar and cook another 5 minutes. Drain, reserving 1 cup of juice. Set apricots aside. Pour 1 cup reserved apricot juice into saucepan and add cornstarch. Add salt and cook until mixture thickens, stirring frequently. Arrange drained apricots in unbaked pie shell. Pour in thickened apricot juice. Dot with butter. Cover with top crust. Slit top and flute edges. Bake at 425¡ for 30 minutes.

JUNE 2001

Lots of weddings around here this month of June. June is the most popular month for weddings. For those new to the column, you might be interested as to some of the details of weddings here. The wedding and wedding lunch have many duties with it before the big day. The house has a thorough cleaning. Weddings are usually on a Thursday. The Saturday before, some of the furniture is carried somewhere to be stored, and some is rearranged. The inside of the home needs to be completely re-done to accommodate and seat the large wedding crowd. Some have wedding tables in a cleaned-out shed. Having the ceremony in an outside shed is lots easier, as this way no furniture has to be moved. When the ceremony is in a house, folding tables are set up with benches to seat the people. Thus far, we have held four weddings in our home for our daughters. We have two sheds on our property; one was used for cooking the meals with some additional seating. The other shed was used for the actual wedding services where the couple was united in marriage.

There are lots of dishes to be taken to the shed from the cupboards: cookware and silverware, and the list goes on and on. All kinds of utensils are in use to prepare the lunch, including potato mashers for the potatoes, cookspoons, peelers and so on.

Usually the cakes are baked on a Saturday or Monday before the wedding. A variety of cakes, perhaps 25 to 30, are frosted after they are baked and cooled. The wedding cake also is nicely frosted and decorated. Decorative coconut is sprinkled on top. Tiny silver ball candies also are put on top to add decoration. The main wedding cake for all our daughters was four layers, each layer about 5 inches thick, so it was a good-sized cake.

There are usually what you call "side cakes" with "good luck" and "best wishes" written on them. The two side cakes are set on either side of the wedding cake in the couple's "wedding corner." The wedding corner is a corner of the room where the married couple and their attendants are seated for lunch. The corner dishes are always kept separate from the other dishes when they're being washed. The dinnerware set for the corner is usually a gift to the bride from the groom.

The Tuesday before the wedding, 20 or more women, usually immediate family and friends, come to bake the pies. Raisin, cherry, oatmeal, pumpkin and rhubarb are popular pies to be served at weddings around here. There are usually at least three or four varieties of pie flavors. The women also make the nothings, and toast bread crumbs for the dressing. Nothings (see recipe in article) are a traditional wedding pastry in our area, a deep-fried dough cooked until a golden brown and sprinkled with sugar. The pastries are tasty, but they also are decorative. The edges of the "nothings" curl up after being deep-fried so they can be stacked on top of each other on plates and placed on the wedding tables. There's usually 60 to 90 pies that are baked in the morning and 13 to 15 batches of nothings made. The most popular pie served is raisin pie, a creamy, raisin-filled pie. Other pies include apple, peach, rhubarb and oatmeal.

The single girls assist the Wednesday before the wedding -- maybe 12 or more girls. They peel potatoes, probably four or five 20-quart cookers full of them. They make the colorful carrot salad, help set remaining tables and do whatever has to be done.

Lately, it has become the women and single girls who have started making their preparations together on Wednesday. I like it this way as everything gets done in one day. Ê

On the day of the wedding, I usually ask more than 30 women to help with the cooking.

NOTHINGS

1 egg
3 cookspoons (large kitchen spoons) cream
Pinch salt
Enough all-purpose flour to make a stiff dough
Shortening for frying

Beat the egg, and then stir in cream and salt. Add enough flour to make a stiff dough. Work it with your hands well. Divide dough into 6 or 7 balls and roll out real flat and very thin. Then cut 3 slits into each flat piece of dough. Have a kettle of hot lard or Crisco ready, and one by one, drop the dough in. Remove when golden. Sprinkle sugar on them, and stack on a plate.

JUNE 2001

𝕴t is now officially summer, so it's a time of working outdoors. Lots of baling hay, and, yes, even barn-raisings take place around here. Ê

The day of the barn-raising has come upon us. How many people will come? The count could be several hundred, with at least 75 or more men and boys to assist with it. In some Amish communities, there are at least 100 to 140 or more men to put up the framework of a barn in one day.

On the day of the barn-raising, some men arrive at dawn with their nail aprons, hammers and other kinds of tools. Other tools include 25-, 50- and 100-foot tape measures, saws and squares. A lot of the men take their toolboxes along so that they have a variety of tools, on hand, whatever they need. These tools will be used throughout the day. The men are usually divided into groups with a leader who will show his group or crew what has to be done.

I think it's a dangerous job if one's not careful enough. The barn-raising crews usually have the barn under roof by evening. Some barn-raisings can be finished in one day's time; some of the larger ones won't be finished in one day. Enough can be put up in one day that a smaller group of family and friends can usually finish the rest on another day.

The materials come from local lumber companies. The size of the barn depends on what the family wants. Some have more cattle, so they need more barn space.

It's remarkable to watch a barn-raising, to see how the barn takes shape, step by step. I've been to several in my lifetime, including our own barn-raising while I was still young. I have lots of memories from it. I must have been about 10 or 11 years old. To see the men put the frame together and put the siding and roof on was quite a memory. It was completed in a day, but it began raining in the evening.

I still remember there were 126 people -- women and children included -- who came to help that day. We thought at the time that 126 was a lot, but compared to nowadays it is not. There are more people around today with all these families, so we might have 250 show up on a day. Ê

A snack of coffee, cookies and a cold drink is served in the forenoon to all the men, women and children. At noon, a good lunch is served. Some women bring in all kinds of desserts, casseroles, baked goods, you name it.

Long tables are set up in the yard where shade is available, and the final preparations of the food is set on the tables. This helped the women with bringing the food to the barn-raising. The tables gave the women a place to set the food and provided a makeshift place to eat the meal. The food is served cafeteria-style. Ê

In the afternoon, another snack, like cold lemonade and cookies, is passed to all present. The boys especially enjoy the break. The snack is taken to them after the dishes have been cleared at noon. In the late afternoon, the workers are served a cold drink to quench their thirst on a hot day. Women are usually kept busy caring for the small children.

JULY 2001

𝕿his is Sunday, June 17, and it seems this month is slipping away too fast.

We spent Saturday night at son Albert's and were there for dinner today. Also there were Paul's (daughter Leah), Joe's (daughter Lovina) and Jacob's (daughter Emma) families. Barbecued chicken was on the menu. ÊÊÊ

232

Later in the day, Joe's family and my daughters Verena, Susan and I with some others had supper at Joe's sister's and family's home also with barbecued chicken on the menu.

Son Albert, Sarah Irene and their eight children were our Friday evening supper guests, and finally plans were made for them to stay for the night. We had an enjoyable breakfast together . Saturday morning. My daughter Susan and Albert's daughter Elizabeth headed to a gathering in Centreville, Mich., for the day.

A finch made its way into one of my hanging flower pots. Looks like six eggs have hatched in it now. Hope they can soon fly and get out of it. Didn't realize there were little birds in it until some of my grandsons saw them in that flowerpot. Several years ago, a finch also had a nest in one. Well, I must hike to bed and get some shut eyes.

This leaves it Wednesday morning already, and I will add some more to this column. The garden is getting a better appearance from those unwanted weeds.

Those pesty plants will soon take over a garden if allowed to grow. They are almost as certain as tomorrow's sunrise and spring rains. Those weeds will destroy or weaken the good plants. All of our hard work and those good seeds will amount to little or maybe nothing when those weeds grow out of control. Nobody sows weed seeds in the garden, but somehow they will still get there.

A hoe or two have felt plenty of elbow grease the last several days. It's good to have Susan back in the garden again as she couldn't the last several years because of her tri-break ankle. She enjoys working in the garden. Glad she does. Verena also has put some time into the garden. I am hoping to put late cabbage and celery into the ground today. Ê

We did the laundry this morning, and Verena is doing the ironing, also cleaning out the shed. Susan is weeding the flowers. My daughter Emma and her children spent the day here yesterday. She was a good helper around here. Always plenty to do without the help of my husband, Ben. We miss his help more and more. But God makes no mistakes and has a purpose for it all.

We went to view a widow (Ben's cousin's wife) last night who had lost her husband nine months ago. He died soon after Ben had died. So it must be hard on those children and families to lose their parents so quick.

On Sunday evening, son Amos and his wife, Nancy, and family had plans to be here for supper but found no one at home. Their first try was to see if we were at son Albert's and found us. Sorry, Amos. Try again!

It is later now, and we are at daughter Liz and Levi's for the night. This way, we'll be closer to attend the funeral services with our horse and buggy. We had just come from our neighbors' north of us who are having a wedding tomorrow. We enjoyed the good supper.

A reader in Federal Way, Wash., asked for my meat loaf recipe. It's a delicious favorite around here. So I'll share it. Thanks to you readers for all your encouraging letters and notes:

JULY 2001

Good old July has appeared on the calendar of 2001, especially for those birthdays out there, including mine.

The six finches have left their home in my hanging flower pot on my porch. As I was giving water to the plant one morning, they flew out, and away they went. The flower needed water even with the birds in there, so I was always careful where I put the water. More and more I could see the feathers on them. Glad they are out of my flower pot.

Garden is doing great with our nice, frequent rains. What would we do without our gardens?

Makes meal planning so much easier -- there's nothing better than taking those vegetables from the ground for cooking, canning and putting them in salads of all kinds. I still miss Ben's company, the times we spent.

Joe's (daughter Lovina) and Jacob's families planned to prepare a breakfast on the grill at Jacob's Sunday morning. So fried eggs, fried potatoes, bacon and buttered toast were put on the grill. Enjoyable cookout.

Then Levi's (daughter Liz) family came here Monday evening, bringing their cast-iron kettle to make vegetable soup on the open fire and barbecued chicken on the grill. The soup was tasty with those fresh vegetables. Joe, Lovina and family, and Jacob, Emma and family members also arrived and enjoyed the outdoors meal.

The cookout was later than we realized, so by then it was decided for all of them to stay here for the night. So we had all those cute little grandchildren sleeping here -- we have plenty of rooms and beds to sleep in. Levi, Liz and their four children; Joe, Lovina and their five children, and Jacob, Emma and their three children all spent the night. Ê
So on Tuesday morning, a big breakfast was fixed; the main meal was a breakfast casserole. Makes life so much more enjoyable when the children and grandchildren come here. What would I do without them, especially Verena and Susan, who still live at home with me? God has plans for us all. We can't question "why." "He" never makes a mistake. What would we do without the help of our Heavenly Father?
Thank you to those readers out there who send me the encouraging cards and notes telling me to continue with this column. It's very encouraging. Rhubarb is still on the list with all the rains we've had recently.
Following are some recipes for our great readers out there:

RHUBARB PASTRY

Crust:
2 cups flour   4 tablespoons sugar
1 cup butter
Mix and press into 9- by 13-inch plan. Bake in 350-degree oven for 10 minutes. Remove from oven.
Filling:
5 cups rhubarb, diced   6 eggs, separated
2 cups white sugar   7 tablespoons flour
1/4 teaspoon salt   1 cup canned evaporated milk
Spread diced rhubarb cuts over crust. Separate eggs. Set aside whites and stir yolks, sugar, flour, salt and evaporated milk until smooth. Pour over rhubarb. Bake at 350 degrees until set (about 45 minutes).
Meringue:
6 egg whites
3/4 cup sugar

3/4 teaspoon salt
1/4 teaspoon cream of tartar
1 teaspoon vanilla
Beat egg whites until stiff. Slowly add sugar, salt, cream of tartar and vanilla. Mix until smooth. Pour on top of baked rhubarb. Brown slightly by cooking at 325 degrees for 10 minutes.

JULY 2001

The Fourth of July passed, so my mind turns to what next year will hold. Only God knows. Tents were set up at Jacob's on Tuesday evening, July 3. So Albert, his wife, Sarah Irene, and their family, along with daughters, Susan, Verena and I camped out. Well, no camping for me. Ha! I slept in the house, but in the morning I went out and tried those tents. They were better, more comfortable, than I thought they would be.
Breakfast was prepared out on an open fire in cast-iron kettles with fried potatoes, scrambled eggs and bacon. Delicious way to begin the day, and spending time with family is the best use of time.
After breakfast, the men and boys went fishing at a nearby pond. So we had some fish on the grill for Fourth of July dinner, as well as hamburgers. A homemade chili soup also was cooked in one of those cast-iron kettles on the open fire. Son Amos, Nancy and family dropped in to enjoy the noon meal. Plenty of food. Was good to see them join the rest of us.
Reckon, Jacob and Emma are tired out by now. For me, things like this just aren't as enjoyable without Ben. But it was enjoyable to spend the Fourth with family.
This morning, I am doing this task of writing, which I can't neglect. Thanks to the many readers who take the time to write to me to tell me that they enjoy this column, worthy or unworthy.
Crops and hay fields, also pasture fields, look so good. Glad for the rains we've had. Gardens look so bountiful this year. Do we appreciate it enough? I must get busy. Always plenty to do. The garden needs more weeding, so I'll send Susan out there when she returns home from work. She enjoys working in the garden, even in that hot sun. Verena has been doing work in the yard also. What would I do without their help?
This is a good recipe to try for a picnic dinner on a holiday:
Barbecued Beef Sandwiches
1/2 cup chopped onion
4 tablespoons sugar
1/2 teaspoon pepper
1/2 cup catsup
3 tablespoons vinegar
1 teaspoon Worchestershire sauce
1/4 cup water
2 pounds cooked, chopped chunk beef

Mix all ingredients except beef and cook over low heat for 5 minutes. Add cooked beef. Serve hot on buns.

28366234R00135

Made in the USA
San Bernardino, CA
27 December 2015